AF818918

Fringe '89

International Workshop
on Automatic Processing
of Fringe Patterns

Physical Research

Volume 10

Fringe '89

edited by

Wolfgang Osten

Ryszard J. Pryputniewicz

Graeme T. Reid

Hans Rottenkolber

Fringe '89

Proceedings of the I. International Workshop on Automatic Processing of Fringe Patterns held in Berlin (GDR), April 25 – 28, 1989

edited by
Wolfgang Osten
Ryszard J. Pryputniewicz
Graeme T. Reid
Hans Rottenkolber

With 90 Figures and 1 Table

Akademie-Verlag Berlin
1989

Editors:

Dr. rer. nat. Wolfgang Osten
Akademie der Wissenschaften der DDR
Zentralinstitut für Kybernetik und Informationsprozesse
Berlin, DDR–1086

Prof. Ryszard J. Pryputniewicz, PHD
Center for Holographic Studies and Laser Technology
Department of Mechanical Engineering
Worcester Polytechnic Institute
Worcester, Massachusetts 01609

Dr. phil. Graeme T. Reid
National Engineering Laboratory
East Kilbride
Glasgow, G75 oqu
Scotland

Dr.-Ing. Hans Rottenkolber
Rottenkolber Holo-System GmbH
D-8011 Kirchheim bei München

Reproduction of the original authors' manuscript

ISBN 3–05–500682–8

Erschienen im Akademie-Verlag Berlin, Leipziger Str. 3–4, Berlin, DDR–1086
© Akademie-Verlag Berlin 1989
Lizenznummer: 202 · 100/446/89
Printed in the German Democratic Republic
Gesamtherstellung: VEB Kongreß- und Werbedruck, Oberlungwitz, DDR–9273
LSV: 1165
Bestellnummer: 763 993 6 (9213)
03200

PREFACE

This volume is a collection of selected papers presented during FRINGE '89 - The First International Workshop on "Automatic Processing of Fringe Patterns" held in Berlin, April 25-28, 1989.

The basic idea of this workshop was born in 1987 during a cooperative work of co-workers of the Central Institute of Cybernetics and Information Processes and the Rottenkolber Holo-Systems GmbH in the field of automatic processing of fringe patterns. The state of the art and the increasing interest in problems concerning that matter have stimulated us to establish a first international workshop with such a special orientation. This workshop provides a meeting place for the exchange of information and ideas among scientists engaged in the development and application of methods for computer aided fringe pattern analysis. We are convinced that the future introduction of interferometric methods to industrial application mainly depends on the problem to what extent the evaluation of fringe patterns can be successfully automated and integrated into the process of testing and manufacturing. By directly orienting towards an efficient combination of modern measurement methods and highly developed computer technique the profile of the workshop FRINGE '89 makes allowance for this requirement. The contributions of the conference contained in this volume provide insights into international trends and show the grown interest in computer-aided optical metrology.

The organizers of the workshop, W. Osten and H. Rottenkolber, have welcomed R. J. Pryputniewicz and G. Reid as further chairmen. We are sure that this decision will contribute immensely to the stimulation of the international information exchange in this field and the future development of the conference.

The editors would like to express their thanks to R. Höfling for his great help during the preparation of this volume and for his supporting the organization of the scientific program. We are very much obliged to Prof. Dr. V. Kempe, Director of the Central Institute of Cybernetics and Information Processes, as the scientific adviser, and to Dr. G. Stanke, the Deputy Director of this institute, for their efforts in helping to organize the workshop. Our thanks are due to Mrs. U. Heilmann and Mrs. H. Höpcke from Akademie-Verlag for providing excellent conditions for the publication of these Proceedings. Finally, we are all very grateful for the untiring efforts made by Mrs. S. Böttcher and Mrs. P. Hänßgen, who

contributed very much to a successful FRINGE '89.
Hoping to have provided good conditions for this Workshop, we are looking forward to FRINGE '93.

W. Osten (local chairman) | R. J. Pryputniewicz

G. T. Reid | H. Rottenkolber

Contents

TABLE OF CONTENTS

INVITED PAPERS

SUBMITTED PAPERS

Invited Papers

IMAGE PROCESSING TECHNIQUES FOR FRINGE PATTERN ANALYSIS

by

G T REID
National Engineering Laboratory
East Kilbride, Glasgow G75 OQU, UK

ABSTRACT

Automatic fringe pattern analysis is now used, with appropriate interferometers, in areas such as optical testing, flow visualisation, nondestructive testing, industrial inspection and medical imaging. This paper describes a cross section of the image processing techniques which can be used as the building blocks for an automatic fringe analysis system. The paper uses simple, non-mathematical, descriptions of the various techniques in an attempt to appeal to first time users of the technology.

INTRODUCTION

The availability of powerful, inexpensive, digital image processing equipment has encouraged many users of interferometry to build systems for automatic fringe pattern analysis. The research community, meanwhile, has devoted growing attention to problems associated with automatic fringe analysis[1]. Many people now regard this area of research as a subject in its own right[2,3] rather than as a specialism within image processing or interferometry. Viewing automatic fringe analysis as an independant subject has the benefit of encouraging the development of concepts and methods which may be applied to the patterns generated by any one of a number of optical methods - the source of the fringe pattern having little or no effect on the analysis algorithm. In this paper, therefore, we will broaden the definition of "interferogram" to include all fringe-like patterns whether or not such patterns have been generated by the interference of optical wavefronts.

THE USE OF PRIOR KNOWLEDGE

When a fringe analysis task contains a series of predictable steps and when the task must be repeated many times (in the testing of mass produced products or in large scale medical screening, perhaps) it may be possible to design a fringe analysis system which exploits the predictability of the task. After identifying the characteristics of the fringe pattern which are peculiar to the task, the capabilities of the analysis may be confined to those required for the work in question.

Robinson and his co-workers, for example, have described a number of specialised fringe analysis procedures[4,5] for use in engineering applications of interferometry. When studying the holographic interferograms produced when testing honeycomb panels it was observed that debrazing of the honeycomb produced

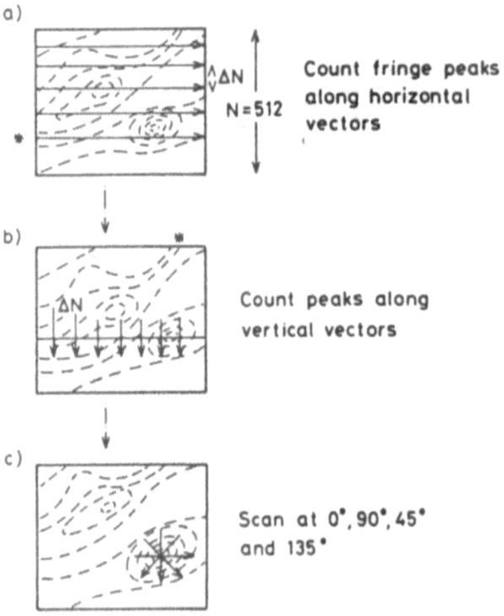

Fig. 1 Processing sequence for the analysis of interferograms for holographic non-destructive testing (courtesy of D W Robinson).

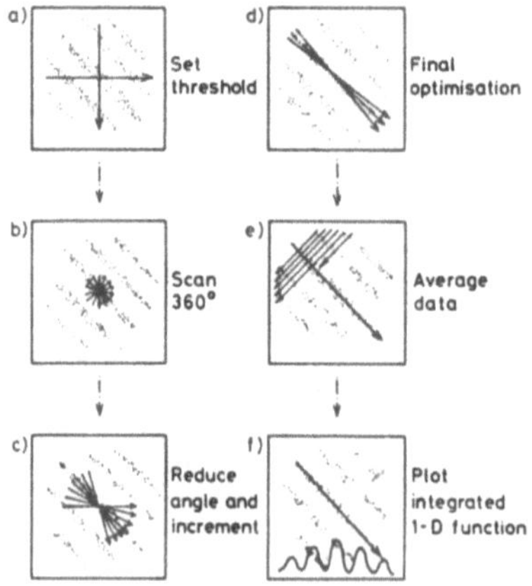

Fig. 2 Analysis sequence for speckle interferograms (courtesy of D W Robinson).

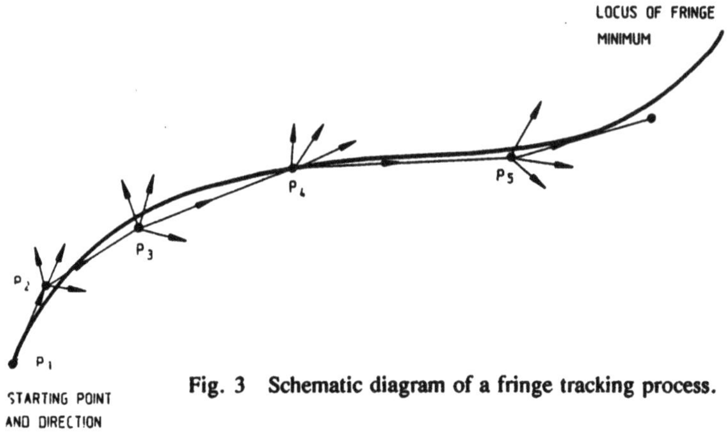

Fig. 3 Schematic diagram of a fringe tracking process.

groups of nearly circular fringes of a particular size and fringe density. Robinson developed a method of automatically searching interferograms for the presence of these pre-specified faults. As shown in Fig. 1, the method involves counting the number of fringes appearing on several horizontal lines through the image. When a comparatively large number of fringes appears on a given line, a flaw is presumed to exist on that line. Short vertical scans about the line are then used to search for the location of the flaw by looking for a comparatively large number of fringes in the vertical direction. Having identified the probable existence and location of a flaw, the system carries out a further check by counting the number of fringes along each of four short vectors, angularly spaced by 45 degrees, centred on the probable flaw site. If the same number of fringes appears on each of the four vectors then the existence and location of the flaw are confirmed.

The interferograms resulting from double exposure speckle photography consist of several parallel fringes, the spacing and orientation of which describe the displacement vector at a point on a deformed object. The spacing and orientation of the fringes could be determined easily were it not for the high level of noise which is inherent in these interferograms. Some degree of filtering or averaging is therefore required before an accurate analysis of the pattern can be performed. The speckle photograph is digitised and, as shown schematically in Fig. 2, intensity values are summed along each of a series of radial vectors which pass through the centre of the pattern. If a bright fringe always passes through the centre of the pattern, the vector giving the largest intensity summation will be most nearly parallel to the fringes. The iterative reduction of the angular separation of the scan vectors allows the fringe direction to be determined. Intensity values are then averaged along the direction of the fringes, thereby reducing the two-dimensional fringe pattern to a one-dimensional function which, in consequence of the averaging, has a comparatively low level of noise. The period of this function is, of course, equal to the spacing of the fringes.

TRACKING AND THINNING OF FRINGES

Perhaps the most obvious approach to fringe pattern analysis involved identifying and subsequently tracking fringes in an interferogram. This approach can be quite general-purpose, requiring little or no prior knowledge of the fringe pattern characteristics. Furthermore, the fringe tracking algorithm may be verified by comparing a graphical representation of the tracked fringes with the original interferogram.

A number of fringe tracking methods have been proposed. These methods differ in detail but they all consist of a series of steps which are similar to the following:

* filter the image[6]

* identify and track the intensity maxima or minima within the fringe pattern[7,8]

Fig. 4 Successive thinning of a thresholded fringe pattern (courtesy of S J Marshall et al).

* assign unique numbers to the fringes - either interactively[9] or automatically[10]

* calculate the measurement parameter from the fringe pattern data.

A typical fringe tracking method is shown schematically in Fig. 3. In this example, loci of minimum intensity are tracked. In principle, the same method could be applied to track the loci of maximum intensity. To begin the tracking process, the operator defines one point on the locus of the fringe minimum. The operator also defines the approximate direction in which the tracking should proceed. As shown in Fig. 3, intensity values are summed along a series of radial vectors which emanate from the starting point. The vectors are concentrated around the starting direction which was specified by the operator. To find the next point along the fringe, it is assumed that the summation with the minimum value must come from the vector which lies closest to the local direction of the fringe. The next point on the fringe is then presumed to lie at the end of that vector. A series of radial vectors is then made to emanate from this second point on the fringe and the process is repeated until the end of the fringe is reached.

An alternative technique[11,12] combines thresholding, thinning and tracing operations to identify fringe centre lines. Firstly, local threshold values are calculated for blocks of pixels over the fringe pattern. An array of threshold levels is formed either by finding average intensity values within blocks of selectable size or by calculating a running average intensity over the field. A 'shrink-expand' operator is then used to remove noise which appears as isolated bright or dark pixels. The fringe pattern is then subjected to repeated passes of a thinning operator which erodes the fringes from all sides, while maintaining continuity, until only the fringe centre lines remain. At this stage, the presence of noise on the original fringe pattern may result in gaps in the fringes, spurious branches emerging from fringes or spurious interconnections between fringes. A tracing routine is then used to refine the fringe pattern. Each fringe is followed separately and when a gap or branch is encountered, a set of rules is invoked to determine the most probable path of the fringe. Fig. 4 shows this technique in operation.

PHASE STEPPING TECHNIQUES

One of the most important developments in automatic fringe analysis was the development of the phase stepping or quasi-heterodyne method[13]. By introducing discrete shifts, or "phase steps" in the position of the fringes within an interferogram and then by analysing a series of interferograms in which the fringe shifts vary systematically from one member of the series to the next, an extremely powerful analysis is possible.

A series of three phase stepped fringe patterns is shown in Fig. 5. The characteristics of the three patterns are identical apart from the 120 degree shift in the phase of each pattern with respect to its neighbour. Analysis of this series of patterns relies on the fact that, at each pixel location, there are three intensity values (one from each of the three fringe patterns) available.

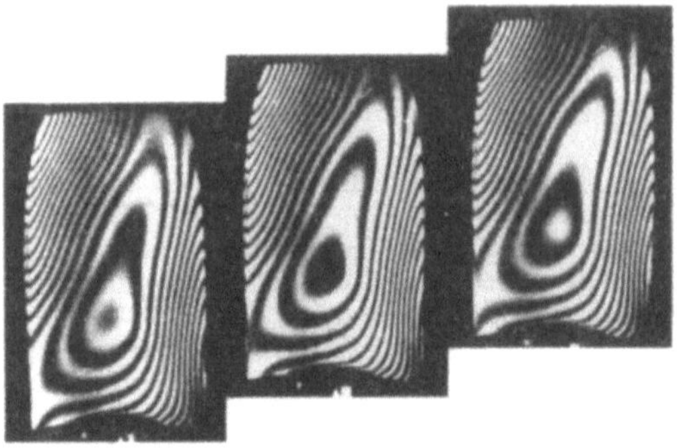

Fig. 5 Three phase stepped fringe patterns.

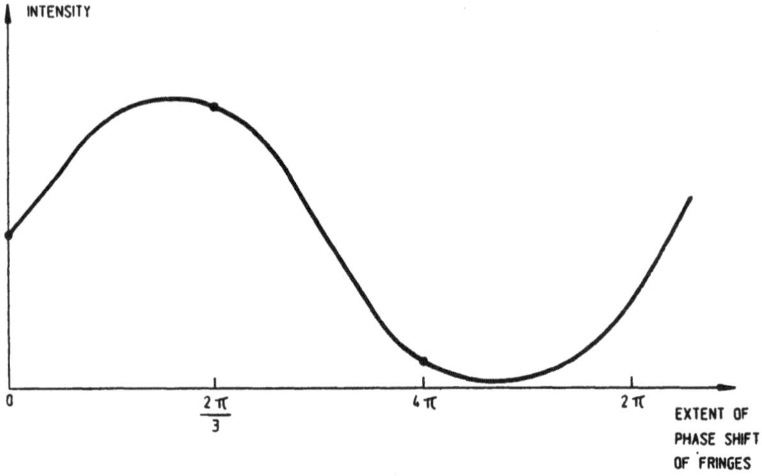

Fig. 6 Amplitude modulation at one pixel location in a series of phase stepped fringe patterns.

Since the series of fringe patterns differ only in the phase of the fringes, the three intensity values must represent points on the continuous sinusoidal curve, such as the one shown in Fig. 6, which results from the translation of the fringe past a stationary detector. By fitting a sine curve to the three intensity values and then by calculating the phase of that curve, the phase of the fringe pattern at one pixel can be determined. When the above calculations are performed in an image processing environment, a two-dimensional array of intensity values is obtained from each fringe pattern. The set of three fringe patterns, therefore, yields three intensity values at each pixel location within the two-dimensional array. Phase values can therefore be calculated at each location in the array. The three fringe patterns, therefore, can be transformed into a "phase image".

The phase image has a number of highly desirable characteristics. Firstly, the phase values are insensitive to changes in contrast of the fringes so that uneven illumination of the workpiece or uneven scattering or reflection of light from the workpiece has little effect on the phase calculation. (Clearly, if the illumination or scattering is so uneven as to saturate the image sensor or to return insufficient light to the sensor then the phase values will be degraded). Secondly, the phase values provide an unambiguous indication of fringe number. According to the conventions used during the phase calculations, the phase values may advance as the fringe number increases and retard as the fringe number decreases. Thirdly, since phase values are available at each pixel location, the measurement parameter (eg wavefront distortion, 3-d shape or deformation) which is evaluated after the analysis of the fringes will be available at a regular mesh of points and not only along the loci of the fringe centres. This format of data is particularly attractive if the results are to be input to numerical analysis software or to computer graphics software. The above features are all embodied in Fig. 7 which shows the result of analysing a series of surface contour maps using the phase stepping method.

PHASE MEASUREMENT FROM A SINGLE IMAGE

We have seen that by measuring the phase, rather than the intensity, of an interferogram, some extremely powerful analysis techniques can be developed. Perhaps the biggest drawback of the phase stepping method its requirement for a series of interferograms to be captured at different instants in time. This feature of phase measurement imposes an ultimate limit on the speed of data capture.

For those applications which require data to be captured in a single image, there exists a number of fringe analysis methods[14-16] which rely on spatial versions of the temporal phase measurement which has already been covered. These spatial phase measurement methods retain many of the advantages of phase- stepping while removing the need to capture a series of fringe patterns. The spatial methods, however, are only applicable to a subset of the interferograms which may be analysed by the phase stepping method. In particular, spatial methods of phase measurement are unreliable if the data has a significant amount of noise and the phase values vary rapidly[17].

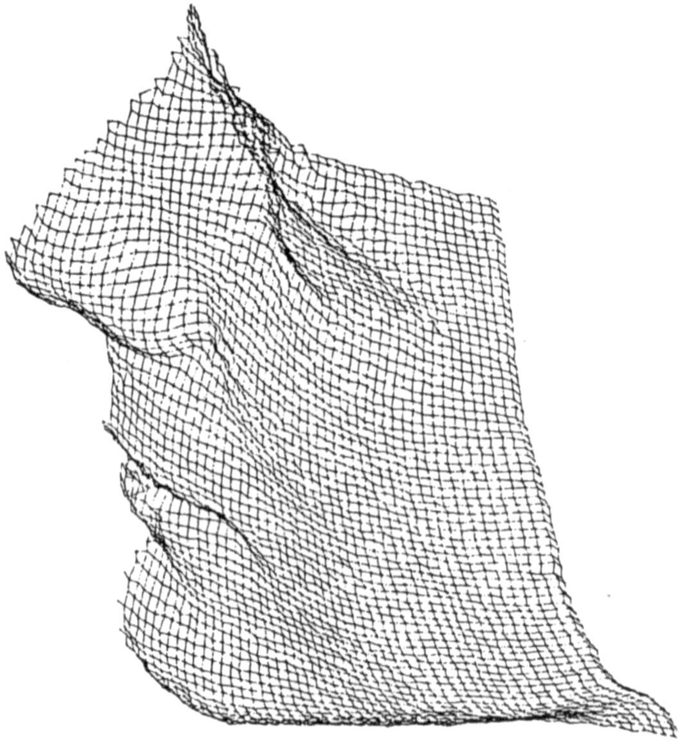

Fig. 7 Wire mesh diagram of a human face resulting from the analysis of a moire fringe contour map of the face (courtesy of S J Marshall and P J Wells).

Spatial phase measurement treats the fringe pattern as a carrier signal which has its shape modulated by the measurement parameter. The null fringe pattern in such a system would be a series of straight parallel fringes. Under the influence of the measurement parameter, the fringes distort (ie the phase of the fringes is modulated by the disturbing influence of the measurement parameter). The task of the fringe analysis system is to demodulate the shape of the fringes and thereby recover the values of the measurement parameter. The best known demodulation technique[18] uses a Fourier transform method to calculate the phase of the fringes. The measurement parameter can be recovered by subtracting the phase bias which is due to the carrier signal so that only the phase modulation remains.

DISCUSSION AND CONCLUSIONS

A "toolbox" of image processing techniques has been developed for the purpose of automatic fringe analysis. In many of the applications which have been addressed so far, a single method from this toolbox has provided a sufficiently robust solution. In future, as ever more demanding applications are attempted, it is likely that several methods from the toolbox will be combined to provide more powerful and more noise-tolerant algorithms for fringe analysis.

We could also imagine a more sophisticated use of prior knowledge in which expert systems would "advise" the fringe analysis software about the specific characteristics of the application. At a more advanced level, we could imagine the expert system helping to analyse incomplete or heavily degraded fringe data by invoking rules (if such rules exist!) governing the way in which fringes "behave" within interferograms in a given application.

By employing ever more sophisticated software and by ensuring that the available fringe analysis techniques are used in appropriate combinations, we can anticipate future capabilities which take interferometry into an even wider sphere of applications.

ACKNOWLEDGEMENTS

This paper is published by permission of the Director of the National Engineering Laboratory, UK Department of Trade and Industry. It is British Crown Copyright.

REFERENCES

1 Reid, G. T., Automatic fringe pattern analysis: a review, Opt. and Lasers in Engng. Vol 7, pp 37-68, 1986.

2 Proc. Int. Symp., Automatic Fringe Analysis, Loughborough, UK, November 1986.

3 Proc. Colloquium, Video Presentations of Fringe Analysis Techniques and Applications, London, UK, November 1987.

4 Robinson, D. W., Role for automatic fringe analysis in optical metrology, Proc SPIE, Vol 376, pp 20-25, 1983.

5 Robinson, D. W., Automatic fringe analysis with a computer image processing system, Appl. Opt., Vol. 22, pp 2169-2176, 1983.

6 Kreis, T. M. and Kreitlow, H. Quantitative evaluation of holographic interferograms under image processing aspects. Proc. SPIE, Vol. 210, pp 196-202, 1979.

7 Schemm, J. B. and Vest, C. M. Fringe pattern recognition and interpolation using non-linear regression analysis. Appl. Opt., Vol. 22, pp 2850-2853, 1983.

8 Yatagai, T., S Nakadate, Idesawa, M., and Saito, H. Automatic fringe analysis using digital image processing techniques. Opt. Engng, Vol. 21, pp 432-435, 1982.

9 Yatagai, T, Idesawa, M. Yamaashi, Y. and Suzuki, M. Interactive fringe analysis system: Applications to moire contourgram and interferogram. Opt. Engng, Vol. 21, pp 901-906, 1982.

10 Cline, H. E., Lorensen, W. E., and Holik, A. S. Automatic moire contouring. Appl. Opt., Vol. 23, pp 1454-1459, 1984.

11 Marshall, S. J., Rixon, R. C., Caulfield, M. M. and Mackenzie, P. M. The application of automatic fringe analysis in fracture mechanics. Opt. and Lasers in Engng, Vol. 7, pp 175-193, 1987.

12 Becker, F. and Yu, Y. Digital fringe reduction techniques applied to the measurement of three-dimensional transonic flow fields. Opt. Engng, Vol. 24, pp 429-434, 1985.

13 Reid, G. T., Rixon, R. C., and Messer, H. I., Absolute and comparative measurements of three dimensional shape by phase measuring moire topography, Opt. and Laser Technol. Vol 16, pp 315-319, 1984.

14 Macy, W. W. Two-dimensional fringe-pattern analysis. Appl. Opt., Vol. 22, pp 3898-3901, 1983.

15 Nugent, K. A. Interferogram analysis using an accurate fully automatic algorithm. Appl. Opt., Vol. 24, pp 3101-3105, 1985.

16 Womack, K. H. Interferometric phase measurement using spatial synchronous detection. Opt. Engng. Vol. 23. pp 391-395. 1984.

17 Green, R. J., Walker, J. G. and Robinson, D. W. Investigation of the Fourier-transform method of fringe pattern analysis. Opt. and Lasers in Engng, Vol. 8, pp 29-44, 1988.

18 Takeda, M. Ina, H. and Kobayashi, S. Fourier-transform method of fringe-pattern analysis for computer-based topography and interferometry. J. Opt. Soc. Am., Vol. 72, pp 156-160, 1982.

SCHNELLE UND ROBUSTE BILDANALYSE VON STREIFENMUSTERN - EIN WICHTIGER SCHRITT DER AUTOMATION VON HOLOGRAFISCHEN PRÜFPROZESSEN

A. Ettemeyer, U. Neupert, H. Rottenkolber, C. Winter,
Rottenkolber Holo-System GmbH, München

Abstract:
Es wird ein neuartiges Auswertesystem für holografische Interferogramme oder andere Streifenmuster vorgestellt. Das Programm basiert auf dem Phasenshift-Verfahren. Durch die Verwendung eines speziellen Demodulationsalgorithmus wird eine extrem hohe Auswertesicherheit erzielt. Der Einsatz der Transputertechnik ermöglicht gleichzeitig eine hohe Auswertegeschwindigkeit. Die Ergebnisse werden benutzerfreundlich aufbereitet und in Form von Pseudo-3D-Plots, Profildarstellungen, Falschfarbendarstellungen, Animationsabläufen etc. zur Verfügung gestellt.

1. Einführung

Die Auswertung holografischer Interferenzmuster und anderer sinusförmiger Streifensysteme ist seit vielen Jahren ein aktuelles Thema. Insbesondere holografische Interferogramme bereiten dabei Schwierigkeiten, da der interessierenden Phaseninformation zusätzliche Hintergrundinformationen durch Objektkonturen, Schatten, Ausleuchtungsunregelmäßigkeiten etc. überlagert sind. Durch die Einführung des Phasenshiftverfahrens wurde ein großer Fortschritt erzielt, jedoch ist eine "vollautomatische" Bildauswertung noch immer Zukunftsmusik. In diesem Beitrag wird ein neuartiges Demodulationsprinzip dargestellt, das einen Schritt weiter in diese Zukunft weist.

2. Prinzip der Hologrammauswertung

Das Prinzip des Phasenshiftverfahrens ist bereits seit mehreren Jahren bekannt, /1/,/2/ und es werden verschiedene kommerzielle Auswertesysteme angeboten.

2.1. Phasenberechnung

Die Hologrammauswertung mit dem Phasenshift-Verfahren erfordert zwei Referenzstrahlen. Die beiden Hologrammaufnahmen werden mit zwei unterschiedlichen Referenzstrahlen aufgenommen und gemeinsam rekonstruiert. Durch Verschieben der beiden Referenzstrahlen gegeneinander werden die beiden Objektbilder gegeneinander verschoben, und die Interferenzstreifen wandern über dem Objekt.
Eine CCD-Kamera registriert die Intensität an jedem Bildpunkt, (Bild 1). Sie läßt sich durch Gleichung (1) beschreiben:

$$I(x,y)=H(x,y)(1 + K(x,y)\cos(phi(x,y) + alfa)) \quad (1)$$

I(x,y)	=	lokale Intensität
H(x,y)	=	lokale Hintergrundhelligkeit
K(x,y)	=	lokaler Kontrast
phi(x,y)	=	lokaler Phasenwinkel
alfa	=	Phasenwinkel der beiden Referenzstrahlen

Durch dreimaliges definiertes Verschieben der beiden Referenzstrahlen um jeweils 90 Grad und Einlesen der jeweiligen Intensitätsverteilungen mit der CCD-Kamera erhält man 4 Gleichungen mit den drei unbekannten Größen H(x,y), K(x,y) und phi(x,y). Daraus kann die gesuchte Phasenverteilung phi(x,y) durch Lösen des Gleichungssystems ermittelt werden:

$$phi(x,y) = \mathrm{atan}\,\frac{I2 - I4}{I3 - I1} \quad (2)$$

Wendet man diesen Algorithmus auf das ganze Interferogramm an, so erhält man die Phasenverteilung an jedem Bildpunkt, bedingt durch die Unstetigkeit der atan-Funktion in 2Pi-modulierter Form, Bild 2.

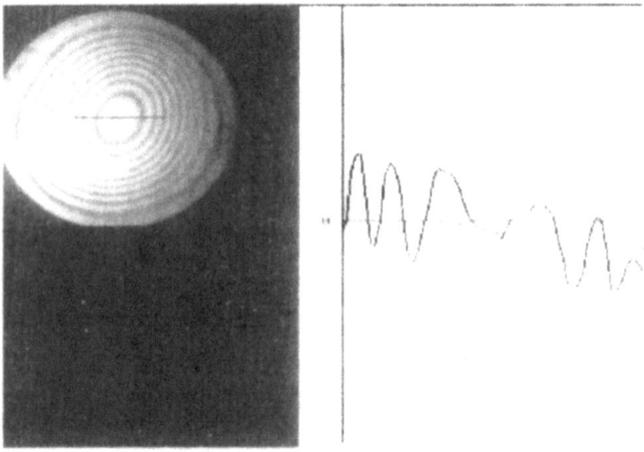

Bild 1: Intensitätsverteilung im Hologramm

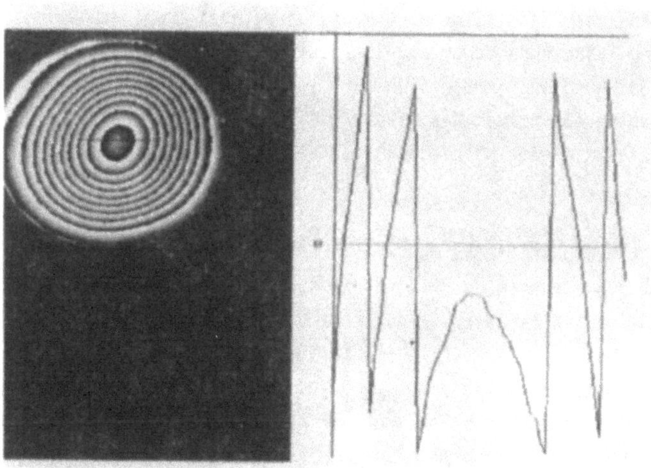

Bild 2: Phasenverteilung des Hologramms

2.2. Prinzip des neuen Demodulationsalgorithums

Bis zur 2Pi-modulierten Phasenverteilung läuft somit ein sehr einfacher Algorithmus ab. Die Schwierigkeiten beginnen bei der Demodulation der Phasenverteilung, d. h. dem Beseitigen der Sprünge im Modulo-2Pi-Bild. Der Rechner muß erkennen, wann ein Phasensprung um 360 Grad (2Pi) vorliegt. Bei optimaler Bildqualität fällt dieser Vorgang sehr leicht, das Modulo-2Pi-Bild muß nur abgescannt werden, und jeweils bei einem Phasensprung, der einen bestimmten Schwellwert überschreitet wird 2Pi addiert bzw. subtrahiert, Bild 3. Haben die

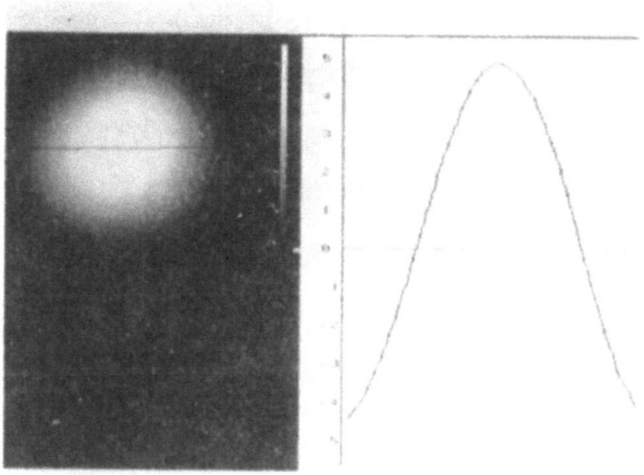

Bild 3: Demodulierte Phasenverteilung

Ausgangsbilder schlechtere Qualität (Specklerauschen, geringer Kontrast, zu große Interferenzliniendichte, etc.), dann kann es leicht passieren, daß beim Demodulieren ein Sprung "übersehen" oder zu viel gesetzt wird. Solch ein Fehler würde sich, da jede Phasenbestimmung sich auf die vorher berechneten Punkte stützt, über den gesamten Rest des Bildes hin fortsetzen. Damit besteht die Möglichkeit, daß einige wenige "schlechte Stellen" im Bild die gesamte Auswertung vereiteln.

Man kann diesem Problem begegnen, indem man eine größere Anzahl von benachbarten Punkten gleichzeitig betrachtet, doch sind dem aus Rechenzeitgründen Grenzen gesetzt. Deswegen wurde in dem hier vorzustellenden Demodulationsalgorithmus ein anderer Weg beschritten:
Ausgangspunkt der Demodulation ist wieder das Mod-2Pi-Bild (Bild 2). Das Grundprinzip der neuen Demodulationsmethode ist, daß vor dem eigentlichen Demodulationsvorgang ein Weg durch das Phasenbild gesucht wird, entlang dem Fehlberechnungen mit größter Wahrscheinlichkeit vermieden werden. Stellen mit sehr schlechter Information sollen erst am Schluß der Auswertung demoduliert werden, so daß mögliche Fehler lokal begrenzt bleiben und nicht weiter über das ganze Bild mitgezogen werden.

Dazu vergleicht der Rechner zunächst sämtliche Nachbarschafen im Mod-2Pi-Bild und sortiert sie nach dem Kriterium "Größe der Phasendifferenz zwischen benachbarten Pixeln". Es wird ein Graph von Kanten (Nachbarschaften) aufgestellt, indem jeder Punkt mit seinem rechten und oberen Nachbarn verglichen wird, Bild 4. Anschließend wird eine Tabelle angelegt, in der diese Kanten so geordnet sind, daß die Kanten mit den kleinsten Werten (Phasendifferenz zwischen den Nachbarpunkten ist möglichst klein) ganz oben stehen und mit zunehmenden Werten unten in der Tabelle angeordnet werden. Wichtig ist dabei die Vorstellung, daß die Phase im Einheitskreis angeordnet ist, daß also die Werte 0 und 360 Grad identisch sind.

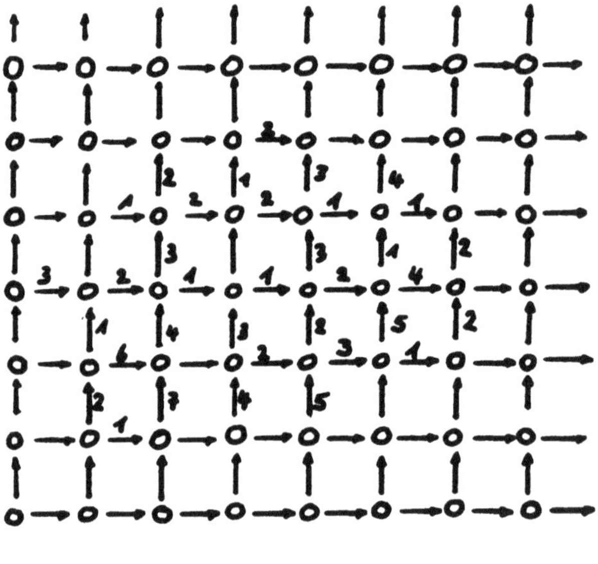

Bild 4: Untersuchung der Nachbarschaften

Mit Hilfe dieser Tabelle wird anschließend ein Auswerteweg generiert, der dem Prinzip des "minimal spannenden Baums" gehorcht, d.h. es werden zuerst alle Nachbarpunkte mit kleinen Kanten verknüpft aufsteigend bis zu den größten Kantenwerten, Bild 5. Dies bedeutet, daß die Punkte mit den größten Nachbarschaften erst am Schluß ausgewertet werden. Da gerade diese aber die Punkte mit der größten Fehlerwahrscheinlichkeit sind, bleiben Fehler lokal auf kleine Stellen begrenzt. Dies macht sich z.B. besonders in Gebieten bemerkbar, wo das Abtasttheorem verletzt ist, d.h. die Liniendichte zu groß ist, bei Rissen im Bauteil (die Interferenzlinien machen Sprünge), Schatten (Information fehlt), etc.

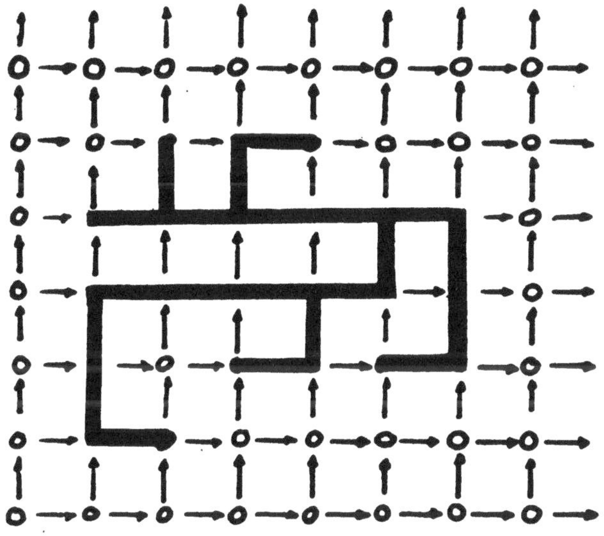

Bild 5: Demodulationsweg in Bild 4

2.3. Hardwarekonfiguration

Um derartige aufwendige Rechenoperationen durchzuführen und gleichzeitig noch eine akzeptable Auswertezeit zu erzielen, wurden auch auf der Hardwareseite einige Maßnahmen getroffen:

Das Auswerteprogramm, das alle Eigenschaften eines modernen Bildverarbeitungsprogrammes aufweist, ist auf einem konventionellen IBM/AT-Rechner oder dazu kompatiblen Computern lauffähig. Durch seinen modularen Aufbau kann es mit wenig Aufwand in die meisten Computersysteme integriert werden (z.B. HP, DEC, etc.). In unserem Hause wird derzeit ein Compaq mit 80386 Prozessor und 25 MHz Taktfrequenz eingesetzt.

Genauso kann das Programm mit vielen Bildverarbeitungskarten verwendet werden. Derzeit werden Bildverarbeitungskarten mit einer Bildspeicherkapazität von

4x512x512 Bildpunkten bei 8 bzw. 12 bit Speichertiefe verwendet. Dies ermöglicht die Option auf das Arbeiten mit Bildgrößen bis 1024x1024 Bildpunkten, falls eine entsprechende CCD-Kamera eingesetzt wird.

Um den oben beschriebenen Demodulationsalgorithmus schnell ablaufen zu lassen, kann zusätzlich eine Transputerkarte verwendet werden. Es handelt sich dabei um einen T800 32bit Transputer mit 4 MByte Speicher und einer Taktfrequenz von 20 MHz. Über seine LINKs wird eine schnelle Verbindung zum Rechner hergestellt. Der Transputer arbeitet als "Rechner im Rechner" parallel zum Hostcomputer, so daß ein deutlicher Geschwindigkeitsgewinn spürbar ist (Faktor 4 - 5 im vorliegenden Fall). Ein weiterer Vorteil der Transputertechnik ist, daß sich praktisch beliebig viele Transputer miteinander verbinden lassen und somit die Rechengeschwindigkeit weiter gesteigert werden kann.

3.Beispiel

Die Leistungsfähigkeit des Auswertealgorithmus soll im folgenden an einem Beispiel demonstriert werden.

Das Hologramm eines laufenden Kompressors (Bild 6) weist einige Probleme auf, die bei der Anwendung der holografischen Meßtechnik häufig vorkommen:

Bild 6: Doppelbelichtungs-Hologramm eines Kompressors

Das Interferenzstreifensystem zeigt eine Unstetigkeit am Übergang Zylinder - Kurbelgehäuse. Diese Stelle muß interaktiv gekennzeichnet werden, da der Rechner von einer stetigen Verformung des Bauteiles ausgeht. Der auszuwertende Bereich wird daher in zwei Teilgebiete aufgeteilt.

Im Bereich der Kühlrippen des Zylinders bestehen viele Schatten. Wie man bereits bei der Modulo-2Pi-Phasenverteilung (Bild 7) erkennen kann, liegt in diesen Bereichen keine Information über die Verformung des Teiles vor. Man kann an diesen Stellen natürlich auch keine korrekte Verformungsberechnung erwarten, sondern müßte sie eigentlich aus dem Auswertungsbereich ausschließen. Dies würde einen erheblichen interaktiven Mehraufwand bedeuten und überdies die großflächige Aussage der Holografie reduzieren.

Die Auswertung des Hologrammes mit dem vorgestellten Auswertealgorithmus führt zu dem Ergebnis in Bild 8 und Bild 9.

Bild 7: Modulo-2Pi-Phasenverteilung im Auswertebereich

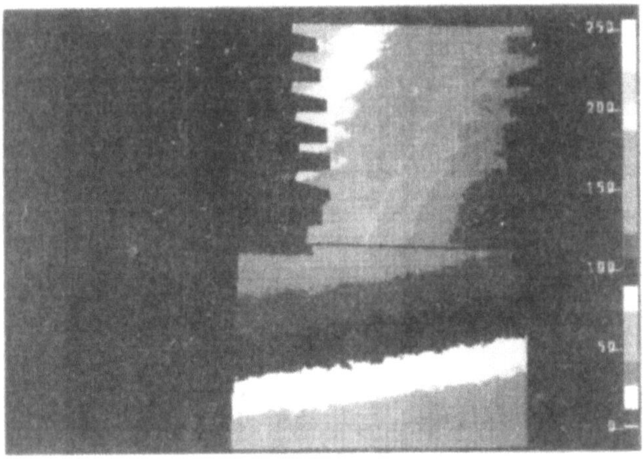

Bild 8: Ergebnis der Verformungsberechnung aus Bild 7

Bild 9: Darstellung der Verformung als Pseudo-3D-Darstellung

Der Algorithmus hat an den Stellen, an denen schon im Modulo-2Pi-Bild keine Information war, fehlerhaft gerechnet, jedoch wurden diese Fehler nicht in die übrigen Bildbereiche mitgezogen, sondern blieben örtlich begrenzt. Somit bleibt die flächenhafte Aussage des Interferogramms erhalten. Die Auswertezeit für ein derartiges Bild beträgt etwa 10 - 20 Sekunden.

Natürlich sind im Anschluß an die Auswertung der Demodulationsweg und alle

Zwischenergebnisse gespeichert. Damit kann das ganze Bild neu aufgebaut werden, um z.B. Relativbewegungen zwischen einzelnen getrennten Auswertebereichen mit anderweitig gewonnenen Meßwerten zu korrelieren, um das Vorzeichen der Auswertung umzudrehen, die absolute Interferenzordnung neu festzulegen etc. Solch ein Neuaufbau des Ergebnisses benötigt nur wenige Sekunden und bringt den Vorteil, daß keine Information durch die begrenzte Speichertiefe von 8 bit verlorengeht.

4.Zusammenfassung und Ausblick

Es wurde ein neuartiges Konzept für die Computerauswertung holografischer Interferenzmuster vorgestellt. Ein speziell entwickelter Demodulationsalgorithmus ermöglicht höchste Auswertesicherheit bei der holografischen Bildauswertung. Damit wird der Anteil der interaktiven Arbeiten bei der Hologrammauswertung weiter reduziert; so ist z.B. die Definition des Auswertebereiches weniger kritisch. Durch Risse, Schatten oder Geometrieeinflüsse hervorgerufene Sprünge im Interferenzlinienverlauf müssen nicht mehr unbedingt vor der Auswertung ausgegrenzt werden.

Damit eröffnen sich für die Zukunft neue Perspektiven: mit Hilfe spezieller Objekterkennungsprozeduren ist nun eine vollautomatische Bildauswertung denkbar.

Durch den Einsatz leistungsfähiger und preisgünstiger Transputer ist eine schnelle Hologrammauswertung möglich, die auch die Anforderungen an Serienuntersuchungen erfüllt.

6.Literatur

/1/ Dändliker,R., Thalmann,R.: Heterodyne and quasi-heterodyne interferometry, Optical Engineering, Sept/Oct 1985, vol. 24, No.5

/2/ Breuckmann,B: Rechnergestützte Auswertung holografischer Interferogramme, Holografie-Seminar, Stuttgart, 4./5.Juni 1985

HOLOGRAPHIC 3D-MEASUREMENT TECHNIQUE BASED ON A DIGITAL IMAGE PROCESSING SYSTEM

D. Vogel[1)], V. Grosser[1)], W. Osten[2)], J. Vogel[1)], R. Hoefling[1)]

1. Introduction

Although basic possibilities of 3D-displacement and shape determination by holographic interferometry had been known since the end of the 60th /1,2/, their practical utilization seemed to be unrealistic for a long time, because of the expensive data acquisition and processing and the low reliability of obtained displacement values. Rapid development of computer techniques, especially of picture processing, has given rise to quantitative analysis of holographic interferograms, too. Improvements were achieved in a two-fold regard. On the one side, fast and effective data acquisition directly from the hologram into picture processing systems and further computer processing allows for the use of the whole field object information. On the other side, computer-aided data processing together with advanced methods of phase extraction, e.g. phase shifting or heterodyne methods, have yielded a higher phase measurement accuracy and so a higher degree of reliability of displacement and deformation values. Nevertheless, complete 3D-deformation analysis of arbitraryly shaped objects has remained a problematic task and demands as sophisticated fringe analysis and processing of extracted interferometric phase data, as extensive interferometric equipment too. This work represents an approach to a full 3D analysis, comprising a conception of computer-aided fringe analysis, holographic geometry, displacement and vibration amplitude determination, and also the respective software and experimental realization.

Analysing the problem we are dealing with, it is useful to start consideration from the optical signal, which is received from the holographic interferogram. The light intensity $I(\vec{r}_o)$ from a particular object point with a position vector $\vec{r}_o$ in a pick-up of a double exposure hologram for displacement measurement can be written in the form of

$$I(\vec{r}_o) = I_o(\vec{r}_o)\ R_{sp}(\vec{r}_o)\ \{\ 1 + V(\vec{r}_o)\ \cos\ [2\pi/\lambda\ \vec{s}(\vec{r}_o,\vec{g})\vec{d}(\vec{r}_o)]\ \} \qquad (1)$$

Obviously, the displacement vector $\vec{d}(\vec{r}_o)$ looked for is covered by several properties, such as the average, i.e. single exposure, light intensity from the object $I_o(\vec{r}_o)$, the speckle noise modulation $R_{sp}(\vec{r}_o)$, the fringe visibility $V(\vec{r}_o)$ and the vector of sensitivity of the interferometer $\vec{s}(\vec{r}_o,\vec{g})$, which all are properties depending on the object position vector

---

1) The Institute of Mechanics, Academy of Sciences of the G.D.R.
P.O.B. 408, Karl-Marx-Stadt - 9010, G.D.R.
2) The Institute of Cybernetics and Information Processes, Academy of Sciences of the G.D.R.
P.O.B. 1298, Berlin - 1086, G.D.R.

$\vec{r}_o$. Therefore, the task to determine the object displacement vector $\vec{d}(\vec{r}_o)$ can be split off into three main problems :

- the extraction of the interference fringe phase $\varphi(\vec{r}_o) = 2\pi/\lambda\ \vec{s}(\vec{r}_o,\vec{g})\ \vec{d}(\vec{r}_o)$ in a fixed point grid of interest from a real hologram, picked up by a TV-camera
- the evaluation of the sensitivity vector $\vec{s}(\vec{r}_o,\vec{g})$ for the given interferometer and object geometry
- the finding out of the displacement vector $\vec{d}(\vec{r}_o)$ with the help of the predetermined $\varphi(\vec{r}_o)$ and $\vec{s}(\vec{r}_o,\vec{g})$

The solution of the whole problem, reported here, bases on a skeleton method for interference phase calculation and makes use of a special architecture processor. Furthermore, displacement measurement is realized in a four illumination point interferometer with only one direction of observation, which permits to treat interferograms without geometry distortion. The established displacement calculation algorithm includes the knowledge of the absolute fringe order number and permits to determine displacement as well as vibration amplitude values. The necessary calculation input data of the sensitivity vector can be provided by a holographic object contouring. The contouring fringe pattern is generated by a multiple illumination point displacement and results in both object shape and object position determination. The rather comprehensive approach to the displacement measurement described above possesses the advantage to be in a wide scope independent on the object surface shape and position and the possibility of their precise predetermination.

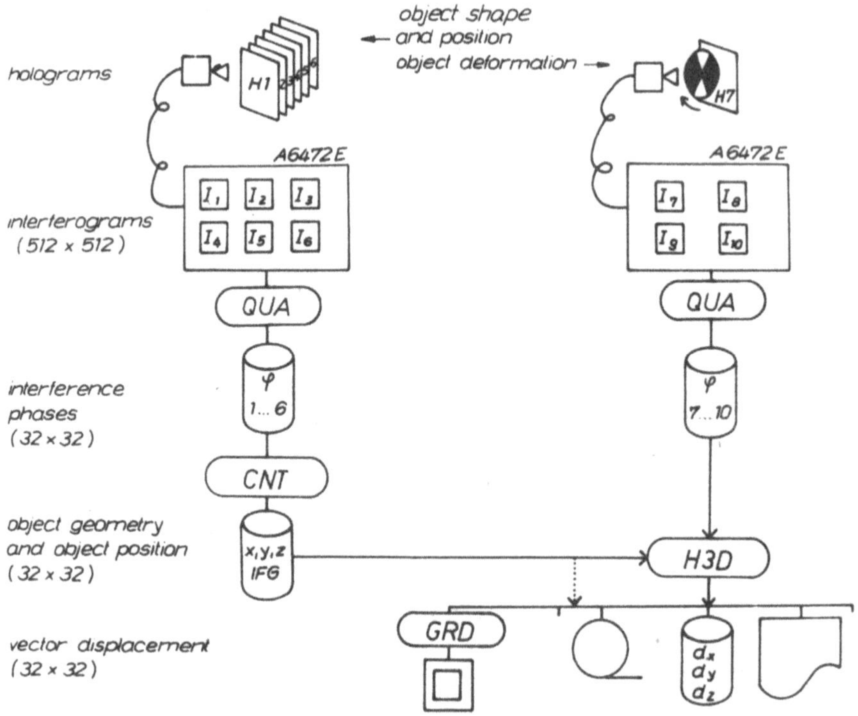

Fig. 1. 3D measurement system QUADRO

The scheme of Fig. 1 illustrates the whole procedure of object contouring and deformation analysis. The designated computer programs are accomplished on a A6472E picture processing system.
The following chapters are devoted to the three particular above considered steps of 3D measurement.

2. The evaluation of phase fields with the skeleton method

The skeleton method is based on the assumption that extreme values of the measured intensity correspond to maximum and minimum positions of the cosine-shaped intensity profile. Depending on the kind of the peak value (maximum/minimum intensity) the phase for such pixels is an even or odd multiple of π. The automatic identification of local intensity extrema and tracking of fringes is perhaps the most obvious approach to fringe pattern analysis, because that method is focused on copying the common visual evaluation process. Different techniques for tracing fringe extrema in two dimensional implementations are known /3-7/. They are all based on several pattern-segmentation methods that involve fast Fourier transforms, adaptive and floating thresholding, and either gradient operators or the piecewise approximation of elementary functions. Some of them fail on interferograms that have sinusoidal intensity modulation, or are inefficient if the shape and the frequency of the fringes varies within the pattern. We use an algorithm for the fast extraction of line structures from interferograms that is based on the detection of valleys, slopes and ridges in the sinusoidal intensity relief by local grey value differences with consideration of characteristic neighbourhood relations /8/. A special feature of that algorithm is its ability for parallel processing on a special purpose processor modelling the SIMD principle. The segmentation procedure produces an image with only four different labels: ridge point, slope point and unrecognized. After that, the ridges and valleys are improved by region growing and binary filtration in order to obtain continuous regions with smooth contours and these regions are thinned to a fringe skeleton /9/. Figure 2 illustrates this process.

The method shows some advantages and disadvantages in comparision with other evaluation techniques as for instance phase sampling /10/. The software expense for automatic fringe tracking is very high because the derivation of skeletons in a suitable time takes a lot of sophisticated image processing routines. During the evaluations of such a skeleton it is difficult to distinguish a positive slope from a negative one and to consider points, where the alteration in phase changes its sign. Consequently sign ambiguities can arise if no a-priori knowledge about the displacement direction is available. Because it is impossible to decide automatically in the skeleton if the fringe number is increasing or decreasing the fringe numbering is done interactively. Over it interpolation is necessary, because the phase is determined on the skeleton lines only.

Depending on the complexity of an interferogram, a fringe number can be given to the skeleton lines automatically or interactively. In each case, a straight testing line is selected crossing as much skeleton lines as possible. Stepping along that line the appropriate fringe order is assigned to all pixels of the skeleton line just crossed using a line tracking routine. Absolute interference order assignment, of course, necessitates the knowledge of the phase at least in one pixel and the consideration of alterations of the fringe order monotony.

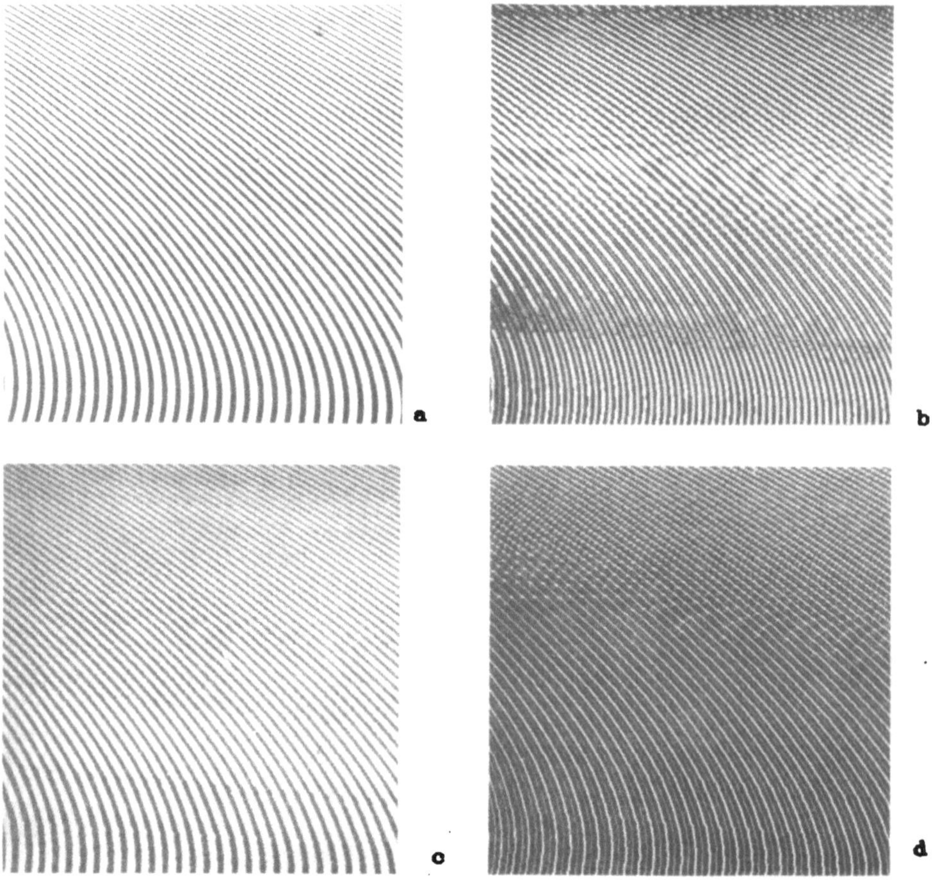

Fig. 2. Processing steps for the segmentation of an interferogram: a) interferogram; b) recognized valleys and ridges (ridges = white, valley = grey); c) improved line structures of ridges and valleys; d) fringe skeleton

In a number of applications a phase field is needed at a given regular mesh. Therefore the phase must be interpolated between adjacent skeleton lines. A sophisticated two-dimensional bilinear interpolation similar to the finite element algorithm has been choosen for this purpose giving better results and running much more faster than one-dimensional cubic spline fitting. The result is a phase field and a displacement field, respectively, plotted as pseudo-three-dimensional figure with 32x32 points .
The whole processing time takes about 5 min including interactions begin-

ning from the interferogram until the phase field.

3. The determination of object shape and position

Successful 3D-displacement or deformation analysis requires information about the position of the investigated object area within the interferometer, i.e. relatively to the illumination and observation points. Commonly, difficulties occur, if the object surface geometry cannot be given in an analytical way. In this case surface shape data has to be transfered pointwise after its determination by other means. Additional, for arbitraryly shaped objects, uncertainty will remain with respect to its position as a rigid body in the interferometer. Therefore, holographic contouring was integrated into our 3D-conception to overcome the described problems.

An object contouring for input data generation of displacement measurements needs the ability to profile relatively deep objects, e.g. objects with a depth comparable to their lateral dimensions. Furthermore it has to allow for the profiling of objects with some hundreds of millimeters lateral extension and with a measurement accuracy of about 1 mm at the same time. And at least a large dynamic region is desirably. To fulfil the mentioned conditions, contouring is carried out by displacement of object illumination points in a double exposure arrangement. Several illumination points are moved in different directions in order to obtain distinguished contouring fringe pattern. In comparison with other contouring techniques this method possesses the following advantages :

- the fringe pattern is located on the object and a good fringe visibility is achievable also for large illumination point displacements
- the fringe distance can be altered in a wide range and so the resolution of the method too
- the method works completely contactless, without immersion media
- it is possible to determine not only the object shape, but also the coordinates of object surface points relatively to the interferometer (in our case to the illumination points)

The interference order number N of the contouring fringes can easily derived from path length differences in the interferometer

$$\lambda\, N = - \frac{1}{L(\vec{s},\vec{x})} \left(\vec{s} - \vec{x} \right) + \text{const.} \tag{2}$$

with $\vec{s}$, $\vec{x}$ as the position vectors of the illumination and object points, respectively, and $L(\vec{s},\vec{x})$ the distance between object and illumination points. Because of the uncertainess of the absolute fringe order number, only relative fringe orders can be considered and so fringe differences between peripheric object points "k" and a central object point have to be used. Consequently, taking into account (2) we get a set of nonlinear equations to solve for the object position vectors $\vec{x}_k$ and $\vec{x}_o$

$$\lambda\, \Delta N^{m,l}_{k,o} = \left[\frac{1}{L^l_k} (\vec{x}_k - \vec{s}^{\,l}) - \frac{1}{L^l_o} (\vec{x}_o - \vec{s}^{\,l}) \right] \vec{u}^{\,m,l} \tag{3}$$

where m and l indicate, that different displacement directions "m" of illumination points and different illumination points "l" for contouring pattern creation have been included.
Noting that K,L,M are the quantities of peripheric object points, different displacement values and different illumination points used, we find equ.(3) solvable, if the condition

$$K > \frac{3}{ML - 3} \tag{4}$$

is fulfiled.
Kohler /11/ has proved the numerical solution of a similar, but simplier set of type (3) for holographic contouring with known absolute fringe order to be reliable. Analogous to Kohler we have used the Newton's method for numerical solution of the nonlinear set of equations, but included an overestimation of the set to improve accuracy. Taking into account accuracy and calculation time consumed, conditions like M=2, L=3 and N=4...8 have been found well suited.
The implemented software permits to scan an object point grid of IxI points (I=8,16,32). Point groups for one solution of (3) are selected considering calculation accuracy. Nondefined points of bad fringe quality are picked out automatically. The output data for the whole point grid of IxI can be used separately or serve as input data for a further object deformation analysis. Finally, the possibility of error simulation corresponding to fringe number, illumination point displacement and position data is provided for.

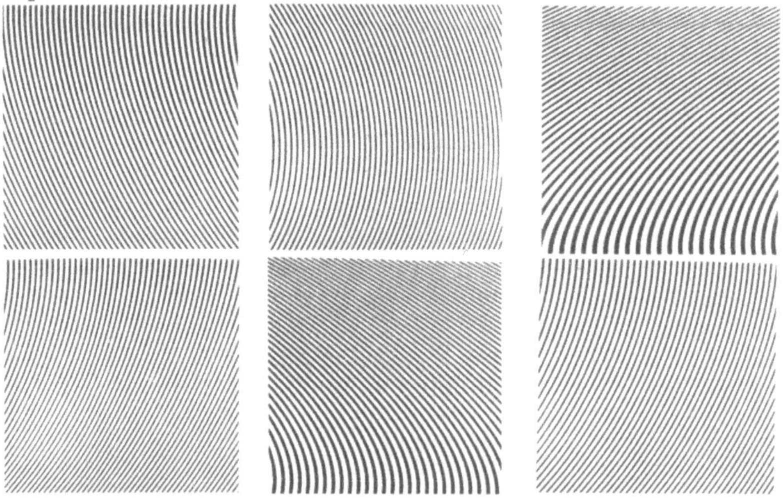

Fig. 3. Holographic contouring fringes on a cylinder
Displacement of 3 illumination points in 2 perpendicular directions

The performance of the geometry evaluation is demonstrated by the Figures 3 and 4. Simulated contouring interferograms have been calculated for a cylinder with a radius of R = 8.0 cm and three different illumination points, which were moved along two independent directions, with $u^{m,l}$ = 200....400 µm (see Fig. 3). The obtained geometry data from the six interferograms after fringe phase extraction and solution of the set of equations (3) is given in a pseudo-three dimensional figure (Fig. 4) for x-, y- and z-coordinates, respectively. Because geometrical imaging distortions were neglected, x- and y-coordinates form planes on the regular point grid. The cylinder form is seen from the z-component within a window of about 10cm x 10cm. The evaluation error, which occurs above all in the z-coordinate can be further suppressed by using more favourable contouring pattern or providing higher phase extraction accuracy, e.g. by the help of phase shifting or other methods.

4. Displacement determination

Displacement measurements are carried out in the same interferometer of at most 4 illumination and 1 observation directions, which is used for object contouring. Absolute fringe order numbers are taken as known, and so the usual linear set of equations for holographic displacement evaluation is to be solved. The slight overestimation of the commonly solved set improves calculation accuracy.

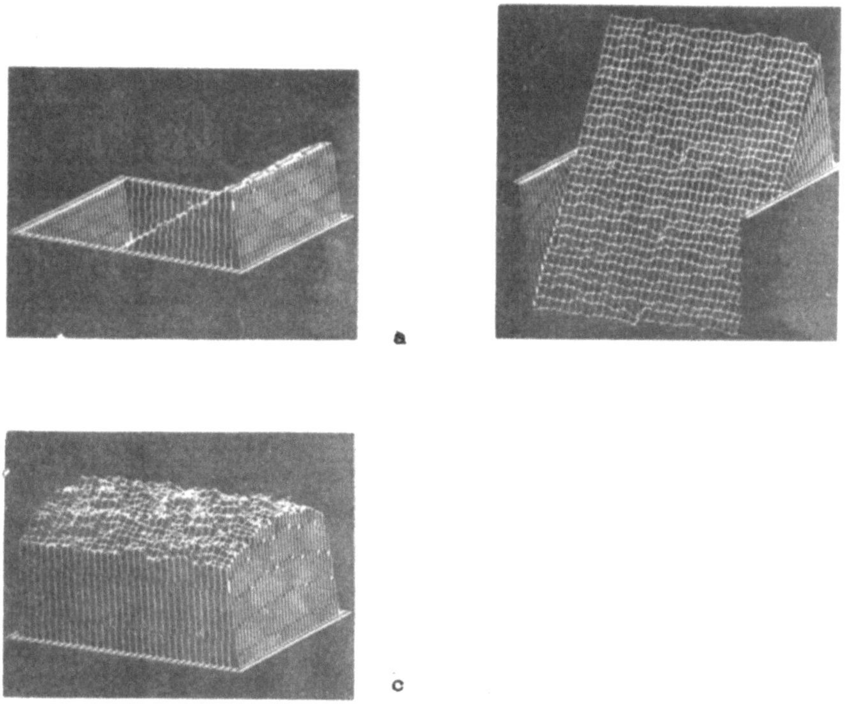

Fig. 4. Object surface coordinates determined by holographic contouring
a,b,c - x-,y- and z-coordinates, respectively

The integrated software can be used for static loading of specimens and also for vibration analysis with the help of the time-average method. For the latter purpose the set of equations to be solved is modified.

Fig. 5 showes the applied holographic experimental arrangement. A He-Ne or an Ar^{+} laser serves as light sources. Analogous to Thalmann /12/ the different directions of illumination are realized by four mirrors and a sectioning diaphragm in front of the hologram plate. The investigated objects are placed in the middle of the holographic table. In the present arrangement it is possible to investigate objects up to 300 mm x 300 mm. Measurement errors are composed by different factors, which errors of object shape and position determination, uncertainess in illumination and observation point location and calculation errors during fringe phase extraction and further data processing are among. To prove the accuracy of the image processing and vector field calculation we have simulated a

Fig. 5. Experimental arrangement

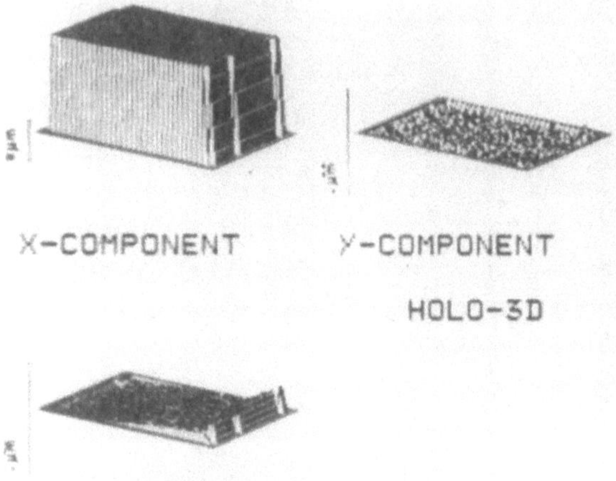

Fig. 6. Evaluation of a plate displacement from simulated holographic fringes

horizontal displacement of 20 μm for an even plate. The evaluation results in displacements of d_x = 20.08 +/- 0.03 μm, d_y = -0.09 +/- 0.04 μm and d_z = 0.03 +/- 0.09 μm (see Fig. 5). It is seen in the figure, that the deviation from the preset displacement is increasing at the boundaries of the plane, where fringe phase extraction is more inaccurate. But generally we have found a good correspondence between the real and the calculated displacement values.

5. Conclusion

A holographic 3D measurement system for displacement and vibration analysis as well as object contouring has been established. Its major advantages the system exhibits with regard to arbitraryly shaped objects of investigation, where object contouring and further displacement analysis are accomplished in the same interferometer and partly with the same software for fringe analysis. Several parts of the experimental arrangement and of the computer-aided evaluation have been tested.

6. References

/1/ Sollid, J.E.: Holographic interferometry applied to measurements of small static displacements of diffusely reflecting surfaces
Appl. Opt. 8(1969) 1587

/2/ Haines K.A.; Hildebrand B.P.: Multiple-wavelength and multiple-source holography applied to contour generation
JOSA 57(1967) 155-162

/3/ Becker, F.; Yung. H.: Digital fringe reduction technique applied to the measurement of three-dimensional transonic flow fields.
Opt. Eng. 24(1985) 429-434

/4/ Nakadate, S.; Magome, N.; Honda, T.; Tsujiuchi, J.: Hybrid holographic interferometer for measuring threedimensional deformations.
Opt. Eng. 20(1981) 246-252

/5/ Mastin, G.A.; Ghiglia, D.C.: Digital extraction of interference fringe contours.
Appl. Opt. 24(1985) 1727-1728

/6/ Cline, H.E.; Holik, A.S.; Lorensen, W.E.: Computer aided surface reconstruction of interference contours.
Appl. Opt. 21(1982) 4481-4488

/7/ Schemm, J.B.; Vest. C.M.: Fringe pattern recognition and interpolation using nonlinear regression analysis. Appl. Opt. 22(1983) 18, 2850

/8/ Eichhorn, N.; Osten, W.: An algorithm for the fast derivation of line structures from interferograms.
J. Mod. Opt. (in press)

/9/ Osten, W.; Höfling, R.; Saedler, J.: Two computer aided methods for data reduction from interferograms.
Proc. SPIE 863(1987) 105-113

/10/Dändliker, R.; Thalmann, R.: Heterodyne and quasi-heterodyne holographic interferometry.
Opt. Eng. 24(1985) 824-831

/11/Kohler H.: Hologramminterferometrische Triangulation: I.Ein Meßverfahren für Entfernungen und Oberflächenkonturen unter Verwendung von Ordnungen
Optik 60(1981) 61-72

/12/Thalmann R.; Dändliker R.: Strain measurement by heterodyne holographic interferometry
Appl. Opt. 26(1987) 1964-1971

Submitted Papers

Fringe Detection Using Mean and n-Rank Filters

K. Andresen, P. Feng and W. Holst*

1 Introduction

Evaluation of moire images has improved substantial since digital image processing systems became available to a reasonable price. In the main, three different methods are used to derive the information from a moire image. The oldest one consists in looking for the centre–line of the dark and white fringes with special algorithms [1] or by means of thresholding, erosion and dilatation [2] in the binary image. The corresponding results, however, were not always satisfying because much interactive input was required or branching structures were calculated and had to be postprocessed with heuristic smoothing routines.

A second group started from a global Fourier–transformation of the intensity distribution yielding the frequency function [3], [4]. After passband filtering and frequency shifting its inverse gives a complex space function from which the phase function can be evaluated in each point of the image. These methods require an image containing a reasonable number of fringes, because the spectrum of the background intensity and that of the fringes must be separated sufficiently , else the phase information becomes incorrect. A slightly different approach is submitted by bandpass and hilbert filtering in the space domain [5] yielding also the above mentioned complex space function. This method is supposed to be more local but it cannot process a certain area around the borders depending on the number of filter constants. Furtheron it needs the same presuppositions as the Fourier–method.

A third kind of methods [6],[7] uses three or more moire images of the same deformation state generated by moving the reference grating in steps of e.g one third of its pitch. From the grey values in corresponding points of the images a simple algorithms delivers the local displacement of the reference grating against the deformed grating. This method works even in the case of very broad fringes but it needs a precise shifting apparatus and two negatives containing the grating lines of the undeformed and the deformed state.

If a moire image is developed by double exposure , then only the first two methods can be taken into account. In this paper a new method looking for dark and white centre–lines within the grey image is presented. First it removes large errors by median filtering. Then it applies a n–rank and a mean filter alternatly until peak values consisting of one pixel are formed. These are assumed to be centre–line of the moire fringes. The method is easy to implement on a personal computer and it can be parallized, if an array processor board is present, yielding very short response times. Furtheron possible artefacts are removed with line following algorithms.

2 Theory

The structure of a moire image containing different fringes in irregular distances can be very complex. Therefore it is often difficult to evaluate the fringes by digital image processing. Besides local errors there are variations in the illumination and there may be areas with not fully developed fringes. The latter ones are hardly derivable with Fourier–Methods but to a certain extent by topologic methods. In the following such a procedure consisting of a median, a mean and a n–rank filter will be investigated. It processes the intensity distribution of each scan line or of an averaged number of neighbouring scan lines.

[1]Mechanik–Zentrum, Technische Universitaet,
D3300 Braunschweig

2.1 Median filter

A median filter with an odd number of elements $N = 2k + 1$ sorts neighbouring elements x_{i+j} $(j = -k, \ldots, +k)$ in ascending order and takes the medium value x_m to be the filter response y_i. Applying this procedure large initial errors are removed.

2.2 Mean filter

A mean filter of the form

$$y_i = \frac{1}{N} \sum_{i=1}^{N} x_i$$

eliminates noisy parts of the signal very effective and yields a low pass filtering of the data. It removes high frequencies, e.g. from the generating grating lines. Compared with a general low pass filter the computing time is substantially shorter, because mainly additions have to be performed.

2.3 n–rank filter

A n–rank filter is sorting neighbouring elements in ascending order like the median filter, but instead of the medium value it takes an arbitrary n–th value $(1 \leq n \leq N)$ of the vector. Fig. 1 shows the variation of a discrete sinusoidal moire fringe when the n–rank filter having a length smaller than half the period of the local fringe is applied several times to it. Obviously the minima become more and more flattend while the maxima are sharpened.

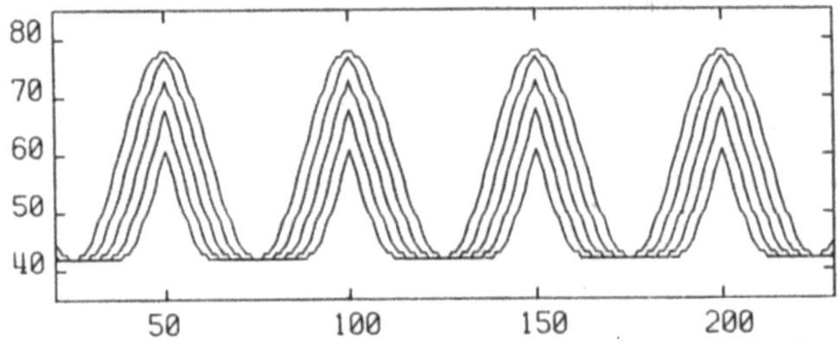

Figure 1: Repeated n-rank filtering of the intensity function in a scan line

The basic idea of the proposed method is to apply this procedure repeatedly until one picture element (pixel) forms the top of the intensity function. This point is assumed to represent the centre–line of the fringe. The method works very stable if the roughness produced by n–rank filtering is smoothed in turn by a mean filter.

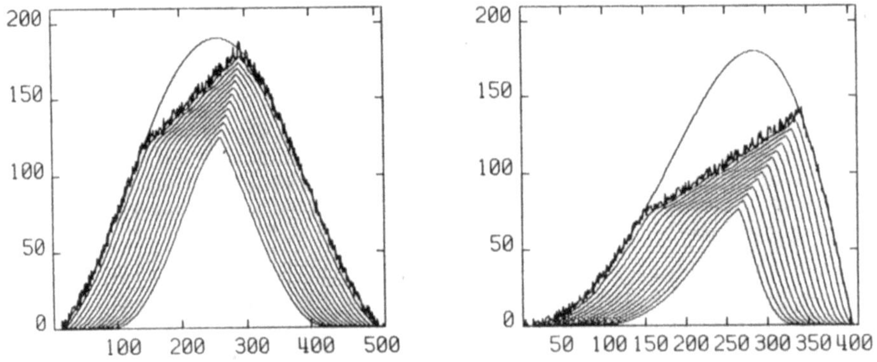

Figure 2: Repeated n-rank filtering of a disturbed function a) sin x–Funktion b) sin x^2–Funktion

2.4 Influence of failures

The influence of failures in the intensity distribution is simulated by the upper half of a symmetrical $\sin x$–signal and a unsymmetrical $\sin x^2$–signal, which are largely flattened on their front part. Fig. 2a shows that the position of the maximum of the $\sin x$–function is determined very accurate even in the case of large flattening. In Fig. 2b it is evident that the coordinates of the maximum, 2, derived by the proposed method are nearer to the real maximum, 1, than e.g. the mean of a section through the curve, 3, or the disturbed maximum, 4, itself.

Varying illumination, a main problem in getting a binary image, does not effect the calculation of the extremal values of the moire fringes, Fig. 3. Different periods of the fringes in a considered line require different length of the filters, because a large filter may extinguish a small period in the first step (cf. Fig. 4). Thus the procedure starts with a small filter, determines the extreme values of small periods, excludes the corresponding parts from further processing and magnifies the filterlength, if necessary, in several steps. This method improves the rate of convergence to a single peak value in the filtered intensity distribution.

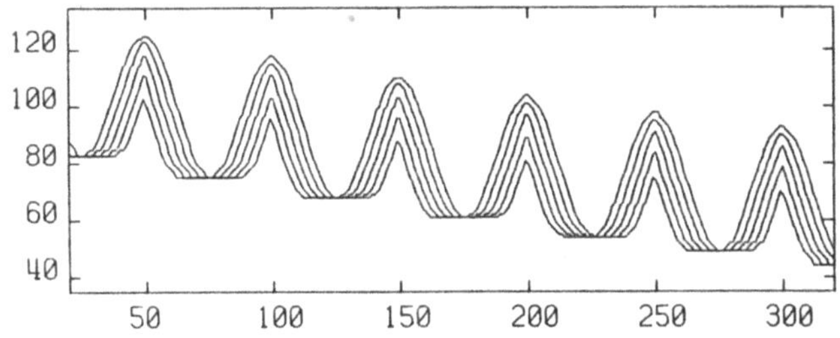

Figure 3: Repeated n-rank filtering of varying illumination (n=1, N=5)

Figure 4: Repeated n-rank filtering on different periods of the fringes (n=1, N=5)

3 Application

As an example a reflection moire pattern is chosen which was derived from a clamped circular plate loaded by constant pressure on the surface. Fig. 5 shows the moire image and the peak values derived from horizontal sections through the intensity distribution. Obviously the method breaks down in those parts where sliding sections through the fringes appear. In consequence the algorithm was applied to vertical sections through the intensity distribution, yielding significant values in those parts where horizontal sections deliver no useful points.

In Fig. 6 the two images with skelettoning points are superimposed proving that apart from minor artefacts the skeletton lines are closed until reaching the border. In practice a line following procedure takes all line segments with slopes of $90° \pm 45°$ from Fig. 5 and from a corresponding image with respect to vertical sections all segments with slopes of $0° \pm 45°$. The areas within the fully

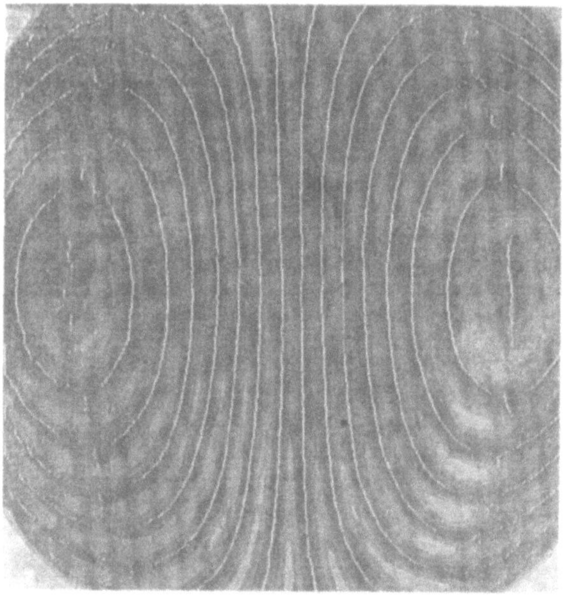

Figure 5: Moire image containing skelettoning points from horisontal sections

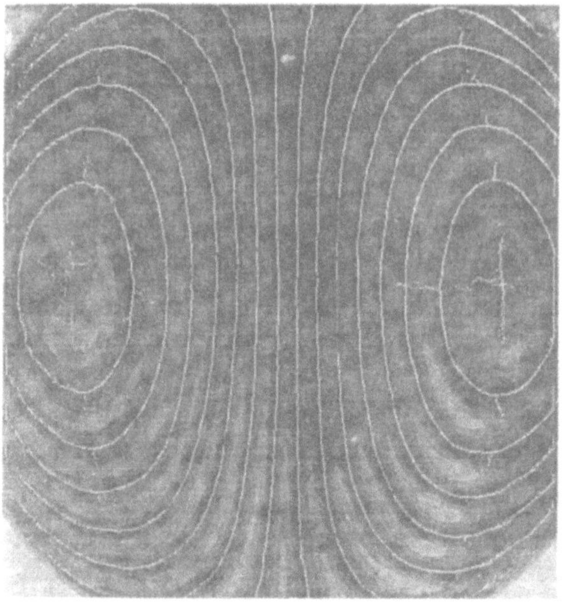

Figure 6: Moire image containing points from horisontal and vertical sections

closed fringes show artefacts which have to be removed interactively. Here the method does not work correctly. On the other hand it is not quite clear from the image wether a full fringe is generated in that area or only a part of a new fringe. The order of the fringes has to be submitted by additional information from the experimental set up.

4 Conclusion

The proposed filter method for calculating moire fringes can be used advantageously when a moire image generated by double exposure is given and, moreover, if fringes give rise to sliding sections in a scan line. Applying the procedure to vertical and horizontal sections through the intensity distribution yields closed fringes even in those parts of the image where sliding sections occur.Here comparable one-dimensional methods like Fourier–or Hilbert–filtering break down.

Generally phase shift procedures or Fourier–filtering are to prefer because they submit the order of the fringes and thus permit a fully automatic calculation of the physical information within the fringes.

References

[1] Mueller,R.K. and L.R.Saackel: Complete Automatic Analysis of Photoelastic Fringes. Exp. Mech. 19 (1979) 245-251

[2] Amiri,H. and R.Ritter: Ein digitales Bildverarbeitungssystem zur praktischen Spannungsanalyse. VDI-Berichte 399 (1981), 5–8

[3] Tekeda, M., H.Ina and S.Kobayashy: Fourier Transform Method of Fringe–Pattern Analysis for Computer–Based Topography and Interferometry. J.Opt.Soc.Am. 72 (1982),156–160.

[4] Kreis, T.: Digital Holographic Interference–Phase Measurement Using the Fourier–Transform Method. J.Opt.Soc.Am. A3 (1986), 847–855.

[5] C.A.Sciammarella a. M.A. Ahmadshahi: Detection of Fringe Pattern Information Using a Computer Based Method. Proc. VIII Int. Conf. Exp. Stress Anal., Mart.Nijhoff Publ., Amsterdam 1986, 359-368.

[6] K.Andresen: Das Phasenschiftverfahren zur Moire-Bildauswertung. Optik 72 (1986), 115-119.

[7] Andresen,K.: Displacement and Strain Calculation by the Phase Shift Method. Appl. Optics 26 (1987), 2747–51

HOLOGRAPHICALLY INVESTIGATED PROPERTIES OF BIOLOGICAL OBJECTS

O.V.Angelsky and P.P.Maksimyak[1)]

To study biological objects such as unicellular algae, blood cells etc., light scattering methods are widely used [1,2] . Many of them are based on studying the changes in coherent properties of optical radiation. Among them are Doppler spectroscopy, the method of self-excited oscillations [2] etc. Such methods cannot however be used to study slow processes in the media with correlation times in excess of several seconds. Thus there is a need in developing new approaches to the problem of optical characterization of disperse media [3].

The present paper demonstrates the possibility of determining the size distribution function of light scattering particles and evaluating their concentrations by measuring the transverse coherence function of the scattered radiation in the particle image plane, or by holographic evaluation of Doppler broadening of the scattered radiation spectrum.

Interference method

The transverse coherence function $\Gamma(\vec{\rho})$ of scattered radiation in the particle image plane carries information on the correlation function $\Psi_2(\vec{\rho})$ of the particle system image. One can write a relation

$$\Gamma(\vec{\rho}) = \Psi_2(\vec{\rho}) + C, \tag{1}$$

where C is the coherent background due to unscattered radiation, $\vec{\rho}$ is the two-dimensional vector in the plane normal to beam propagation.

A normalized function $\psi(\vec{\rho}) = \frac{\Psi_2(\vec{\rho})}{\Psi_2(0)}$ is the convolution of the transverse correlation function of single particle image with the particle size distribution function. An integral equation for $\psi(\vec{\rho})$ for a case of spherically shaped particles has the form

$$\psi(\vec{\rho}) = \int_0^{R_{max}} \psi_0(\vec{\rho}, R) f(R)\, dR \tag{2}$$

where

$$\psi_0(\vec{\rho}, R) = \frac{2}{\pi R^2} \int_{\rho/2}^{R} \sqrt{R^2 - x^2}\, dx = \tag{3}$$

$$= \frac{2}{\pi R^2} \left[\frac{\pi}{2} R - \frac{\rho}{2} \sqrt{R^2 - \frac{\rho^2}{4}} - R^2 \arcsin \frac{\rho}{2R} \right]$$

Here $f(R)$ is the particle radius distribution function.

Thus by using eq.(1) and solving eq.(2) one can obtain the particle size distribution function from the measured particle image coherence

1) Chernovtsy State University, 2 Kotsyubinsky Str., 274012 Chernovtsy, USSR.

function. To solve eq.(2), the regularization method was used involving minimization of the functional, which takes into account the precision of assignment of the measured quantity and the kernel of the integral equation [4]. The proposed approach enables one to evaluate the scattering particle concentration and find the difference in refraction indices between the scattering particles and the medium using the relations

$$C = \left(\frac{1-\Gamma_\infty}{2-\Gamma_\infty}\right)\frac{1}{\pi \bar{R}^2 d} \quad (4)$$

$$\Delta n = 4 \arcsin \frac{\lambda}{\rho} \quad (5)$$

where ρ is the $\Gamma(\vec{\rho})$ function halfwidth, Γ_∞ is the value of $\Gamma(\vec{\rho})$ for $\rho > R_{max}$; $\bar{R}$ is the average particle size, and d is the geometrical thickness of the medium.

The experimental studies were performed using an arrangement shown in Fig.1.

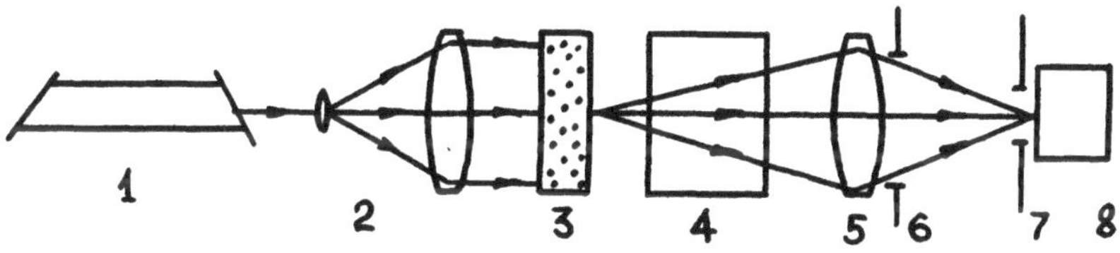

Fig.1. 1-laser, 2-collimator, 3-specimen, 4-Mach-Zehnder interferometer, 5-objective, 6-aperture diaphragm, 7-field diaphragm, 8-photodetector.

The transverse coherence function was obtained by measuring the contrast of the interference pattern for different relative displacements of the beams. Measurements were carried out on lycopodium spore suspension and unicellular blue-green Microcystis aeroginosa algae. The results are in good agreement with those of other, more labour-consuming, microscopic measurements. The disagreement is less than 15%.

Holographic method

The idea of the holographic method is based on forming the selected spatial component of the radiation scattered by a non-steady medium by superposition of signals of different frequency. The Doppler shift for each of the signals is determined by the mobility of a particle which in turn depends on its size. Moving interference structures are thus formed in the hologram plane resulting in erasure of information on the particles. Varying the exposure time of the hologram one can obtain information on particle subsets with different mobilities. Knowing the rules of the information erasure in the process of holographic recording of moving interference structures, one can obtain estimates of the fractions of particles with different mobilities [3,5] . To carry out a correct holographic experiment, the scattering angle must be chosen so that the intensities of partial signals scattered from different particles be close to each other.

Our experimental results are in good agreement with those of independent measurements by other methods. The efficiency of the holographic method is demonstrated by the measurements of Microcystis aeroginosa cell division (see Fig.2).

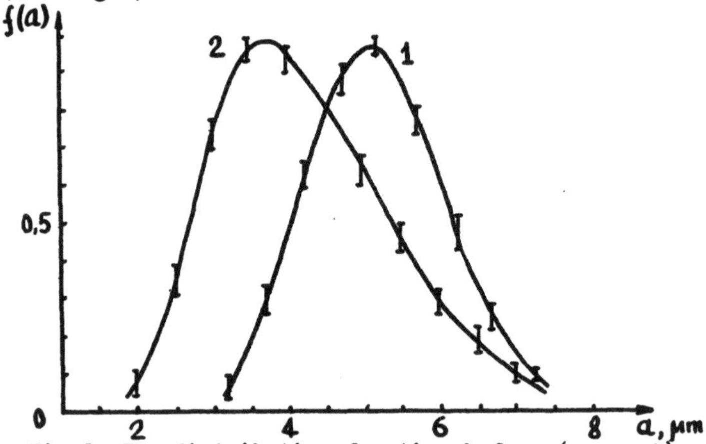

Fig.2. The distribution function before (curve 1) and after (curve 2) Microcystis aeroginosa cell division.

[1] Shifrin, K. and E.Chayanov: Determination of particle spectrum from scattering indicatrix. Izv.Akad.Nauk SSSR, 2 (1966) 2, 149-163.

[2] Royer, H.: Holographic velocimetry of submicron particles. Opt.Commun. 20 (1977) 1, 73-75.

[3] Angelsky, O. and P.Maksimyak: Informativeness of holographic method in studying Brownian movement of scattering particles. Optika i Spektroskopiya 3 (1985) 623-628.

[4] Tikhonov, A. and V.Arsenin: Methods for Solving Ill-Conditioned Problems. Nauka, Moscow 1986.

[5] Sirenko, A., O.Angelsky, P.Maksimyak et al.: Movement of microphytic algae in water. Dokl.Akad.Nauk Ukr.SSR, 5 (1984) 68-69.

OPTICAL CORRELATION SYSTEMS FOR STUDYING WEAK SURFACE ROUGHNESS

O.V.Angelsky, P.P.Maksimyak and T.O.Perun[1)]

Optical systems for studying weak surface roughness are based on the relationship between statistical structure parameters of a sample and corresponding correlation parameters of the radiation reflected by the surface. One of the above systems is realized in the method of speckle optics in which the relationship between the surface irregularity phase dispersion $\sigma^2_{\varphi_0}$ and the object field intensity fluctuations [1,2] . The realization of the above method requires measurements of local field characteristics and their subsequent computer processing. A scanning system and computer data processing in the electronic channel are time consuming. It seems therefore reasonable to design a system in which statistical processing of the results would be performed within the optical channel.

The present paper suggests some ideas for realization of such systems based on the measurements of transverse coherence function and amplitude and phase dispersion.

In the discussion that follows, a model of the arbitrary phase screen for infinitely extended objects [3] is used. We consider a coaxial interference between the object and the reference waves at the interferometer exit in the XY plane orthogonal to the beam propagation

$$J_p(x,y) = A_0^2 + A^2(x,y) + 2A_0 A(x,y)\cos\varphi(x,y) \qquad (1)$$

where $J_p(x,y)$ is the resulting field intensity at (x,y) ; $A(x,y)$ is the object wave amplitude, A_0 is the reference wave amplitude, and $\varphi(x,y)$ is the phase difference between the object and the reference waves.

The minimum intensity of the resulting field will be observed when the average phase of the object wave is opposite to the phase of the reference wave, and the average amplitude of the object wave is equal to the amplitude of the reference wave,

$$\varphi(x,y) = \pi + \tilde{\varphi}(x,y) \qquad (2)$$

$$\langle A(x,y)\rangle = A_0 \qquad (3)$$

where $\tilde{\varphi}(x,y)$ is the fluctuation of the object field phase about the average value $\bar{\varphi} = \pi$. Assuming the fluctuations of the object wave phase to be small ($\tilde{\varphi} < 10^\circ$) and averaging in eq.(1) over the beam cross section, one gets

$$\frac{\langle J_p(x,y)\rangle}{J_0} = \frac{\langle A^2(x,y)\rangle - \bar{A}^2(x,y)}{\bar{A}^2(x,y)} + \langle \frac{\tilde{A}(x,y)}{\bar{A}(x,y)} \tilde{\varphi}^2(x,y)\rangle + \langle \tilde{\varphi}^2(x,y)\rangle \qquad (4)$$

1) Chernovtsy State University, 2 Kotsyubinsky Str., 274012 Chernovtsy, USSR.

where $\tilde{A}(x,y)$ are the fluctuations of the object field amplitude. It follows from eq.(4) that direct measurements of the field phase dispersion which is equal to the phase dispersion of surface irregularities are possible for the case where the field amplitude fluctuations are absent in the region of the boundary field,

$$\frac{\langle J_p(x,y)\rangle}{J_0} = \langle(\varphi-\bar{\varphi})^2\rangle = \sigma_\varphi^2 = \sigma_{\varphi_0}^2 \qquad (5)$$

In the same coaxial interference arrangement, weak surface roughness studied can be made by measuring the field amplitude dispersion. For this one can make use of the well known equality which is valid in the far field[3] ,

$$\sigma_A^2 = \sigma_\varphi^2 = \frac{1}{2}\sigma_{\varphi_0}^2 \qquad (6)$$

where σ_A^2 is the field amplitude dispersion.

The field amplitude dispersion can be measured as follows. The resulting field intensity for coaxial mixing of light beams will be minimal if conditions (2) and (3) are met, and the field amplitude dispersion is then defined by

$$\sigma_A^2 = \frac{\langle A^2(x,y)\rangle - \langle A(x,y)\rangle^2}{\langle A(x,y)\rangle^2} \qquad (7)$$

where $\langle A^2(x,y)\rangle = J_{0б}$ is the scattered intensity averaged over the sample surface area. Direct measurement of $\langle A(x,y)\rangle^2$ is not possible. However, when the condition (3) is fulfilled, $\langle A(x,y)\rangle^2 = A_0^2 = J_0$, i.e. is equal to the wave intensity J_0 .

We thus conclude that direct interference measurement of the field amplitude dispersion is quite possible.

The method based on the measurement of the transverse coherence function $\Gamma_\perp(\rho)$ employs the relation[3]

$$\Gamma_\perp(\rho) = \exp\left\{\sigma_{\varphi_0}^2\left[K(\rho)-1\right]\right\}, \qquad (8)$$

where $K(\rho)$ is the correlation coefficient of the sample phase. It follows from eq.(8) that by measuring $\Gamma_\perp(\rho)$ for $K(\rho)=0$, one can obtain the $\sigma_{\varphi_0}^2$ value of the sample.

Experimental studies were made on plane-parallel germanium single crystals with surface roughness parameters as given in Table 1.

Parameters \ No.	1	2	3	4
R_q (μm)	0.015	0.024	0.047	0.060
$\sigma^2_{\varphi h}$	0.053	0.115	0.422	0.720
$\sigma^2_{\varphi A}$	0.047	0.125	0.400	0.620
$\sigma^2_{\varphi \varphi}$	0.049	0.102	0.386	0.605
$\sigma^2_{\varphi K}$	0.052	0.120	0.390	0.670

The measurements of amplitude and phase dispersion were carried out using interference configuration shown in Fig.1.

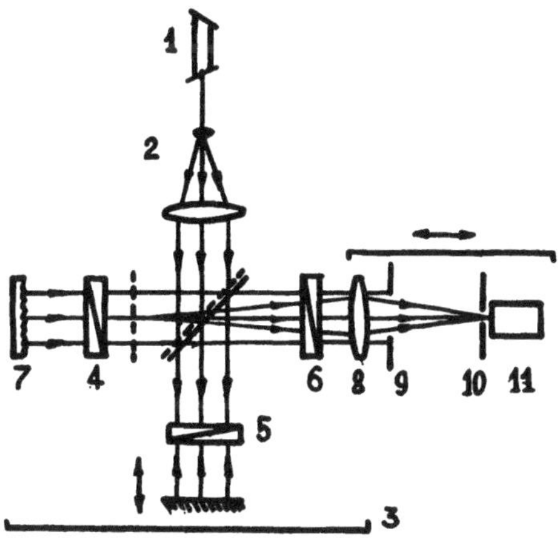

Fig. 1. An experimental arrangement for measuring the field amplitude dispersion using a Michelson interferometer. 1-laser; 2-telescopic system; 3-interferometer; 4,5,6-polarizers; 7-sample; 8-objective; 9,10-aperture and field diaphragms; 11-photodetector.

Such a configuration ensures the validity of the infinitely extended object assumption, and makes possible the measurements both in the near and far fields.

The transverse coherence function was measured using an arrangement shown in Fig.2.

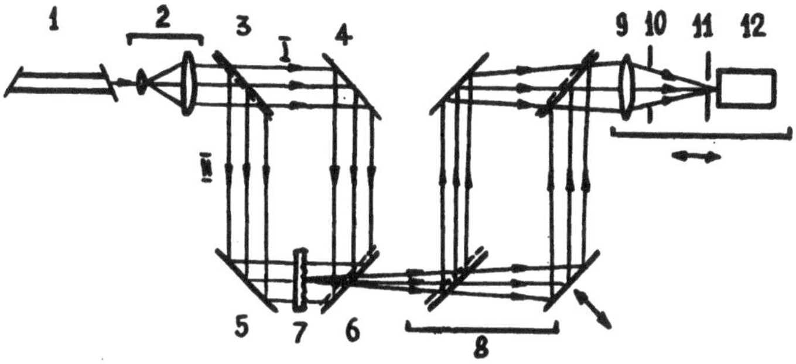

Fig.2. An experimental arrangement for measuring the transverse coherence function. 1-laser; 2-telescopic system; 3,6-beamsplitters; 4,5-mirrors; 7-sample; 8-Mach-Zehnder interferometer; 9-objective; 10,11-aperture and field diaphragms; 12-photodetector.

The sample was illuminated by a beam having a plane wave front. Radiation scattered from the sample was split into two components of equal intensity. Their consequent relative displacement and mixing were made in the interferometer. At the interferometer exit, the mixed beams propagated collinearly. The transverse relative displacement ρ of the split beams was achieved by one of the interferometer mirrors. The coherence of the resulting field was determined by measuring the intensities I_{max} and I_{min} for beam path differences in the interferometer arms $2m\frac{\lambda}{2}$ and $(2m+1)\frac{\lambda}{2}$, respectively, m being an integer.

Optical arrangements shown in Fig.1 and 2 featured automatic adjustment to infinite interference band by means of a four-element photodetector, automatic control of I_{min} and I_{max}, and computer data processing.

The results are given in Table 1, where comparison is made of the phase dispersion values obtained by profile measurements $\sigma^2_{\varphi h}$, phase dispersion measurements $\sigma^2_{\varphi\varphi}$, amplitude dispersion measurements $\sigma^2_{\varphi A}$, and transverse coherence function measurements. The results are in good agreement, indicating usefulness of the above described methods.

In conclusion, the proposed optical correlation systems for studying weak surface roughness ensure high precision and speed of the measurements.

References

[1] Fujii,H., F.Asakura, and Y.Shindo: Measurements of surface roughness properties by means of laser speckle techniques. Opt.Communs 16(1976) 1, 68-72.

[2] Ohtsuba, J. and T.Asakura: Statistical properties of speckle intensity variations in the diffraction field under illumination of coherent light. Opt.Commun. 14 (1975) 1, 30-34.

[3] Rytov, S., Yu.Kravtsov, and V.Tatarsky: Introduction to Statistical Radiophysics. Nauka, Moscow 1978.

INTERFEROMETRIC FLATNESS TESTING OF SILICON WAFERS

R. Feitscher, H. Fritz and K. Körner [1)]

Abstract:

In the paper a 5"-flatness-testing-system with a resolution of 0.01 µm and an accuracy of 0.1 µm is described. The optical arrangement is based on the principle of a Fizeau-interferometer with grazing incidence combined with a follow-up Moire-interferometer that produces two-beam-interferences. By phase sampling and digital signal processing the surface profiles of silicon wafers are evaluated and plotted.

1. Introduction

The importance of silicon wafer flatness is continuously increasing in the field of very large scale integrated circuit production where patterns with line width of 1 µm or less are usual. To realize this demand very flat wafers are required with a local flatness on the order of 1 µm. To adapt to this flatness testing devices with high resolution and accuracy are necessary.

Such a device was developed in the Centre of Scientific Instruments of the Academy of Science of the GDR and is named "Real-Time Interferometer EIF 130". Some essential contributions as to theoretical ideas, experimental assistance, and software modules have been provided by the Central Institute of Optics and Spectroscopy. The instrument facilitates the inspection of hight variations of 5"-wafers and the analysis of the surface profile of any other nearly plane object with a diameter up to 125 mm. It features international device parameters as to a resolution of 0.01 µm and an accuracy of 0.1 µm.

2. Optical configuration

The optical configuration of our interferometer is based on the principle of a Fizeau-interferometer with grazing incidence as shown in Fig. 1 according to Abramson (1969). It is followed up with a special variant of a Moire-interferometer that produces two-beam-interferences.

[1)] AdW - ZWG GDR-1199 Berlin Rudower Chaussee 6

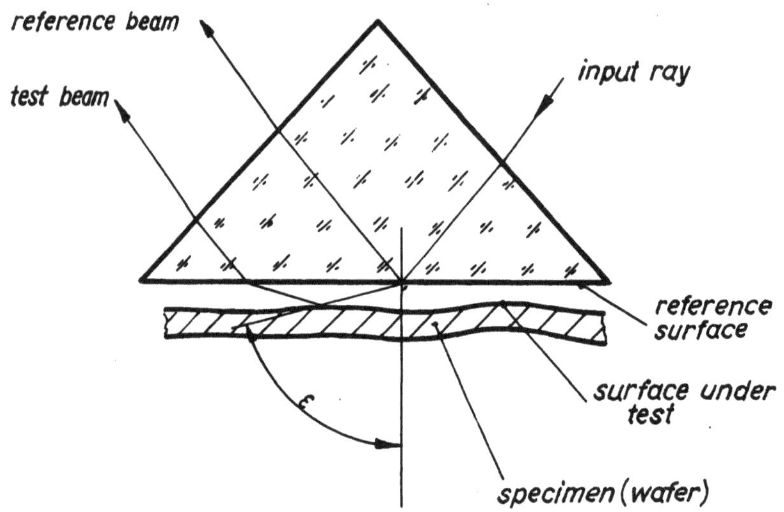

Fig. 1. Grazing incidence interferometer

This arrangement was proposed and tested by Schwider et al.(1983 and 1986).

The main advantage of the grazing incidence is the reduced interferometer sensitivity. This facilitates a measuring range on the order of the maximal surface deviations of silicon wafers (±25 μm). In our case a interference phase step of $\Delta\phi = 2\pi$ corresponds to a hight step of $\Delta h = 3.16$ μm, being equivalent to the surface deviation. This hight step is evaluated according to

$$\Delta h = \frac{\lambda}{2\cdot\cos(\varepsilon)}\cdot\frac{\Delta\phi}{2\pi} \tag{1}$$

where the wavelenght $\lambda = 633$ nm and the incident angle $\varepsilon = 84.3^\circ$.

The necessary incident plane wave front is produced by an astronomical objective (⌀ 110 mm, f = 750 mm) supported by a beam expanding optical system. Due to the grazing incidence in the measuring plane a projective distortion of the plane wave front with a circular cross-section arises. The appropriate use of an anamorphotic double wedge system as shown in Fig. 2 provides for two advantages (Körner et al., 1985): the projective distortion is compensated and the beam diameter in the measuring plane is increased; this means in our case an increase from 100 mm to 134 mm.

After being reflected at the test object the expanded beam is processed in the opposite way, is being passed on in a Moire-interferometer with an amplitude grating, and is imaged on to the CCD matrix camera.

By shifting the amplitude grating the four or five reference phases, necessary for the phase-sampling-method, are adjusted (Schwider et al., 1983).

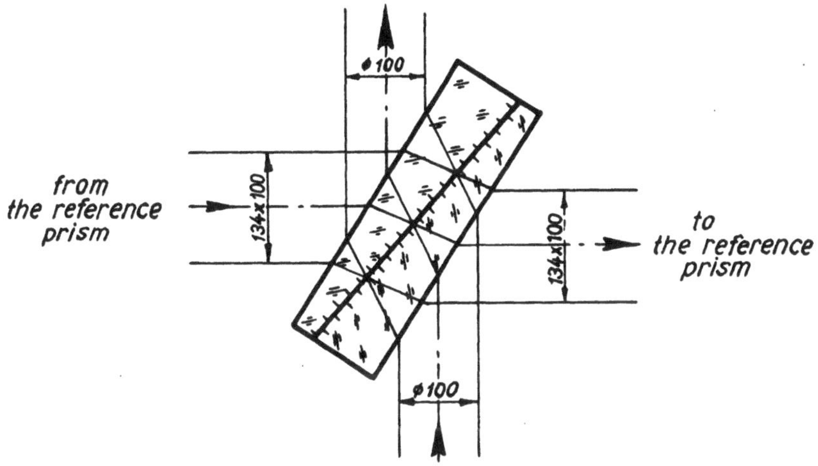

Fig. 2. Double wedge system

In the case of four reference phase steps the phase function is given by

$$\varphi_{r_i} = 0,\ \frac{\pi}{2},\ \pi,\ 3\cdot\frac{\pi}{2} \quad : \quad \phi(x) = \arctan\left[\frac{I_3 - I_1}{I_0 - I_2}\right] \bmod 2\pi \qquad (2)$$

and in the case of five reference phase steps by

$$\varphi_{r_i} = -\pi,\ -\frac{\pi}{2},\ 0,\ \frac{\pi}{2},\ \pi \ : \ \phi(x) = \arctan\left[\frac{2\cdot(I_1 - I_3)}{2\cdot I_2 - I_4 - I_0}\right] \bmod 2\pi \qquad (3)$$

3. Evaluation and plotting

Hardware

The interferometer dealt with in this paper is operating in real-time. So all processes as drive control, camera control, evaluation, and plotting are in our case done by only one Z80-microprocessor. There is no doubt that this processor with a clock frequency of 2.5 MHz is not very rapid, but it is sufficient under the aspect of producing a single prototype flatness testing system for research, not for wafer production.

The interferograms are taken by a 64x64-pixel CCD matrix camera. The analog values coming from the camera are processed by sample-and-hold-circuits, are converted from analog to digital signals with a resolution of maximal 10 bit, and then they are transmitted by the parallel interface to RAM places. The transfer of one frame from the CCD matrix to the computer needs a time of 250 ms.

The computing system consists of
- the central processing board
- the 128 kbyte RAM board
- control boards for: * alphanumerical display (80x24 characters)
  * graphic display (512x256 pixel)
  * keyboard and daisy wheel printer
- the parallel input/output interface board (32 bit) for data transfer from and to the interferometer

All drives for positioning the wafer and the phase grating are realised by stepping motors getting their control pulses from the Z80-processor.

Software

The whole software is working under an operating system that is compatible to CP/M 2.2. Apart from this operating system the software package consists of:
- the self-explaining communication program written in BASIC;
- the evaluation and plotting programs written in assembler;
- the control programs for camera and drives written in assembler.

The digital signal processing comprises the following computations: The 64x64 pixel intensities coming from the camera are compressed to 32x32 values to reduce computation time and storage needed. From these reduced intensities taken at four or five reference phases the evaluation of hight variations is done. After that the plane of the best fit is calculated by least squares approximation, and it can be subtracted from the surface profile to eliminate the tilt. A correction of interferometer errors is possible by subtracting a surface profile that is evaluated from a calibration object of very high planity.

Menu controlled the computer may display the surface profile in different ways:
- as a pseudo-3D-plot;
- as a contour line plot;
- as a x-y-cut plot.

According to the intended application of our flatness testing system for silicon wafers several typical flatness quantities in this branch are calculated:

- MPD: mean plane deviation;
- FPD: focal plane deviation;
- RMS: root mean square;
- LSF: local site flatness;
- PUA: percent usable area;
- PUS: percent usable sites.

Furthermore differences can be formed between any surface profile measurements. To eliminate random errors of the arrangement a chosen number of accumulations of the intensities or of the calculated surface profiles can be selected. It is possible to store measured surface profiles at a mass store for later use. Extended variants of printing value matrices and getting hardcopies from the alphanumerical and from the graphic display, and self-test routines for the interferometer complete the program package.

4. Summary

In this paper a special 5"-testing-flatness-device for research applications was explained. The optical arrangement was discussed and the advantages of an anamorphotic double-wedge-system are pointed out. The wide application range of the dedicated software package is based on a single Z80-processor.

5. References

Abramson, N., 1969, "The interferoscope - a new type of interferometer with variable fringe separation", Optik, 30/1:56-71

Körner, K., Puder, J., Stadthaus, W., Holota, W., 1985, "Anordnung zur interferometrischen Messung der Ebenheit von Oberflächen", DDR-Wirtschaftspatent DD-WP 242 473

Schwider, J., Spolaczyk, R., and Elssner, K.-E., 1983, "Anordnung zur interferometrischen Ebenheitsprüfung technischer Oberflächen", DDR-Wirtschaftspatent DD-WP 219 565

Schwider, J., Burow, R., Elssner, K.-E., Grzanna, J., and Spolaczyk, R., 1986, "Semiconductor wafer and technical flat planeness testing interferometer", Appl. Opt., 25/7:1117-1121

VERGLEICHENDE UNTERSUCHUNGEN UNTERSCHIEDLICHER TRÄGERFREQUENZMETHODEN ZUR INTERFERENZSTREIFENAUSWERTUNG IN EINEM DIGITALEN INTERFEROMETER

Frankowski, G., Schillke, F., Stobbe, I., Tischer, W.[1], Nadeborn, W.[2]

Zusammenfassung

Für die interferometrische Messung von Maß-, Form- und Lageabweichungen wurden in ein Signalanalysesystem zur automatisierten Bildauswertung Trägerfrequenzverfahren implementiert und in zwei Stufen getestet. Kriterien der Testung sind Schnelligkeit, Genauigkeit und Empfindlichkeit hinsichtlich verschiedener Störeinflüsse.

1. Allgemeine Zielstellung der Anwendung interferometrischer Methoden

Die Anwendung interferometrischer Verfahren bietet die Möglichkeit, Maß, Form und Lage sowie Oberflächenrauheiten und -welligkeiten qualitativ und quantitativ zu erfassen. Voraussetzung ist, daß es sich um nicht diffus reflektierende, sondern spiegelnde Oberflächen handelt, wie sie zum Beispiel bei der Ultrapräzisionsbearbeitung entstehen. Hier lassen sich sowohl makro- als auch mikroskopische Größen erfassen /1/. Insbesondere für eine qualitative Erfassung von Oberflächenabweichungen aus der interferometrischen Aufnahme ist eine exakte Ermittlung der Phasenlage zwischen den interferierenden Wellenfronten erforderlich. Um dies zu erreichen, wurden bereits eine Reihe von Auswerteverfahren entwickelt, die auf der Basis von Phasenschiebeverfahren /2/ oder unter Verwendung von Bildauswerteverfahren (Skelettierung) /3/ arbeiten. In verschiedenen Einrichtungen international entwickelt und angewandt, jedoch in der DDR bis zum gegenwärtigen Zeitpunkt nicht praktiziert, sind die sogenannten Trägerfrequenzverfahren, bei denen durch die Aufmodulation des Nutzsignals auf eine räumliche Trägerwelle (spatial carrier frequency) eine näherungsweise Linearisierung der Interferenzstreifenmuster erfolgt. Ziel der vorliegenden Arbeit ist es, eine Reihe häufig eingesetzter Trägerfrequenzverfahren in ein optisches Signalanalysesystem zu implementieren, z.T. weiterzuentwickeln sowie anhand simulierter und realer Intensitätsmuster hinsichtlich ihrer Leistungsfähigkeit zu testen.

2. Theoretische Grundlagen

In die Analyse wurden folgende Trägerfrequenzverfahren einbezogen :

a) Sinusoid-fitting-Methoden
   - nach MERTZ /4/ mit einem Korrekturterm, wenn die Abtastschrittweite ungleich $1/(3\ f_o)$ ist.
   - nach RANSOM /5/ mit Korrekturterm.

b) Fourier-Transformations-Methoden
   - nach TAKEDA /6/, mit verschiedenen Fensterfunktionen.
   - nach WOMACK /7/, (Transformation im Ortsbereich).

c) Parameterschätzverfahren /9/
   - mit expotentieller Wichtung (RECLS).
   - mit Rechteckfenster-Wichtung (EXFENST, EXFENST3).

Die Bearbeitung erfolgte in zwei Stufen :
   - Implementierung der Auswertesoftware und Testung an Simulationsbeispielen /9/,
   - Testung anhand einer Meßaufgabe mit einem Michelson-Interferometer.

---

1) Akademie der Wissenschaften der DDR, Institut für Automatisierung, Rudower Chaussee 5, Berlin 1199

2) Akademie der Wissenschaften der DDR, Zentralinstitut für Kybernetik und Informationsprozesse, Kurstrasse 33, Berlin 1086

Gemeinsamer Ausgangspunkt aller Verfahren ist eine digitalisierte Intensitätsverteilung einer interferometrischen Aufnahme in einem gegebenen Koordinatensystem :

$$I(x,y) = I_0(x,y)\,[1 + V(x,y)\cos(\Phi(x,y)-\Phi_0)]\,R_m(x,y) + R_a(x,y) \qquad (1)$$

Dabei bedeuten $I_0(x,y)$ die ortsabhängige mittlere Intensität, $V(x,y)$ den Streifenkontrast, $\Phi(x,y)$ und Φ_0 - die Phasenwinkel der Prüflings- und Referenzlichtwelle. R_m stellt einen multiplikativen Rauschterm (Speckle-Rauschen) und R_a ein additives (elektronisches) Meßrauschen dar. Die Referenzphase wird in der Form $\Phi_0 = \varphi_0 - 2\pi f_0 x$ gewählt mit f_0 als Orts-Trägerfrequenz. Die x-Richtung ist senkrecht zu den Interferenzstreifen der Trägerphase festgelegt. Eine eindeutige Bestimmung der Phasenverteilung $\Phi(x,y)$, ihres Vorzeichens und der Änderungsrichtung ist bei Erfüllung der Bedingung

$$2\pi f_0 > \max |\mathrm{grad}(\Phi)| \qquad (2)$$

durch die Monotonie der Gesamtphase gewährleistet. Eine weitere Bedingung an die Größe der Trägerfrequenz f_0 ist mit der maximalen Abtastrate $h = x_{i+1} - x_i$ verbunden :

$$f_0 < f_{max} = \frac{1}{2h} \qquad (3)$$

Es wird vorausgesetzt, daß die angestrebte Genauigkeit des Experiments (der Messung) durch eine hinreichend große Abtastrate gesichert ist : Die Bedingungen (2) und (3) sind erfüllt, wenn der maximale Phasenabstand zwischen zwei benachbarten Punkten des Phasenfeldes kleiner als π ist. (4)

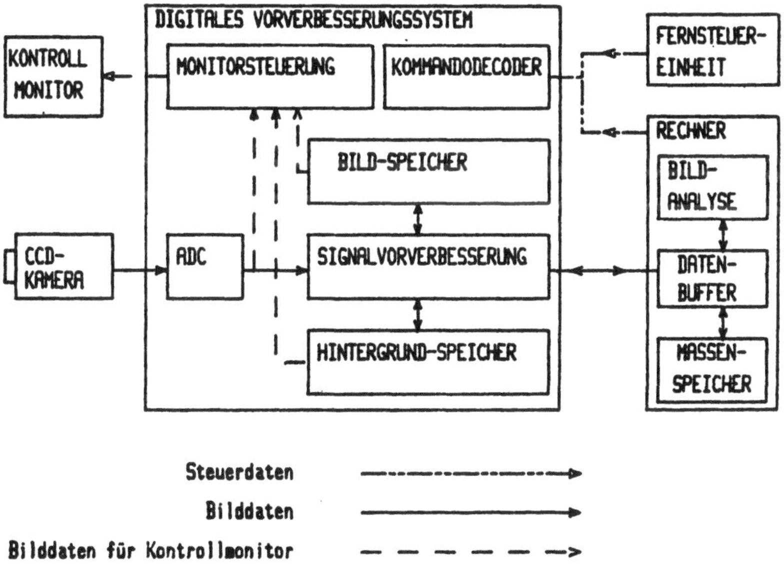

Abb. 1 : Komponenten des Signalanalysemoduls

3. Experimentelle Basis

In der Abb. 1 wird das funktionelle Zusammenwirken zwischen CCD-Camera, digitalem Vorverarbeitungssystem und Host-Computer mit implementierter Auswertesoftware gezeigt. Zur Erzeugung der Interferenzstreifen wurde ein Michelson-Interferometer genutzt, wobei im Interferometerarm der Referenzwelle mittels Phasenstellen die Trägerfrequenz erzeugt wurde. Als Sensor fand eine hochauflösende CCD-Matrix-Kamera mit 582x500 Bildpunkten Verwendung. Das digitale Vorverarbeitungssystem verfügt über einen Bildspeicher von 1024 x 512 Bildpunkten (genutzt 688 x 512 Bp.) und 16 Bit Bildtiefe sowie einen 8 Bit tiefen Hintergrundspeicher und ermöglicht eine Reihe von Bildverarbeitungsoperationen zur Verbesserung des Signal-Rauschabstandes und eine interaktive, ohne mechanische Stellelemente auskommende Bildauswahl. Die vorverarbeiteten Intensitätsdaten werden vom Host-Computer übernommen und wahlweise dem Auswertealgorithmus zugeführt bzw. auf Massenspeicher abgelegt. Der Datentransfer vom DVS in den Arbeitsspeicher des Host-Computer benötigt bei voller Bildgröße (688 x 512 x 16 Bit) 6.2 Sekunden ohne, und 3.1 Sekunden mit DMA-Betrieb.

4. Simulation und Anwendungsbeispiel

Um eine Vergleichbarkeit der Resultate bei den Verfahren untereinander und mit den in der Literatur /5,8/ angegeben zu gewährleisten, wurde als einheitliches Testbeispiel der Astigmatismus gewählt: $\Phi(x,y) = 2\pi\,\Phi_\lambda\,(x^2 - y^2)$, mit dem Koordinatenursprung im Bildzentrum. Als Meßrauschen wurde ein gaußverteilter "weißer" Zufallsprozeß verwendet, die Quantisierungseffekte aus dem Bildaufnahme- und Übertragungsprozeß wurden durch entsprechende Rundung der Bildintensität erreicht. Als einheitliches Gütekriterium wurde die maximale (über alle Bildpunkte bestimmte) Standardabweichung σ(=Sigma) der Differenz von berechneter und simulierter Interferenzphase verwendet. Die folgenden Abbildungen zeigen einen Vergleich der Methoden, wobei am rechten Bildrand die Verfahren mit Ziffern bezeichnet sind : 1.. MERTZ, 2.. WOMACK, 3.. RANSOM, 4.. TAKEDA, 5.. EXFENST, 6.. EXFENST3, 7.. RECLS . Die Abb. 2 zeigt die Abhängigkeit des Interferenzphasenfeldes von der Pixelzahl je Streifen ($1/f_o$).

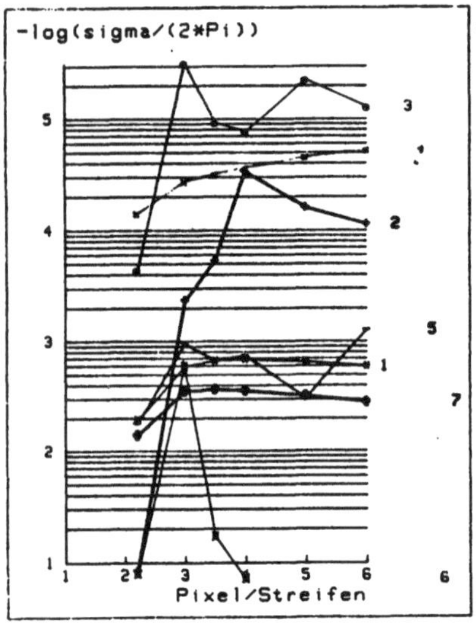

Abb. 2: /9/

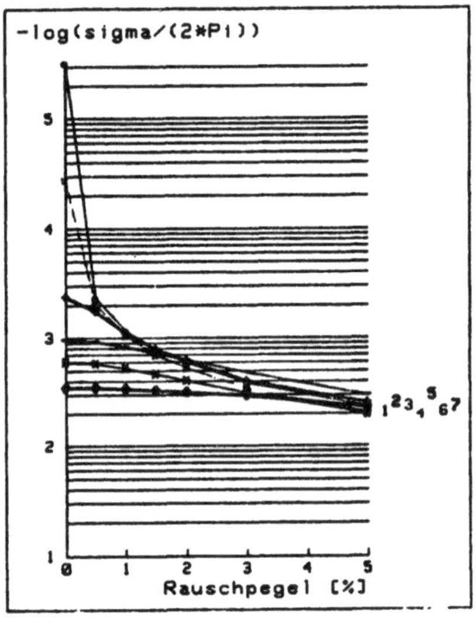

Abb. 3: /9/

Erwartungsgemäß erhält man für den unverrauschten Fall mit "RANSOM", "TAKEDA" und "WOMACK" die besten Ergebnisse, bei "RANSOM" auf Grund der Wirkung des Korrekturterms bis zu $\lambda/300000$. Die Schätzverfahren "EXFENST" und "RECLS" berechnen hier bereits Ausgleichslösungen, was zu größeren Fehlern führt. "EXFENST3" ist auf den Spezialfall $f_o = 1/3$ zugeschnitten. Bei $f_o \rightarrow 1/2$ (Nyquist-Frequenz (4)) steigen die Fehler stark an.

Die Abhängigkeit des Interferenzphasenfehlers vom Rauschpegel ist in Abb. 3 dargestellt. Bereits bei etwa 1% Rauschpegel sinkt die Genauigkeit der im "unverrauschten" Fall exakteren Verfahren auf etwa $\lambda/1000$ und fällt mit zunehmendem Rauschpegel weiter ab. Dagegen zeigen die Parameterschätzverfahren relativ geringe Genauigkeitsänderungen im untersuchten Bereich. Als Verfahren mit den geringsten Fehlern bei stärkerem Meßrauschen erweist sich "EXFENST". Ähnliche Aussagen treffen für den

Einfluß veränderlicher Signaltiefe zu; bereits bei einer Verarbeitungsbreite von weniger als 8 Bit ist eine deutliche Annäherung aller Fehlerkurven zu erkennen, bei 4 Bit sind die Werte von "EXFENST" am besten.

Weiter konnte am Simulationsbeispiel nachgewiesen werden, daß die Verfahren (mit Ausnahme von "RANSOM") von der Ortsabhängigkeit der Grundintensität $I_o(x,y)$ und des Streifenkontrastes $V(x,y)$ unabhängig sind.

Durch eine nachträgliche Filterung der gewonnenen Interferenzphase können die Ergebnisse im Sinne einer geringeren Standardabweichung noch verbessert werden, sie dient der Unterdrückung verfahrensbedingter oder aus dem Meßrauschen resultierender hochfrequenter Störanteile. Dabei ist bei der Wahl der Grenzfrequenz des Tiefpasses zu beachten, daß keine Nutzsignale ausgelöscht werden. Die erreichbare Genauigkeitsverbesserung liegt bei höheren Rauschpegeln z.B. für die Verfahren "MERTZ" u. "RANSOM" etwa in der gleichen Größenordnung.

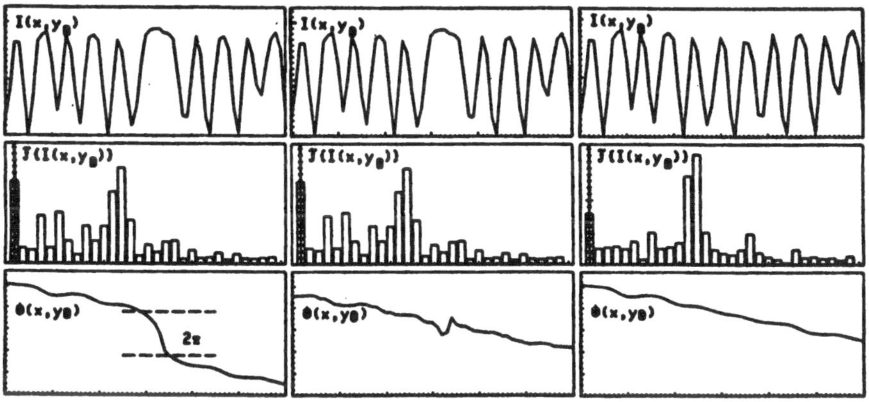

Abb. 4 a) b) c)
Intensitätsverlauf, Leistungsspektrum und berechnete Phase der detektierten Zeile. a) mit Meßfehler, Phase nach "WOMACK", b) mit Meßfehler, Phase nach "EXFENST", c) korrigiert durch Interpolation von Elementen der vorhergehenden und nachfolgenden Zeile, Phase nach "WOMACK"

Bei der Analyse gemessener Intensitätsdaten wurden Auswirkungen des Meßrauschens u.a. Fehlerquellen untersucht. Als Beispiel ist in Abb. 4 die Auswirkung eines Aufnahmefehlers in einer Zeile des Intensitätsbildes dargestellt. Beim Verfahren "WOMACK" tritt ein nicht dem realen Phasenverlauf entsprechender 2π-Sprung auf; das Schätzverfahren "EXFENST" (Abb.4b) bewirkt bei ausreichender Fensterbreite ($> 1/f_o$) den Fehlerausgleich an dieser Stelle. Die Korrektur der Intensitätsdaten (Abb. 4c) im Rahmen einer Bild-Vorverarbeitung, wie sie auch in kommerziellen Bildverarbeitungssystemen üblich ist, führte ebenfalls zum Erfolg. Insgesamt ist im Experiment darauf zu achten, daß die Bedingung (4) auch bei stärkerem Rauschen erfüllt ist.

Als Resultat der implementierten Auswertealgorithmen entstand im realen Versuch das in den Abb. 5 dargestellte Interferenzphasenbild der gegenseitigen Verkippung zweier "ebener" Spiegel mit dem maximalen Abstand zwischen Phasenmaximum und -minimum von 0.31 µm bei einer abgebildeten Fläche von 10 mm x 8 mm.

5. Schlußfolgerungen

Da die Verfahren unterschiedliche Leistungseigenschaften besitzen, sind Einsatzzweck (Form- oder Rauhigkeitsmessung) und Versuchsbedingungen (Rauschpegel und Signaltiefe) genau zu bestimmen. Das theoretische Leistungspotential an sich genauerer, aber aufwendiger Verfahren wie

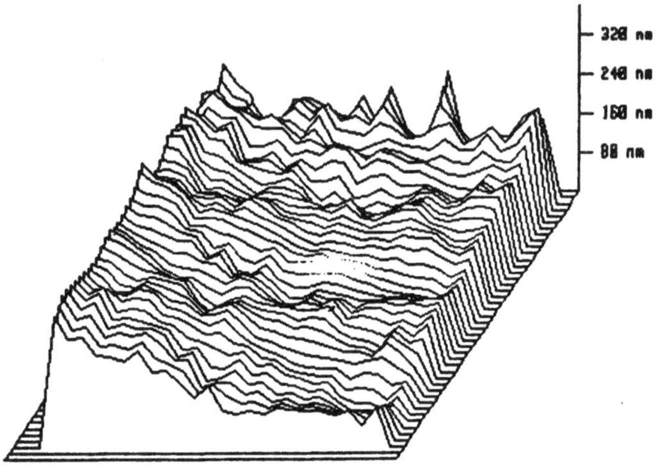

Abb. 5 :

"TAKEDA" oder "RANSOM" läßt sich praktisch nur dann nutzen, wenn die Störeinflüsse wie Rauschen u.a. durch geeignete Bildvorverarbeitung weitgehend unterdrückt werden. Minimale Auswertezeiten sind bei Benutzung einfachster Verfahren (z.B. "MERTZ") und anschließender angepasster Tiefpassfilterung des ermittelten Phasenwinkels erreichbar, insbesondere bei hardwaremäßiger Umsetzung beider Komponenten.

Die Bildauswertung erfolgt für ein ausgewähltes Verfahren ohne weitere interaktive Handlungen. Auf der Basis der ermittelten Phasenbilder sind weiterführende Auswertungen, z.B. statistische Oberflächenbewertungen, in der Software implementiert /10/.

6. Literatur

/1/ LANGENBECK, .:
Optical acceptance testing for ultra precision air bearing machines. SPIE-Proceedings 802, 1987

/2/ DÄNDLIKER, R.,THALMANN, R.:
Heterodyne and quasi-heterodyne holographic interferometry. Optical Enginering, Nr.5, 1985

/3/ OSTEN, W.,SAEDLER, J.,WILHELMI, W.:
Schnelle Auswertung von Interferogrammen mit Verfahren der digitalen Bildverarbeitung. LASER MAGAZIN, Nr.2, 1987

/4/ MERTZ, L.:
Real-time fringe-pattern analysis. Applied Optics, Vol.22,Nr.10,1983.

/5/ RANSOM, P.L., KOKAL, J.V.:
Interferogram analysis by a modified sinusoid fitting technique. Applied Optics, Vol.25, Nr.22, 1986.

/6/ TAKEDA, M., INA, H., KOBAYASHI, S.:
Fourier-trasform method of fringe-pattern analysis for computer-based topography and interferometry. J.Opt.Soc.Am.,Vol.72,Nr.1,1982.

/7/ WOMACK, K.H.:
Interferometric phase measurement using spatial synchronous detection Optical Engineering, Vol. 23, Nr. 4, 1984.

/8/ MACY, W.W.:
Two-dimensional fringe-pattern analysis. Appl.Opt. Vol.22,Nr.23, 1983

/9/ TISCHER, W., NADEBORN, W., STOBBE, I.:
Computergestützte Signalanalyse/ Digitale Auswertung von Interferogrammen. Bericht LMAD 6/88, Akademie der Wissenschaften der DDR.

/10/ FRANKOWSKI, G., SCHILLKE, F., STOBBE, I.:
Surface testing and inspection of pieces in manufacturing using computer-aided methods of lasermotrology. Proceedings of the 12 th WCNDT, Amsterdam, April 1989 (in Vorbereitung)

MODEL CALCULATION FOR THE PHASE SAMPLING INTERFEROMETRY

H. Fritz and K. Körner [1)]

1. Introduction

Due to the intensive development of modern detectors and powerful computers over the last few years, optical methods for measuring form error and roughness has become a very important technique. In our opinion the coupling of interferometric methods with the phase sampling technique is of special importance. Therefore this paper deals with the investigation of two error sources: errors in reference phase shifting and in intensity measurements.

2. The basic idea of the phase sampling technique

If the known intensity distribution of two-beam-interferometry

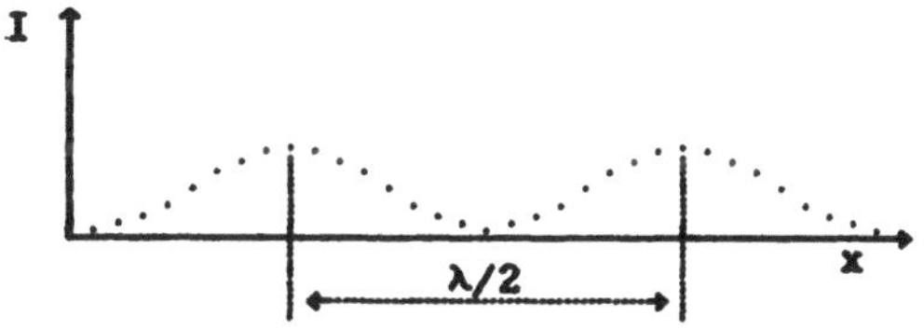

$$I(x) = I(x_o)\{1 + V(x)\cos[\phi(x)]\} \quad (2.1)$$

$I(x)$: intensity
$I_o(x)$: mean intensity
$V(x)$: Visibility
$\phi(x)$: interference phase

Fig. 2-1 : Intensity distribution of two-beam-interferometry

is made to vary in some known manner by introduction of a so-called reference phase φ_r, the interference phase can be derived from three or more intensity measurements. The reference phase is changing between 0 and 2π either in discrete steps (*phase stepping*) or continuously with time (*integrating bucket*).

The only effect of integrating the interferogram while changing the phase is to reduce the modulation of the fringes recorded in the interferogram data set. Therefore we deal only with the more simple *phase stepping* method.

From (2.1) the intensity is therefore:

$$I_i(x) = I_o(x)\{1 + V(x)\cos[\phi(x)+\varphi_{r_i}]\} \quad (2.2)$$

[1)] AdW - ZWG GDR-1199 Berlin Rudower Chaussee 6

At any given point x, the measured intensity will vary sinusoidally with φ_r, so that the interference phase $\phi(x)$ can be determind by fitting the data obtained to a sine curve of known period but unknown phase and amplitude.

3. Algorithms

The concrete form of an algorithm follows from the choice of the reference phase. Here are the most usual algorithms:

- 3 reference phase steps of $\pi/2$ *Wyant* /2/:

$$\varphi_{r_i} = \frac{\pi}{4},\ 3\cdot\frac{\pi}{4},\ 5\cdot\frac{\pi}{4}: \qquad \phi(x) = \arctan\left[\frac{I_2 - I_1}{I_0 - I_1}\right] \bmod 2\pi \qquad (3.1)$$

- 3 reference phase steps of $2\cdot\pi/3$ *At* /3/:

$$\varphi_{r_i} = 0,\ 2\cdot\frac{\pi}{3},\ 4\cdot\frac{\pi}{3} \quad : \quad \phi(x) = \arctan\left[\frac{\sqrt{3}\cdot(I_2 - I_1)}{2\cdot I_0 - I_1 - I_2}\right] \bmod 2\pi \qquad (3.2)$$

- 4 reference phase steps of $\pi/2$ *Wyant* /2/:

$$\varphi_{r_i} = 0,\ \frac{\pi}{2},\ \pi,\ 3\cdot\frac{\pi}{2} \quad : \quad \phi(x) = \arctan\left[\frac{I_3 - I_1}{I_0 - I_2}\right] \bmod 2\pi \qquad (3.3)$$

- 5 reference phase steps of $\pi/2$ *Schwider* /4/:

$$\varphi_{r_i} = -\pi,\ -\frac{\pi}{2},\ 0,\ \frac{\pi}{2},\ \pi : \phi(x) = \arctan\left[\frac{2\cdot(I_1 - I_3)}{2\cdot I_2 - I_4 - I_0}\right] \bmod 2\pi \qquad (3.4)$$

- Calibration insensitive algorithm by Carré /5/:
  For four reference phase steps of the same amount follows for the interference phase by *Cheng* /6/ :

$$\phi(x) = \arctan\left[\frac{\sqrt{[(I_1 - I_2)+(I_0 - I_3)]\cdot[3(I_1 - I_2)-(I_0 - I_3)]}}{(I_1 + I_2) - (I_0 + I_3)}\right] \bmod 2\pi \quad (3.5)$$

4. Model calculation

The algorithms (3.1) to (3.4) require that all reference phase steps φ_{r_i} are equal to the rated value, but algorithm (3.5) requires only that all φ_{r_i} are equal to each other.

Real phase shifters, for instance the often used piezoelectric transducer (PZT), fulfil only partly this approximation.

For the *integrating bucket* technique the phase characteristic is given as

$$\varphi_r(t) = 2\pi A\cdot t/T + 2\pi B\cdot t^2/T^2 \qquad (4.1)$$

T is here the period within which the N integrating intensities are measured. A is the linear coefficient and B the quadratic coefficient.
In an ideal case A should be equal to 1 and B should be zero.
With $t_1 = 1/4\cdot T$, $t_2 = 1/2\cdot T$ (for instance) and so on we obtain the phase steps for *phase stepping*.
Now let $A \neq 1$. Substituting then the reference phases from (4.1) into (2.2), the resulting phase ϕ differs from the initial phase ϕ_o .
Varying the phase ϕ_o from 0° to 360° in steps of 1° and evaluating the phase error $\Delta\phi = \phi - \phi_o$, a nearly sinusoidal function is obtained, as illustrated in Fig. 4-1. Because the absolute phase value is not important, the dc bias for each phase error curve is removed. Therefore we have introduced as error the quantity

$$\Delta\phi = \frac{1}{2}\left[|\Delta\phi_{max}| - |\Delta\phi_{min}|\right] \qquad (4.2)$$

Fig. 4-2 shows the compiled results.

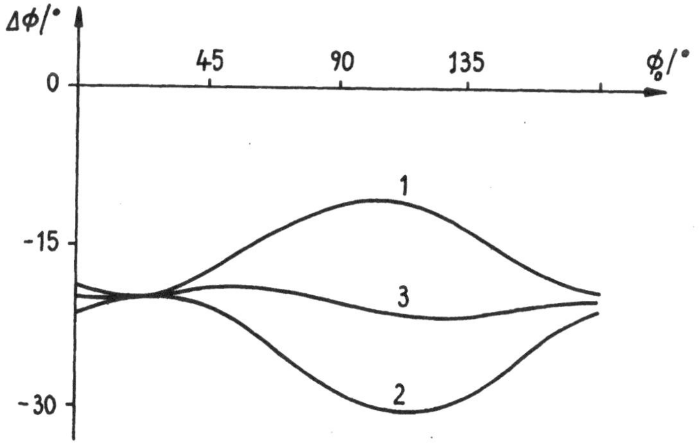

1 : $\varphi_{r_0} \dots \varphi_{r_3}$
2 : $\varphi_{r_1} \dots \varphi_{r_4}$
3 : mean value

curve	Δφ / °
1	10.04
2	10.04
3	1.91

Fig. 4-1 : Phase error of the 4 reference phase algorithm (3.3) with reference phase steps of 80°

For $180° \leq \phi_o \leq 360°$ we obtained the same curves like in the case of $0° \leq \phi_o \leq 180°$.

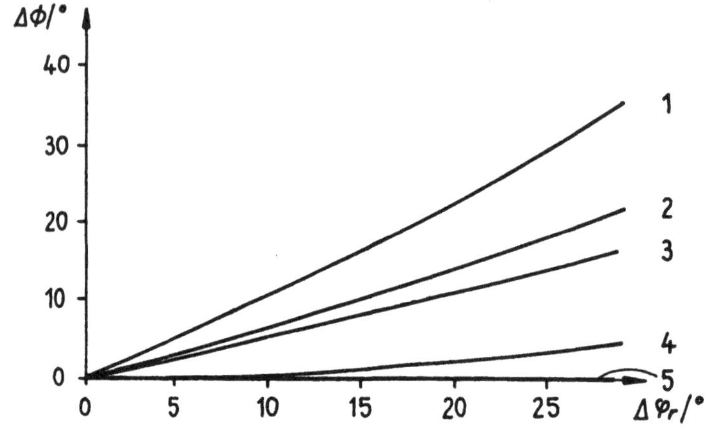

Fig. 4-2 : Error of the phase sampling algorithms in dependence of the error of the reference phase
1: (3.1) 2: (3.2) 3: (3.3) 4: (3.4) 5: (3.5)

The amplitudes of the phase error curves 1 and 2 in Fig. 4-1 are not equal, but they are ≈ 180° out of phase. Therefore averaging two measurements made from the first intensities (number 0 to N-1) and the last intensities (number 1 to N) will considerable reduce the phase error. This is more or less true for all of the considered algorithms, like Fig. 4-3 shows.

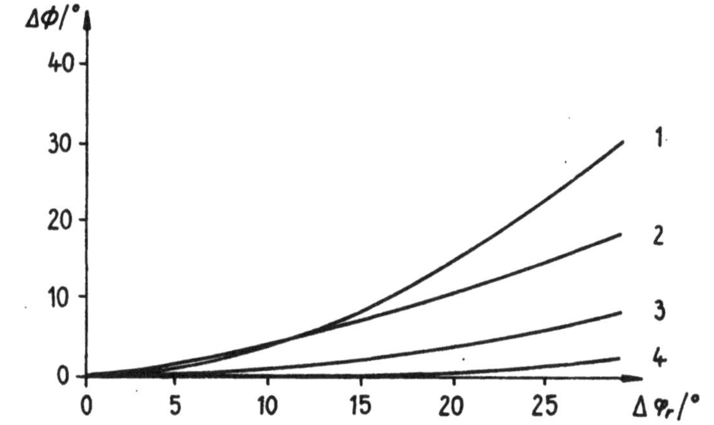

Fig. 4-3 : Error of the phase sampling algorithms with averaging measurements in dependence of the error of the reference phase
1: (3.1) 2: (3.2) 3: (3.3) 4: (3.4)

Similar investigations we have carried out for the nonlinear case with A = 1 but B ≠ 0. The results are shown in Fig. 4-4.

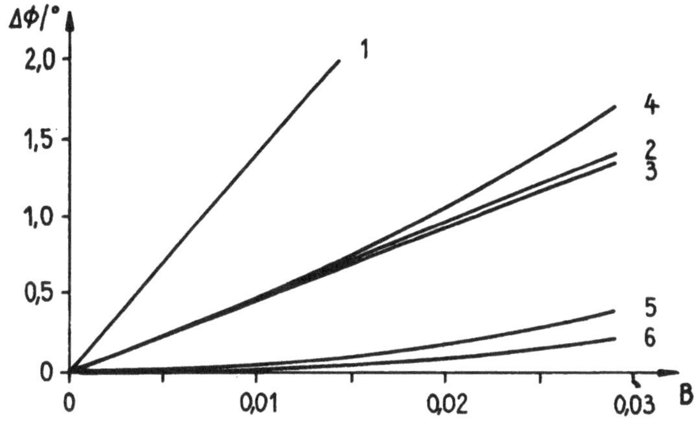

Fig. 4-4 : Error of the phase sampling algorithms in dependence of the quadratic coefficient B
1: (3.3) 2: (3.4) 3: (3.5)
4 - 6: like 1 - 3, but with averaging

It's not possible to convert the intensity into infinitesimal steps and this leads to considerable errors in some cases. This error was calculated analytically. In addition to it we obtained this error by a computer simulation.

The following table shows the formulas and values for $\Delta I = 1$. I_{max} is the maximum number of intensity steps. For 8 bit analogue to digital converting I_{max} is 256.

Algorithm	Error formula	Value /°	Simulation /°
3-reference phases of 90°	$\lvert\Delta\phi\rvert \le \sqrt{3/2}\cdot\Delta I/I_{max}$	0.27	0.27
3-reference phases of 120°	$\lvert\Delta\phi\rvert \le 2/\sqrt{3}\cdot\Delta I/I_{max}$	0.26	0.29
4-reference phases of 90°	$\lvert\Delta\phi\rvert \le \sqrt{2}\cdot\Delta I/I_{max}$	0.32	0.25
5-reference phases of 90°	$\lvert\Delta\phi\rvert \le \sqrt{3}\cdot\Delta I/I_{max}$	0.39	0.21
Algorithm by Carré	———	———	0.27

5. Literature

/1/ J.E.Greivenkamp, Opt. Eng. 23(1984)350-352
/2/ J.C.Wyant, Proc. 38th Annual Meeting of the ASLE (1983)
/3/ Chiayu Ai and J.C.Wyant, Appl. Opt. 26(1987)1112-1116
/4/ J.Schwider et al., Appl. Opt. 22(1983)3421-3432
/5/ P.Carré, Metrologia 2(1966)13
/6/ Y.-Y.Cheng and J.C.Wyant, Appl. Opt. 24(1985)3049-3052
/7/ A.G. Worthing and J.Geffner, *Treatment of Experimental Data*, Wiley, New York, 1943, S.208

ABSOLUTE TESTING OF OPTICAL FLATS ON A QUADRATIC GRID

Juergen Grzanna, Andreas Vogel [1)]

1. Introduction

Tests for flatness are of fundamental importance. For instance the calibration of a digital interferometer needs such a test. When comparing different flats,one distinguishes between relative and absolute methods. Using relative methods, one can only obtain the sum of the deviations of the two surfaces from ideal planes. Absolute methods provide knowledge of the surface itself e.g. of its deviations from a mathematical plane. For absolute testing a summary of available methods is given in /3/.Some methods use a liquid mirror as flatness standard.Other methods determine the deviation from flatness by combining relative measurements between unknown surfaces in a suitable way /3/,/1/. In the following, methods of of the latter case will be considered.
If a digital interferometer is used to get the relative measurements, the measured values are located at the knots of the quadratic grid defined by the detector array. Using the known methods, it is necessary to interpolate between the measured values on the quadratic grid and the needed values at certain points at defined diameters.
A possibility to avoid this interpolation is to develop a method for absolute testing on a quadratic grid.

2. Absolute Testing on a quadratic grid

2.1 Reference plane defined by three points

The following method tests three flats absolutely. In order to determine the deviation from flatness on a quadratic grid it is necesarry to add a fifth position /2/ to the four positions used by known methods. The four positions are the three basic positions and a rotating position, where the flat C is rotated about an angle of 90 degree in the mathematical positive sense after tilting (see Fig. 1). The fifth position requires a translation of the flat C relativ to the flat A about the distance between two pixels of the detector array along the positive x axis after tilting.

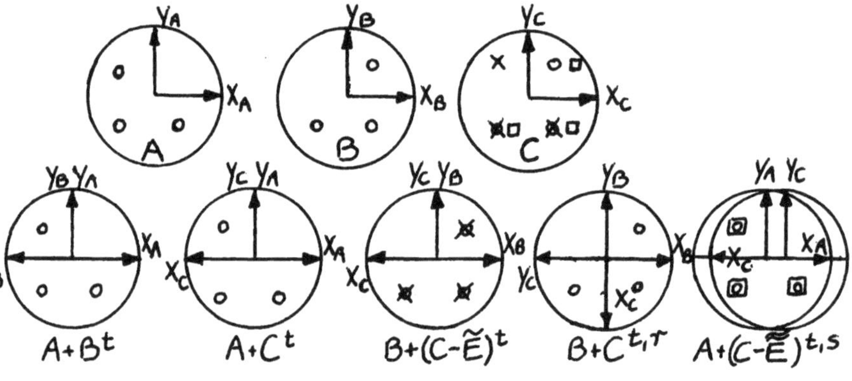

Fig. 1. Positions of the quadratic grid method, using the reference plane defined by three points, where
t - denotes the tilting of a flat around the y axis,
r - denotes the rotation of a flat about an angle of 90 degree in the mathematical positive sense,
s - denotes the shifting of a flat about the distance between two pixels along the positive x axis.

1) AdW ZOS 1199 Berlin-Adlershof Rudower Chaussee 6

The reference plane coincides with the flat at three points (see o Fig. 1). The problem consists in guaranteeing that the sum of two reference planes are computable by analysing each of the five interferograms There are no problems with the first, second and fourth interferogram. Here the zero points of one flat coincide with the zero points of the other flat. In order to solve the problem at the third and fifth interferogram it is necessary to introduce mathematical planes $\tilde{E}$ and $\tilde{\tilde{E}}$ in such a way that the zero points of flat B coincide with the zero points of $(C-\tilde{E})^{t}$ and that the zero points of flat A coincide with those of $(C-\tilde{\tilde{E}})^{t,s}$ (see Fig. 1). Altogether the mathematical reference planes E_A, E_B and E_C are defined by

$$A(o)=A^{*}(o)-E_A(o)=0,\quad B(o)=B^{*}(o)-E_B(o)=0,\quad C(o)=C^{*}(o)-E_C(o)=0,$$

where A^{*}, B^{*} and C^{*} are deviations from flatness and o denotes any one of the defined three zero points of the corresponding flat.
$\tilde{E}$ is determined by $C(x)-\tilde{E}(x)=0$, where the three points (defined by x see Fig.1) are located at the flat C in such a way that the zero points of $(C-\tilde{E})^{t}$ coincide with the zero points of the flat B. In the same manner $\tilde{\tilde{E}}$ is defined at ◘ (see Fig. 1).
With these statements it is possible to compute the sum of two reference planes by analysing each of the five interferograms. This is done by substracting a plane, which coincides at the common three zero points with the values of the interferogram.
In order to determine the unknown deviations from flatness the corresponding set of equations must be solved in the least square sense (l.s.) :

$$\begin{pmatrix} I & T & 0 \\ I & 0 & T \\ 0 & I & T+\tilde{M} \\ 0 & I & R \\ I & 0 & S+\tilde{\tilde{M}} \end{pmatrix} \begin{pmatrix} \vec{a} \\ \vec{b} \\ \vec{c} \end{pmatrix} \overset{l.s.}{=} \begin{pmatrix} \vec{m1} \\ \vec{m2} \\ \vec{m3} \\ \vec{m4} \\ \vec{m5} \end{pmatrix} \qquad (1)$$

Set of equations for the computation of the deviation from flatness using the reference plane defined by three points.

The matrix I denotes the unit matrix. T describes the changing of I after tilting the flat around the y axis. The matrix R reflects the defined rotation of a flat after tilting and S reflects the corresponding shift. $\tilde{M}$ and $\tilde{\tilde{M}}$ denote matrices, which reflect the influence of the planes $\tilde{E}$ and $\tilde{\tilde{E}}$. $\tilde{M}$ and $\tilde{\tilde{M}}$ consist of zeros with the exception of one column for $\tilde{M}$ and three columns of $\tilde{\tilde{M}}$. $\vec{a}$, $\vec{b}$ and $\vec{c}$ denote the vectors of the unknown deviations to be determined (row for row of the flat) and $\vec{m1}$, $\vec{m2}$, $\vec{m3}$, $\vec{m4}$ and $\vec{m5}$ are vectors of the values of the five measured interferograms relative to the corresponding zero points.
This set of equations is solvable with the known CHOLESKY Algorithm, if the equation is multiplied with the transposed matrix from the left.

Here, the error propagation is not influenced by the form of the deviations as in the case with previous methods. The zero points at the interferograms, however, are sensitive with respect to great measuring errors.

2.2 Reference plane defined by the least square plane

A better reference plane for the three flats is the least square plane. But there is a problem.The interferogram with the shifting position does not allow to determine the true sum of the two least square planes of the corresponding flats. This is due to the fact, that the area for the least square algorithm is smaller, than in the other interferograms.

At first it is possible to unite the rotating and the shifting position in one position in such a way that only four interferograms must be analysesd (see Fig. 2). This would,on principle,be possible also for latter method.

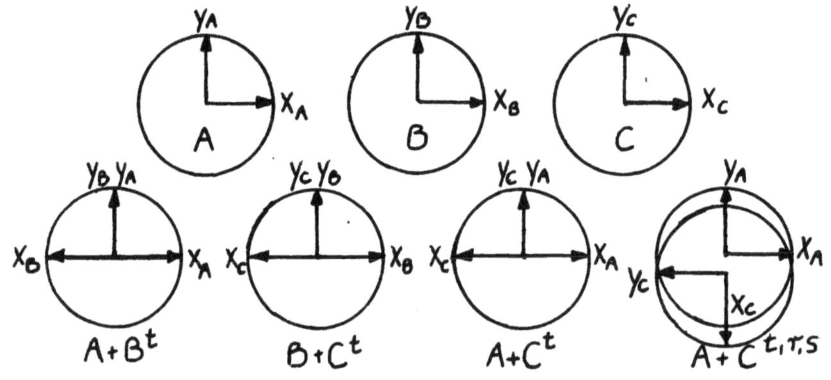

Fig. 2 Positions of the quadratic grid method, using the least square plane as reference plane, where
t – denotes the tilting of a flat around the y axis,
r – denotes the rotation of a flat about an angle of 90 degree in the mathematical positive sense,
s – denotes the shifting of a flat about the distance between two pixels along the negative y axis.

The resulting set of equations (analogously to (1)) has the form

$$\begin{pmatrix} I & T & 0 \\ 0 & I & T \\ I & 0 & T \\ I & 0 & P \end{pmatrix} \begin{pmatrix} \vec{a} \\ \vec{b} \\ \vec{c} \end{pmatrix} \overset{l.s.}{=} \begin{pmatrix} \vec{m1} \\ \vec{m2} \\ \vec{m3} \\ \vec{m4} \end{pmatrix} \quad (2)$$

Set of equations to determine the deviation from flatness using the least square plane as reference plane.

or in abbreviated notation

$$D \quad \vec{z} \overset{l.s.}{=} \vec{m} \ .$$

I, T ,$\vec{a}$, $\vec{b}$, and $\vec{c}$ are the same as in Equ. (1). The matrix P reflects the changing of I after tilting, rotating and shifting the flat C. $\vec{m1}$,$\vec{m2}$,$\vec{m3}$ and $\vec{m4}$ are determined relative to the least square plane of the corresponding interferogram. But $\vec{m4}$ differs from the correct vector $\vec{m4}$ by an unknown error plane

$$E(x,y) = k1\ x + k2\ y + k3 \ .$$

The problem is now to determine the unknown vector $\vec{k} = (k1,k2,k3)$.
To solve this problem the error function of (2) is considered

$$f(\vec{k}) = \| D\,\vec{z}(\vec{k}) - \vec{m}(\vec{k}) \|^2,$$

where $\vec{m}(\vec{k})$ means that $\vec{m4}$ is varied by the unknown plane $k1\,x + k2\,y + k3$. $\vec{z}(\vec{k})$ is the solution of the least square problem $D\,\vec{z}(\vec{k}) = \vec{m}(\vec{k})$, i.e.

$$\vec{z}(\vec{k}) = [D^T D]^{-1} D^T \vec{m}(\vec{k}) .$$

$\| . \|$ denotes the norm, which is defined by

$$\|\vec{z}\| = \sqrt{(\vec{z}, \vec{z})} \quad \text{and} \quad (\vec{z}, \vec{z}) = \sum_{i=1}^{n} z_i^2 .$$

$f(\vec{k})$ is a quadratic function of the unknown k1, k2 and k3, but f has no unique minimum. The reason for this is explained in the following. If at $\vec{m4}$ an added plane has the form

$$E(x,y) = c\,(x + y - 1), \qquad c - \text{arbitrary real number},$$

i.e. if k1 = c, k2 = c, k3 = -c and $\vec{m1}, \vec{m2}, \vec{m3}$ and $\vec{m4}$ are arbitrary, then a plane of the form c y is added to the deviation of flatness of A, B and C. In order to prove this, it is assumed that the three flats A, B and C have deviations of the form c y in each case. Thus

$$\vec{m1} = \vec{m2} = \vec{m3} = 0, \quad \vec{m4} = \begin{bmatrix} \vdots \\ c\,(x + y - 1) \\ \vdots \end{bmatrix}$$

all x and y at the apertur (row for row) and

$$D(\vec{z}(\vec{k})) = \vec{m}(\vec{k}) .$$

Moreover

$$f(\vec{k^*} + \vec{k}) = f(\vec{k^*})$$

for an arbitrary $\vec{k^*}$ and all values of c of the vector $\vec{k} = (c, c, -c)$. Because $f(\vec{k_0})$ is a quadratic function in k1 and k2, where $\vec{k_0} = (k1, k2, 0)$, the minimum of f lies along the straight line

$$\vec{k}(c) = (k1^m, k2^m, 0) + c\,(1, 1, -1), \qquad (3)$$

where $k1^m$ and $k2^m$ are the coordinates of the minimum of $f(\vec{k_0})$ and c is arbitrary.
This uncertainty is uniquely solvable, if a second criterion

$$g(\vec{k}(c)) = \| \vec{z}(\vec{k}(c)) \|^2 = \min$$

is used. g is a quadratic function in c and g has only one minimum along the straight line $\vec{k}(c)$ (see Equ. (3)). This minimum determines the unknown k1, k2 and k3 of the error plane $E(x,y) = k1\,x + k2\,y + k3$ exactly.

Literatur

/1/ Fritz, B.S., "Absolute calibration of an optical flat", in Contemporary Methods of Optical Manufacturing and Testing, G.M. Sanger, ed., Proc. SPIE 433, 123-130 (1983).
/2/ Grzanna J., Burow R., Schulz G., Vogel A., "Absolute Ebenheitsprüfung über einem Quadratgitter", 20. Frühjahrsschule Optik Suhl, Beiträge zur Optik und Quantenelektronik, S. 93, (1988).
/3/ Schulz G., Schwider J., "Interferometric testing of smooth surfaces", in Progress in Optics XIII, E. Wolf, ed., Chap. IV, (1976)

USING INTEGER PROPERTIES FOR AUTOMATIC PROCESSING OF FRINGE PATTERN

Guschov V.I., Solodkin U.N.[1]

The interferometry is aimed at obtaining the total difference of the wave front a two-dimensional interference pattern or from a periodic variation of brightness at the given points. The decoding techniques based on controlled phase shift have been applied recently. The primary reasons for the acceptance of the phase-shifting interferometry (PSI) are the ease of data analysis and the extreme precision to which measurements can be made. Other advantages of this technique are the ability to determine the phase difference at any point of the field being analyzed. The phase difference, however, is determined to the precision of the wave length as with other interference techniques. The total phase will be correctly reconstructed only if the phase difference between adjacent measurement points is a half wave or less. This condition dramatically limits the type of the wave fronts being measured. To overcome this they use null lenses, computer-generated hologramms, the increased number of pixels in detector arrays of the interferogram input devices, the longer wavelengths of the light sources, the two-wavelength techniques. However these techniques either make the system much more complex or lead to its decreased precision.

The purpose of this paper is to describe a new method of interferogram analysis based on the use of the natural number properties which allows determination of the total phase at effective wave length variation.

The method is based on divisibility treated by the number theory.

If the integers leave the same remainder r on division by m, they are called congruent modulo m. To express this fact one writes:

$$a \equiv b \pmod{m}. \qquad (1)$$

The numbers congruent modulo m make the number class modulo m, all the class numbers being obtained from the expression mq+r, where q takes on the values all the integers.

Any class number is called the residue modulo m. The residues giving all possible values of r make the whole residue system modulo m.

If in comparison (1) one of the numbers, say, a, is unknown, then by calling it X one can write

$$x \equiv b \pmod{m}. \qquad (2)$$

---

[1] Novosibirsk institute of electrical engineering
Novosibirsk 630092 K.Marks, 20

The expression (2) is a comparison of the 1st order with one unknown. To solve this comparison means to find all the satisfactory X values. If an $X=X_0$ satisfies the comparison (2), it will satisfy all the numbers compared with X_0 modulo m. Hence the whole class of numbers determinated by the comparison

$$X \equiv X_0 \pmod{m} \tag{3}$$

will be the solution of comparison (2).

Consider the solution of the simultaneous comparisons of the 1st order

$$\begin{aligned} x &\equiv b_1 \pmod{m_1}, \\ x &\equiv b_2 \pmod{m_2}, \\ &\dots \\ x &\equiv b_k \pmod{m_k} \end{aligned} \tag{4}$$

moduli being not equal to each other and being prime numbers. The solution of the simultaneous comparison (4) is the number class (3) which satisfies all the comparisons simultaneously. It's necessary to find X_0 and m. In the number theory a theorem is proved according to which

$$x_c = M_1M_1'b_1 + M_2M_2'b_2 + \dots + M_kM_k'b_k, \tag{5}$$

$$m = m_1 \, m_2 \dots m_k, \tag{6}$$

where M_k and M_k' are the numbers found in the conditions

$$M_S m_S = m_1 \, m_2 \dots m_k, \tag{7}$$

$$M_S M_S' \equiv 1 \pmod{m_S}, \tag{8}$$

where S takes on the values from 1 to k in succession.

The properties of simultaneous comparison solution (4) are the basis of the interferogram technique proposed. By approaching the result obtained in the number theory to the task being solved in the interferometry it can be interpreted as follows. If linear periodic functions are given by their entire values and their periods are mutually prime numbers, then a linear periodic function with the period equal to the product of the periods of these functions can also be put them in a single-valued correspondence.

Let's determine the phase difference by phase-shifting interferometry (PSI) with one effective wave length. The phase difference values within a period can be put in correspondence to the integers b with the same valid digits and with the number of digits depending on the measurement accuracy. The period determined by the effective wave length can be put in correspondence to the integer m with the same number of digits.

A series of measurements with other effective wave length values such as their periods can be put in correspondance to mutually prime numbers being carried on. X_0 (5) corresponding to the total phase can be unambiguously be found within the dynamic range determined in (6).

The effective wave length can vary due to variation in the wave length, the refractive index of medium and that of angle at wave front interference.

Let's consider a condition when measurements are carried on with two wave length values. They are 0.529 m and 0.633 m. We put the integers 529 and 633 to their correspondence. They are mutually prime numbers. Then the measurement range is determined by tne number of 529 633=334857 which makes 529 times 633 periods. If we consider more decimals or carry on measurements with three or more period values, the gain can be higher.

The main advantage of the method proposed is a substantial increase of the dynamic range thereby high accuracy of measurements characteristic of the phase-shifting interference techniques and independance of the resalts from measurements at adjacent points are maintained. The technique doesn't require introduction of additional elements into the interferometer circuit and allows complete automation of the interferogram decoding.

Interferometrical Microprofilometry
Methods, Resolution and Computersimulation of the Measuring Process

Harnisch, Bernd [1]

Introduction

The optical interferometrical microprofilometry is a fast growing field in the contactless measurement of the profiles of technical and optical surfaces. Optical interferometrical profilers are subdivided by the kind of the reference surface, of the phase measurement and of the measuring process - point by point or parallel with a CCD-row or matrix.

The aim of profilometric methods is the measuring of the surface profile, that means the measuring of the typical surface wavelengths and of the typical surface heights. It isn't possible to fullfill this demand exactly because of the limited resolution of the measuring process.

The vertical resolution depends on the accuracy of the phase measurement (optical heterodyne, phase-shifting-interferometry, phase-lock-interferometry) in the interference pattern. This resolution is typical in the range of $^{1}/_{1000}$ of a fringe distance, and correspondends to a vertical resolution of about 5Å.

The lateral resolution is limited by the diffraction in the optical system and by the scanning length of the measuring process, so that the measurement is bandlimited.

With optical profilers it is possible to calculate the surface heights in dependence on the measuring point distance, so that we will get a discrete profile.

[1] Friedrich-Schiller-Universitaet Jena, Sektion Technologie, Wissenschaftsbereich Technische Optik

Two special optical interferometrical profilers

The optical profilers are commonly two wave interferometers. In any case the measured phase is the difference between object and reference wave. That's why it is important to distinguish the profilers with respect to the reference wave.

Interferometer with a real reference plane and a CCD-row [1]

The principle of this method is shown in figure 1. The basic type of the interferometer is a Linnik-interferometer. The interference fringes are measured in the focal plane of the tubus lense with the help of a CCD-row. The point spacing of the measurement is determined by the magnification. The diffraction limited resolution of the optical system and the resolution and the pixel area are of the same dimension because of the sampling theorem.
The calculated surface profile appears as the pointwise difference between object and reference surface. That's why it is necessary to use a reference surface, which is at least one order of magnitude smoother than the surface to be measured.

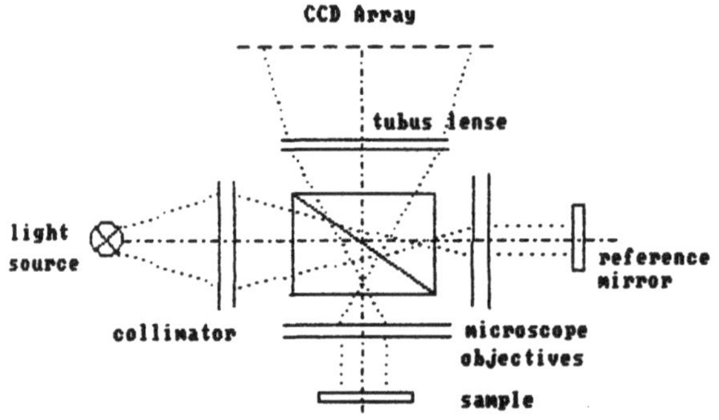

figure 1 Linnik interference microscop

Interferometer with a virtual reference plane created by averaging over a large surface area [2]

The principle of this method is shown in figure 2. The surface is sampled with two linear polarized coaxial beams with orthogonal polarization states One of the beams is

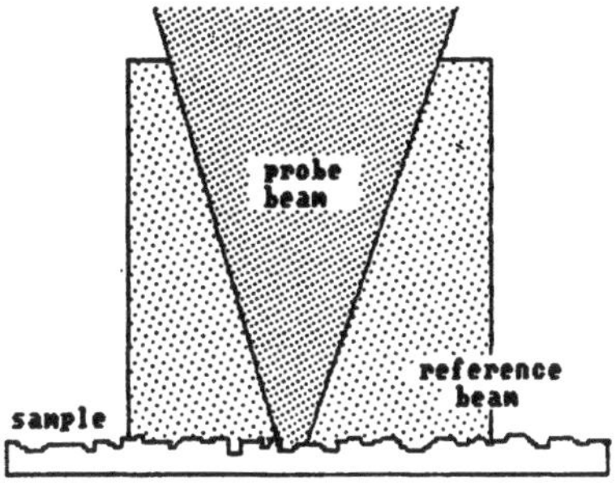

figure 2 reference and probe beam

collimated to a relatively large diameter, while the other is focused on the surface coaxially to the reference beam. The reflected collimated beam carries information about the averaged surface height distribution within the illuminated area, and can be used as a reference. The other beam carries the information about the averaged surface height within the focal spot area. The phase measurement is realized by an optical heterodyne. The measurement is bandlimited by the size of the focal spot diameter and the scanning length.

Surface profile and statistical calculations

The result of the profilometric measurement is a discret surface profile h_i. This profile is a superposition of the geometrical form, the waviness (low spatial frequencies) and the roughness (high spatial frequencies). The measuring of the surface roughness demands the fitting of the profile with a polynom of the order of two and substracting the low frequency part from the profile.

The roughness of the profile can be calculated by using first- and higher-order statistical methods. The first-order statistics leads to the roughness parameters, par example height parameters (rms-height R_q), lateral parameters (S_m) and hybrid parameters (surface slope).

$$R_q = \left[\frac{1}{N} \sum_{i=1}^{N} (h_i - \langle h_i \rangle)^2 \right] \qquad \langle h_i \rangle = \frac{1}{N} \sum_{i=1}^{N} h_i$$

(h_i is the surface height of the i-th from N measuring points)

The use of higher order statistics leads to the statistical functions These are the autocovariance function (ACF), the power spectral density and the higher statistical moments [3].

Computersimulation of the measuring process

In literature many papers deal with the comparison of different techniques for measuring the roughness of optical surfaces. The different techniques have different band limits and so the result depends strongly on the distribution of the spatial frequencies. To make clear the influence of the band limits, the measuring process was computersimulated.

The algorithm used for generating the profile was taken from Whitehous [4]. The profile has a gaussian distribution function with the variance 1 and a defined correlation between adjacent points. The correlation length is about three points (arbitrary units).

The measuring process was simulated for the two interferometers described above. For the measurement with the CCD-row the surface height of the n-th pixel (CCD_n) was calculated by:

$$CCD_n = \frac{1}{int} \left[\sum_{j=1}^{int} h_{int*n+j} \right]$$

In this notation h_i is the i-th point in the generated profile and int is the number of points per pixel.

The integration of the profiler with the two coaxial beams was calculated using

$$P_n = \frac{1}{int} \left[\sum_{j=1}^{int} h_{n+j} \right]$$

The surface height of the n-th point of the measurement is P_n.

In figure 3 the generated profile and the calculations of the measurements with the two profilers are shown. The integration length is twice of the correlation length of the generated profile.

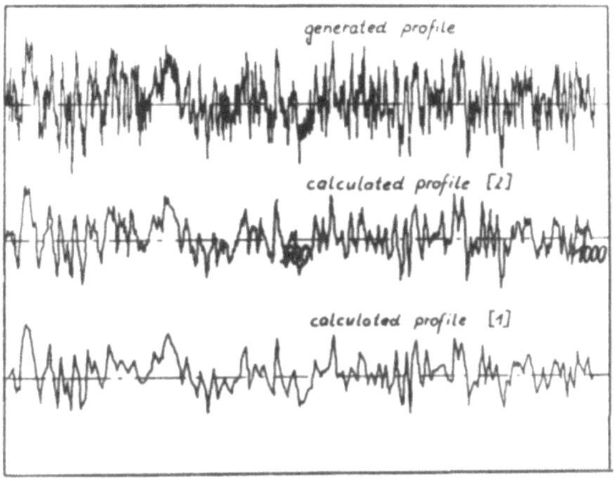

figure 3

The difference between the two principles is the distance of adjacent measuring points. The interferometer with a CCD-row has a distance that is determined by the pixel spacing. The profiler with the two coaxial beams has the possibility to measure the surface with a distance between two points, that is smaller than the diffraction limited resolution. That's why this profiler is able to measure spatial wavelengths, which are smaller than the resolution, but with reduced vertical heights.

[1] Bhushan, B., Wyant, J.C., Koliopoulos, C.L. : "Measurement of surface topography of magnetic tapes by Mirau interferometry" . Applied Optics 24(1985)10,1489-97.

[2] Huang, C.C., "Optical heterodyn profilometry". Optical Engineering 23(1984)4,365-70.

Pantzer, D., Politch, J., Ek, L., "Heterodyne profiling instrument for the angstrom region". Applied Optics 25(1986)22,4168-72.

[3] Nayak, P.R., "Random process model of rough surfaces". J. Lubr. Techn. 93(1971)398-407.

[4] Whitehous, D.J., Phillips, M.J., "Sampling in a two dimensional plane". J. Phys. A: 18(1985)2465-77.

AUTOMATIC ANALYSIS OF YOUNG'S FRINGES IN SPECKLE PHOTOGRAPHY BY HIGH-SPEED IMAGE FITTING

Roland Höfling[1)]

Abstract

Videoprocessor programs have been designed for fast fringe pattern generation. In this way, a new fringe analysis method has become feasible - automatic image fittig. The technique is applied to speckle photography fringes which depend upon two parameters - the speckle displacement vector components. We optimize these parameters until the fringes match.

Introduction

Speckle pattern photography is going to be more and more accepted now in experimental mechanics. Usually, double exposure recordings are analysed point by point in order to measure displacement fields. A thin laser beam is diffracted and yields the so called Young's fringes. The fringes are of simple geometry: straight, parallel and equally spaced. The problems in automatic fringe analysis arise from fringe quality, the fringes are degraded by strong speckle noise and sometimes they have low contrast due to experimental conditions. Nevertheless, a reliable automatic analysis algorithm is the key for a wide application of speckle photography.

Different approaches have been reviewed elsewhere /1,2/. In this paper, we describe a new analysis method that involves a minicomputer system and a videoprocessor of pipeline architecture. Although the software has been designed for a special device /3/, the basic algorithm is portable to systems with similar principles of operation which increasingly come into use. Synthetic fringe patterns are created by the algorithm described below and they are fitted to the Young's fringes originating from the measurement. The shape of synthetic fringes depends upon the simulated displacement $\underline{d} = (d_1, d_2)^T$ and so a best fit yields the desired result. This is a global, non-local method with respect to the image and accordingly, the influence of speckle noise is expected to be considerably suppressed.

It is shown, that this algorithm does still work if few fringes are formed within the diffraction halo and even if the halo is slightly deformed only. This means a shift of the lower sensitivity limit of speckle photography and is an important destinction to other methods.

---

1) Academy of Sciences of the GDR, The Institute of Mechanics P.O.Box 408, Karl-Marx-Stadt, 9010, GDR

Theoretical considerations

For the analysis of a given fringe pattern $I(\underline{d}_0)$ by fitting a synthetic image $I_S(\underline{d})$ to it, we need a measure of conformity and choose the crosscorrelation function c for this purpose

$$c = \frac{\langle I \cdot I_S \rangle}{\sqrt{\langle I \rangle \cdot \langle I_S \rangle}} \tag{1}$$

Synthetic fringes may be calculated starting from the well known formula for the Young's fringes in speckle pattern photography analysis /4/. An example of the fringe pattern is given in fig.1 where a synthetic speckle pattern acts as multiplicative noise /5/. The videoprocessor program described in the next section makes it possible to undertake computer experiments in order to gain some knowledge of the correlation surface $c(d_1,d_2)$. For this purpose, given noisy fringe patterns $I(d_{01},d_{02})$ obtained either experimentally or by computer simulation have been compared with large sets of synthetic fringe patterns $I_S(d_1,d_2)$ and the correlation is calculated as

$$c(d_1,d_2) = \frac{\sum_{ij} I_{ij}(d_{01},d_{02})\; I_{Sij}(d_1,d_2)}{\sqrt{\sum_{ij} I_{ij}(d_{01},d_{02}) \quad \sum_{ij} I_{Sij}(d_1,d_2)}} \tag{2}$$

where i and j denote a location in the discrete image and the double sums are taken over all 512x512 picture elements.

We have varied both d_1 and d_2, independently. The result is given as a grey level representation of $c(d_1,d_2)$ in a 128x128 pixel image. The isolines of such correlation surface are shown in figs.1 and 2.

In the case of large displacements ,three well seperated peaks are found in the correlation function. They are located at $\underline{d} = \pm \underline{d}_0$ and $\underline{d} = \underline{0}$, respectively. An example is given in fig.1.

Fig.2 represents the subfringe case, the diffraction halo is slightly deformed only because the displacement is smaller than the speckle size of about 4 µm. The correlation surface isolines in fig.2 prove the feasibility of peak detection in this difficult case, because the central peak at $\underline{d} = \underline{0}$ is merged in. This makes up a main difference to Fourier transform techniques that will fail in this case. Another important feature of fringe fitting is the inherent noise suppression. This has been proved by comparing correlation surfaces derived from smooth and noisy fringes: we could not find essential differences in the surface shape /6/.

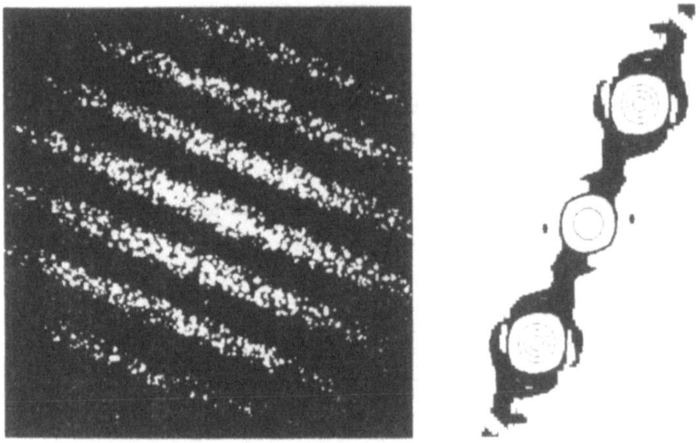

(a) (b)

Figure 1: a) Young's fringes $I(d_{01}=8\ \mu m,\ d_{02}=6\ \mu m)$, computer simulation
b) Lines of equal correlation $c(d_1,d_2)$ in the area
$-60\ \mu m \leq d_1,d_2 \leq 60\ \mu m$

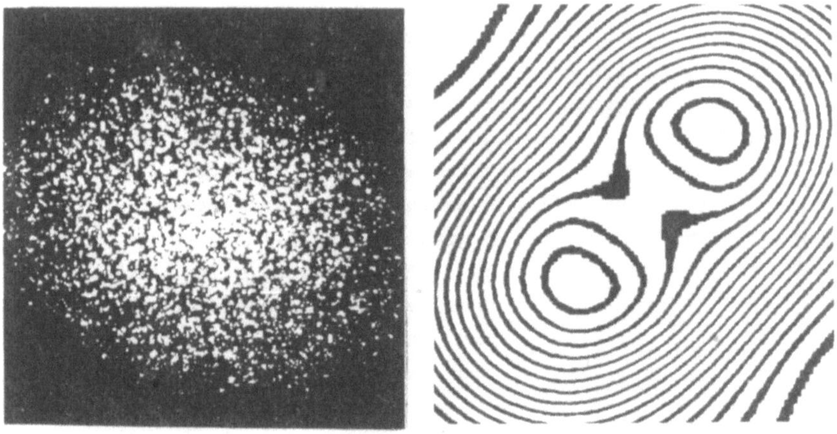

(a) (b)

Figure 2: a) Young's fringes $I(d_{01}=0.5\ \mu m,d_{02}=1\ \mu m)$, computer simulatien
b) Lines of equal correlation $c(d_1,d_2)$ in the area
$-4\ \mu m \leq d_1,d_2 \leq 4\ \mu m$

Implementation

We have already mentioned the importance of a programmable videoprocessor equipment for a fast image fitting procedure. The method itself does not depend upon a certain processor architecture although the algorithms may somewhat differ for various systems. One of the processing channels of our system is sketched schematically in fig.3.

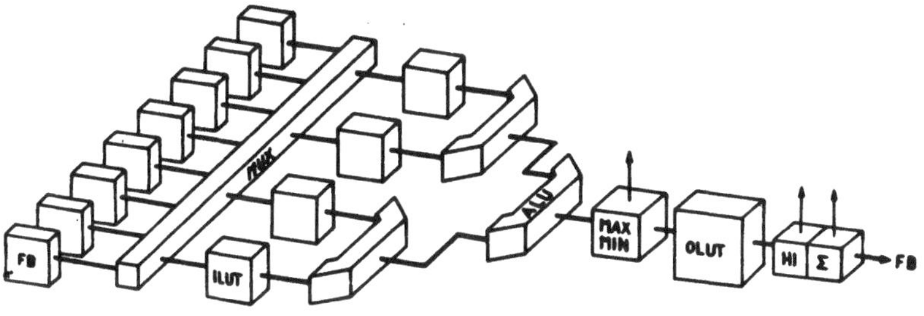

Figure 3: Schematic of one processing channel of the videoprocessor

FB ... frame buffer,	MUX ... input multiplexer
ILUT ... input look-up table,	OLUT ... output look-up table
ALU ... arithmetic logical unit	HI ... histogram extracter

The general concept of image generation by a videoprocessor is to transform grey values into image locations by grey wedges. In a first video cycle, the phase plane of Young's fringes is constructed according to the current displacement vector $\underline{d}$. A second cycle gives the pure cosine fringe pattern by look-up table processing. The last step is to introduce the halo modulation by an image multiplication. The search path for the correlation maximum should be started with a reliable estimate. Moving from one scanning point at the specklegram to the next, the Young's fringes do not vary essentially. This is true for almost all points except for e.g. surface cracks or material boundaries within compounds crossing the scanning path. So we can calculate a good estimate by extrapolating the previousely measured displacement field. The displacement search is based on the correlation values at single points in the d_1-d_2 plane instead of calculating the full correlation surface. The evaluation of equ.(2) for one test point requires more than 1.5 million instructions, we get them executed during one TV cycle by virtue of the videoprocessor performance. All together, it takes us 4 TV cycles to get the correlation value for a test displacement vector. Nevertheless, we had to look for a search algorithm that requires a minimum of test points to find the peak centre. We have implemented a search algorithm that determines the correlation surface tangential plane by a three-point test and steps into the direction of maximum slope.

Test

Simulated fringes have been found to be very useful in developing pattern analysis algorithms and we apply them to accuracy and reliability checks of software products. So we obtain error quantities from test series with simulated displacement vectors. We have carried out a number of such tests and found the algorithm to fail only when starting estimate and solution differ more than 50%. The result of one test is plotted in fig.4 where we have varied both displacement components simulating a position change in the specklegram and found the evaluation results to differ from the simulated displacements with a standard deviation of 0.11 µm and 0.15 µm for d_1 and d_2, respectively. The subfringe case has been tested by simulating $d_2=0$ and low d_1 values and it turned out that reliable pattern analysis is possible for displacements of about 20% speckle size /6/. The correlation search is finished after typically 4 ... 20 steps where the algorithm allows about 2 steps per second.

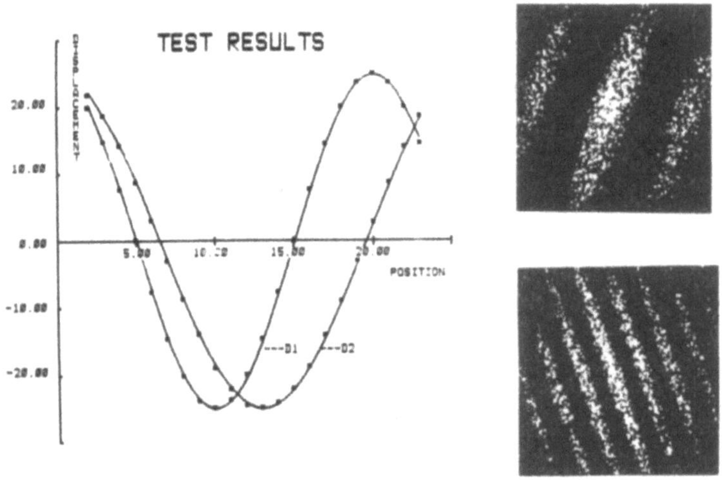

Figure 4: Test results for a series of simulated Young's fringes (left) with various displacement vector components D1 and D2 (in µm) and two example patterns from position 6.0 (above) and 16.0 (below)

First experimental experiences gave surprising reliable operation with good accuracy not only for an in-plane rotation test /6/ but also for poor quality fringes originating from thermally stressed specimens and displacement fields around crack tips.

Conclusion

A new method has been proposed for the analysis of images which content depends upon a few global parameters only but may be seriousely degraded by noise : fitting of synthetic images. The concept has been applied to speckle pattern photography and the feasibility of such approach is proved theoretically and by computer experiment. It could be shown that the crosscorrelation function provides an efficient measure for the best fit search also in the subfringe case where the diffraction halo is only slightly deformed.

Series of simulated Young's fringes have been used to check the algorithms and to give experiences on errors. We have found standard deviations of 0.1 ... 0.2 µm for displacements in the region of 1 ... 25 µm with a halo extension that corresponds to about 4 µm mean speckle size. Fringe synthesizis and correlation are speeded up by a commercial high performance videoprocessor and appropriate software developments.

Depending on the starting estimate and the number of search steps, the analysis of one fringe pattern is accomplished after 2 ... 10 seconds and so the algorithm can also compete from this point of view. The application of fringe fitting analysis to practical problems encourages for further improvements in this field.

References

1	C.J.D.Pickering N.A.Halliwell	Automatic Analysis of Young's Fringes in Speckle Photography and Particle-image Velocimetry, Opt. Lasers Eng., 7 (1986/87) 227-242
2	E.Diez D.Chambless J.Turner	Image processing techniques in laser speckle photography (with application to hybrid stress analysis) Exp. Mech. 26 (1986) 230-237
3	V.Kempe F.Kenner B.Rebel W.Schulze W.Wilhelmi	Interaktives Bildverarbeitungssystem robotron A647x Neue Technik im Büro, 26 (1982) 131-137
4	I.Yamagushi	Fringe formations in deformation and vibration measurements using laser light Progr. in Opt. 22 (1985) 271-340
5	R.Höfling W.Osten	Displacement measurement by image processed speckle patterns J. Mod. Opt. 34 (1987) 607-617
6	R.Höfling	Fringe analysis by automatic image fitting and its application to speckle pattern photography (submitted to Opt. and Lasers in Eng.)

AUTOMATED FRINGE MEASUREMENT BY LINEAR CCD IN VIBRATION ANALISIS BY SPECKLE TECHNIQUES.

Kober V.I., Kotova S.P., Mnatsakanyan E.A., Chupakhin V.N., Shevyakov N.A. [1]

Introduction.

One of the methods of contactless determination of lateral vibration amplitude is the speckle photography method. Fringe obtained as a result of this method, containing the information on the vibration amplitude are one-dimensional, therefore it is convenient to record fringes by means of a receiving camera on the basis of a photosensitive linear charge-coupled device (CCD).

In the offered paper the results of the fulfilled experiments on vibration amplitude measurements for diffuse scattering objects, carried out by the time average speckle photography method are presented. For the experiments automation a computer complex for semimodel simulation of optical measuring systems on the basis of minicomputer and additional CAMAC equipment was used [1].

1. Basic part.

In speckle photography methods of the vibration analysis for the recording of speckle pattern appearing as the result of a laser radiation dispersion by a diffuse object as a rule a photorecording mediums are used that require additional processing (development). In this paper as well as in [2] a liquid crystal spatial ligth modulator (SLM) was used that allows to carry out these measurements in real-time scale. Fig. 1. represents a schematic set arrangement. A diffuse scattering aluminium plate oscillating in the plane perpendicular to the beam was lighted up by He-Cd laser (λ=0.44 μm). The scattered radiation was recorded on the SLM and then was read by means of He-Ne laser radiation (λ = 0.63 μm). With the aid of an objective O a spatial frequency spectrum of image read off from the SLM was formed. In this plane the CCD was mounted. Vibrations were excited by means of a portable electrodynamic vibrator (PEV) onto which a piezoelectric accelerometer was mounted in order to control the vibration amplitude. SLM represented a photoresister liquid crystal structure operating as a reflector. The reflected ligth modulation was achieved owing to the twist effect in the liquid crystal lay-

---

[1] Lebedev Physical Institute of the USSR Academy of Sciences, Kuibyshev Branch. 443020 Kuibyshev, Sadovaya Street, 61.

er. The structure sensitivity was 10^{-5}J/sm^2, the resolution was 45 mm^{-1}.

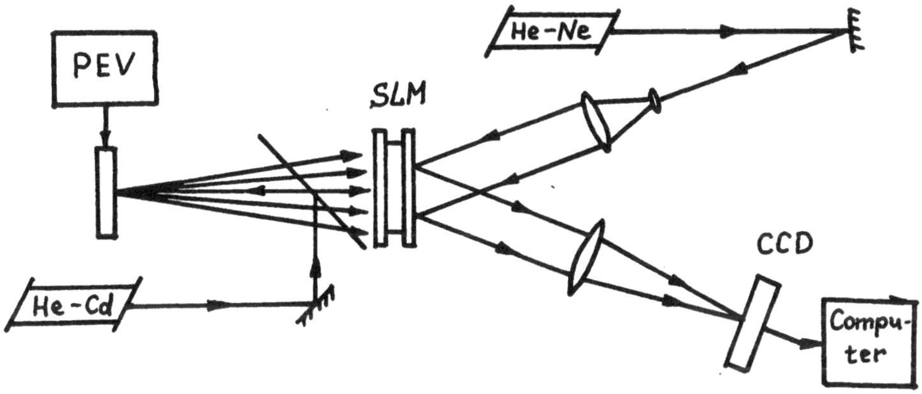

Fig. 1

In the presence of vibrations the speckle pattern in the output plane becomes modulated by fringes oriented perpendicularly to the vibration direction and the distance between the fringes is inversely proportinal to the vibration amplitude. If the object is vibrating under the harmonic law, then the intensity distribution at Fourier plane [3] is described by the following function :

$$I(x,y) = I_o(x,y)\cdot J_o\left(\frac{2\pi L}{\lambda F}x\right), \qquad (1)$$

where $I_o(x,y)$ – the intensity of the wave diffracted at the speckle photograph and obtained from a fixed object, J_o – zero order Bessel function, λ – radiation wave length, F – focal distance of the objectiv fulfilling Fourier trasformation, L – amplitude of the object vibration, x – coordinate parallel to the motion direction.

It follows from equation (1) that the vibration amplitude can be determined by the following formula :

$$L = 0.76\,\frac{F\lambda}{d}, \qquad (2)$$

where d – is the distance between the first minima. The intensity distribution in the direction perpendicular to the fringes was recorded by means of the CCD photosensitive camera, the signal from which was received by the computer complex for its processing through the worked-

-out conjunction module disposed in the CAMAC crate. Together with the mentioned module and number of service ones in the crate there was mounted the module for the reflection of television monitor data, that allowed to put to the screen half-tint and graphic images of the size 256x256 points. In Fig. 2A the standard initial intensity distribution, recorded by receiving camera, is shown. The software part of the complex has a number of subroutine sets : a set of interaction with the modules in the CAMAC crate, a set of processing of one-dimesional and two-dimesional images, a set of data structural transformations, etc. Each section of the processing allows to fulfill different transformations, including statistical, spectral, by-pixel, local and other ones of the corresponding images.

In the present work during the processing the averaging operations by 20 signal interpretations were carried out in order to lower the influence of random interferences. For the impulse interference suppression the median filtering was used, than for obtained signal smoothing an optimal linear correlation with the local window was used, the weighting coeffitients of the window were calculated by an optimal method on assumption that : the signal is the realization of a random stationary process with the exponential correlation function; the calculation criterion is mean squared; the noise is "white", additive. In Fig. 2B the form of the signal after its processing is shown. Than a program determination of the signal first minima coordinates was made and the vibration amplitude was calculated on the basis of equation (2).

The vibrations have the amplitude from 20 to 100 μm and the frequency from 0.1 to 2 kHz. The lower frequency threshold was set by the SLM speed. The minimal vibration amplitude that can be measured by this method must exceed the speckle size in its turn was limited by the SLM resolution. The maximal amplitude measured by means of the speckle photograph method must not exceed such a value depending on the size of a spot ot the object that can result in the disturbance of the speckle pattern correlation at the illuminating of different surface regions. The calculated I and experimental II measured diagrams of the maximum of the speckle pattern cross-correlation function dependence on the shift in case of a round aperture having 5 mm diameter are shown in Fig. 3. The divergency between the experimental and theoretical curves can be explaind by the presence of ligth background at the exposure, resulting in the deterioration, and also by the conditions of the photosensitive medium processing.The accuracy of measurements was limited by the accuracy of the fringe minima determination and a mounted to ~15%. The amplitude values in the error range coincided with the reading of the check out piezopickup.

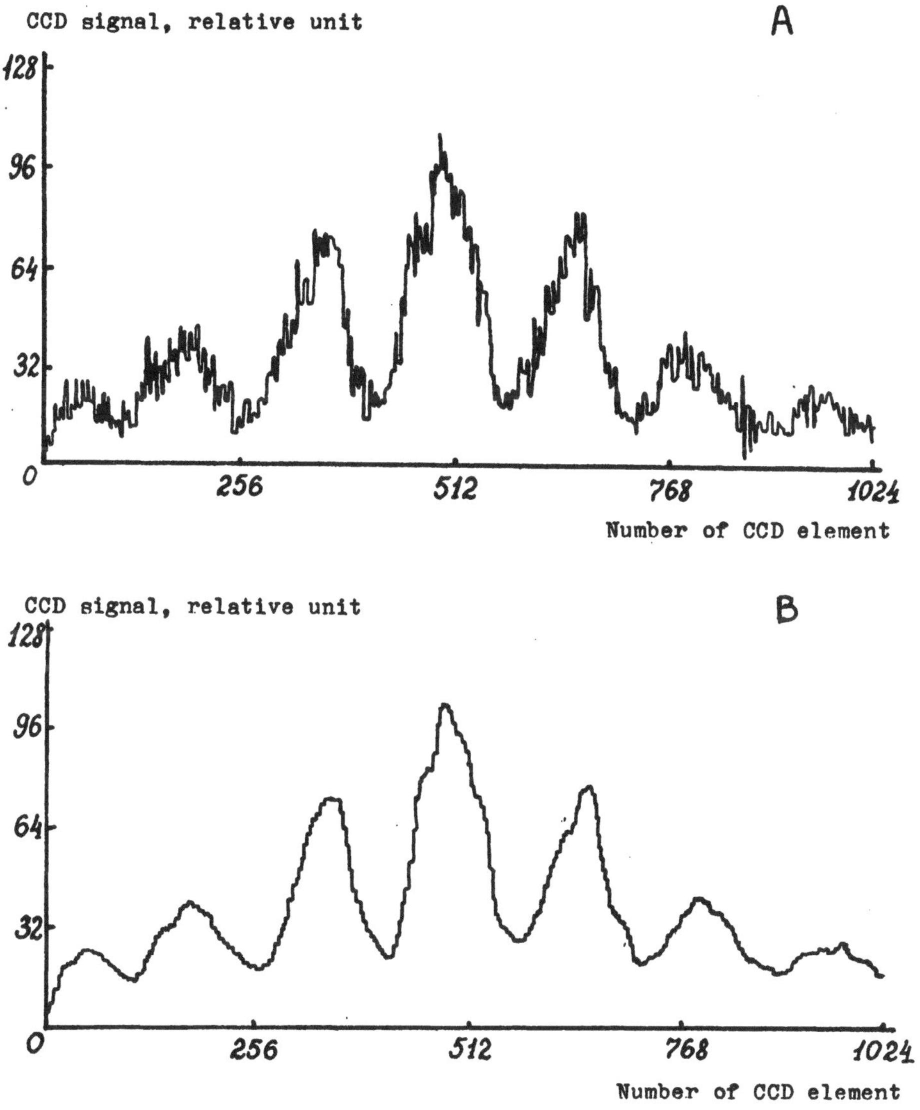

CCD signal, relative unit
A
128
96
64
32
0
256
512
768
1024
Number of CCD element
CCD signal, relative unit
B
128
96
64
32
0
256
512
768
1024
Number of CCD element

Fig. 2.

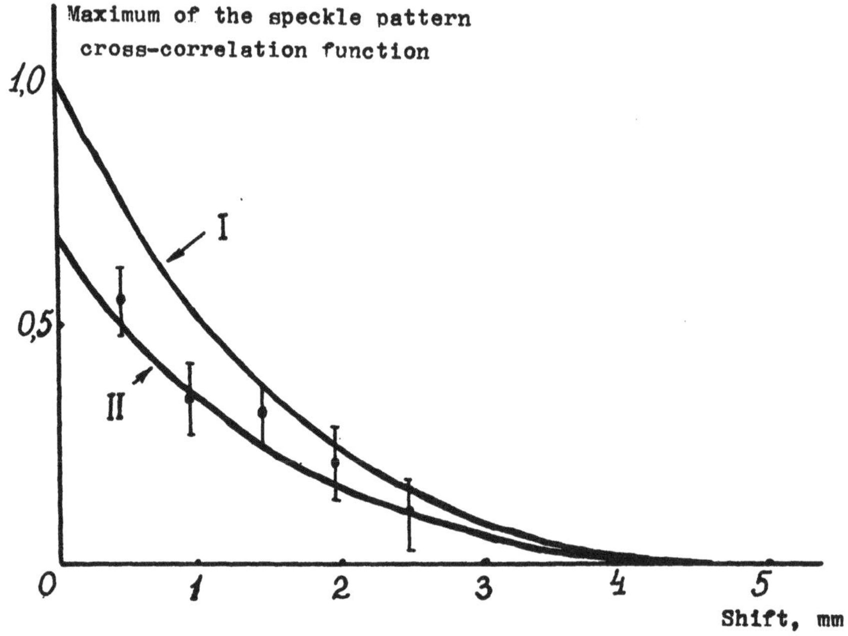

Fig. 3.

References.

[1] Abrosimov A.A., Kotova S.P., Mnatsakanyan E.A.: Development of Spetial Measuring Systems on the Basis of CCD. Laser Technology & Experiment Automation. 198, Proceedings of P.N. Lebedev Physical Institute USSR Academy of Sciences. Science, Moscow 1982.
[2] Dergachyov D.I., Koryakovtsev V.S., Kotova S.P.: Vibration Measurement by Means of Liquid Crystal SLM. Abstracts of the 3-rd Science-Technic Seminar "Optical Propertis of Liquid Crystals & their Application". State Optical Institute, Leningrad 1983, p.85.
[3] Jones R., Wykes C.: Holographyc and Speckle Interferometry. Cambridge University Press 1983.

EVALUATION OF INTERFERENCE PATTERNS BY THE FOURIER-TRANSFORM-METHOD

Thomas M. Kreis [1)]

Abstract

The Fourier transform method accurately determines the interference phase distribution from holographic or other interference patterns. The method pointwisely calculates a phase distribution with sub-wavelength resolution from a single interference pattern. Disturbances like non-uniform background illumination, spurious diffraction patterns, and speckle noise may be filtered out by properly defined bandpass-filters.

Introduction

Quantitative evaluation in interferometric metrology consists of two steps: The first and crucial one is the determination of the interference phase distribution from the recorded and stored interference pattern, the second is the combination of the phase data with data describing the optical arrangement to yield the displacement vector field, the optical path differences, the surface heights or the refractive index field.

The fringe counting methods /1/ for interference phase determination search for local brightness extrema, that correspond to phase values being integer multiples of π. This method gives no uniform sampling, sub-wavelength variations may be overseen.

Phase-stepping /2,3/ pointwisely evaluates with high accuracy, but requires a set of three or more interferograms, reconstructed with a constant mutual phase shift.

Best accuracy is obtained with heterodyne interferometry, where the beat frequency of two interfering optical waves, differing by a mutual frequency shift, is analysed /4,5/. This method requires a high amount of precision mechanics and electronics. Thus it is restricted to laboratory environments.

The Fourier-transform method with additional carrier frequency /6/ requires a shift or tilt in one of the interfering wavefronts to produce a carrier of equidistant parallel fringes. This is not generally possible with all interferometric methods.

The Fourier-transform method as presented in this paper /7,8,9/ requires no additional carrier. It determines one interference phase distribution belonging to the given interference pattern. The method works on a single interference pattern, no multiple phase shifted interferograms are needed. The Fourier-transform method evaluates pointwisely and achieves an accuracy and a resolution in the same range as the phase step methods.

Bremer Institut für angewandte Strahltechnik - BIAS
Ermlandstr. 59, D-2820 Bremen 71, BRD

Numerical analysis

Interferometric metrology today is performed with the aid of digital image processing systems. The reconstructed interference pattern is recorded by a TV-camera, digitized into a rectangular array of pixels, quantized to discrete gray values normally ranging from 0 to 255, and stored.

The measured intensity $i(x,y)$ at the pixel with discrete spatial coordinate (x,y) may be written in the form

$$i(x,y) = a(x,y) + b(x,y) \cos\varphi(x,y) \tag{1}$$

where $a(x,y)$ describes the additive disturbances, mainly the varying background intensity and $b(x,y)$ contains the multiplicative noise related to local contrast variations and speckles. $\varphi(x,y)$ is the interference phase distribution that has to be determined.

Since the cosine is a periodic and even function, each interference phase distribution determined from $i(x,y)$ in Eq. (1) is indefinite to an additive integer multiple of 2π and to the sign /7/.

$$\cos\varphi = \cos(s\varphi + 2\pi n) \qquad s \in \{-1,1\}, \quad n \in \mathbb{Z} \tag{2}$$

The sign correction and determination of the additive term in the phase-unwrapping or demodulation procedure must be based on extra knowledge about the applied loading or deformation.

The Fourier-transform method is based on Eq. (1) expressed as

$$i(x,y) = a(x,y) + c(x,y) + c^*(x,y) \tag{3}$$

with $c(x,y)$ defined by

$$c(x,y) = \frac{1}{2} b(x,y) \exp(j\varphi(x,y)) \tag{4}$$

In Eqs. (3) and (4) * denotes complex conjugation, j is the imaginary unit. The numerical Fourier-transform applied to $i(x,y)$ gives

$$I(u,v) = A(u,v) + C(u,v) + C^*(u,v) \tag{5}$$

Since $i(x,y)$ is a real distribution in the spatial domain, $I(u,v)$ is a Hermitean distribution in the spatial frequency domain, that means

$$I(u,v) = I^*(-u,-v) \tag{6}$$

$A(u,v)$ contains the low-frequency components of the background and is concentrated around the zero-peak. $C(u,v)$ and $C^*(u,v)$ are placed symmetrically to the origin and carry the same information due to Eq. (6) .

Bandpass-filtering in the spatial frequency domain eliminates $A(u,v)$ and one of $C^*(u,v)$ or $C(u,v)$. The remaining spectrum $C(u,v)$ or $C^*(u,v)$ alone is no longer Hermitean, so the inverse Fourier-transform applied to $C(u,v)$ gives a complex $c(x,y)$ with non-vanishing imaginary part. From this $c(x,y)$ the interference phase is calculated pointwisely by

$$\varphi(x,y) = \arctan \frac{\mathrm{Im}\ c(x,y)}{\mathrm{Re}\ c(x,y)} \tag{7}$$

with values between $-\pi$ and $+\pi$, the principal values of the arctan-function. The inverse transform of $C^*(u,v)$ would yield $-\varphi(x,y)$.

A one-dimensional example of the method is shown in Fig. 1. The processed intensity distribution with Gaussian background, varying contrast, speckle noise, quantization to only 4 bit and nonlinear response with local saturation is shown in Fig. 1a. The amplitude spectrum is given in Fig. 1b. The remaining spectrum after filtering is displayed in Fig. 1c, the determined interference phase modulo 2π is shown in Fig. 1d.

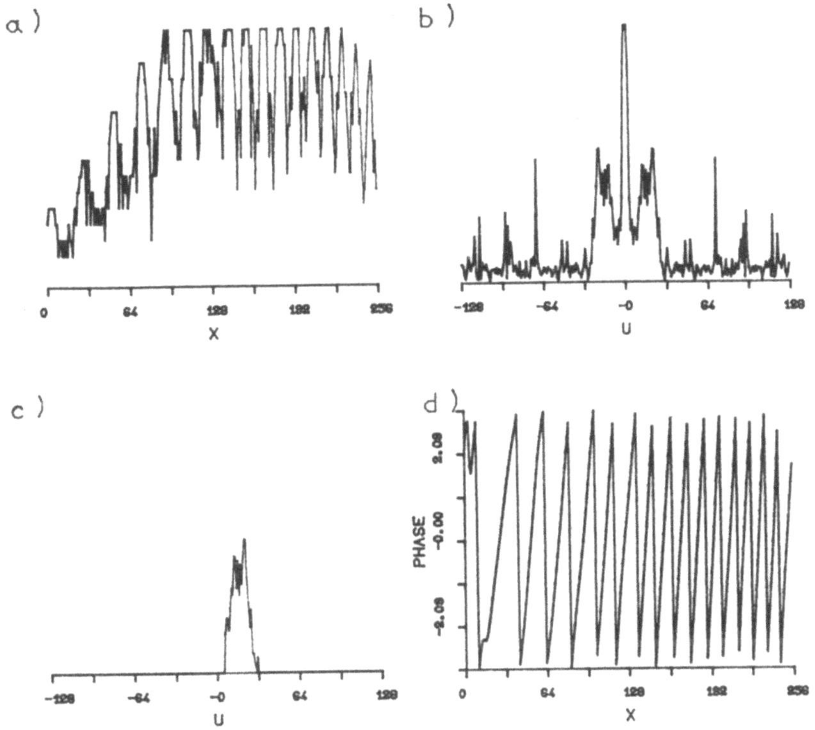

Fig. 1. Fourier-transform evaluation in one dimension

Filtering in the spatial frequency domain

The bandpass-filtering in the spatial frequency domain not only makes the spectrum non-Hermitean, but performs an inherent image enhancement, as shown in Fig. 1. Even better results are achieved, if the tested surface carrying the illumination variation and spurious patterns is recorded before the interference fringes are generated. In holographic interferometry this can be done by recording the surface illuminated by the object wave with a blocked reference wave. In real-time holographic interferometry this pattern can be produced as a holographic reconstruction by the reference wave while the object wave is blocked.

Fig. 2a shows the holographic interferogram of a thermally loaded composite panel, consisting of an internal aluminium honeycomb structure and a surface layer of carbon-fiber reinforced plastic. The recorded background illumination is shown in Fig. 2b. The Fourier-spectrum of the background is normalized to have the same amplitude at the zero-peak as the spectrum of the interferogram, and then is subtracted from this spectrum.

In the two-dimensional spatial frequency domain there are manifold ways to eliminate one halfplane to destroy the Hermitean property. With a passband only in the +u-halfplane, where only positive spatial frequencies in the horizontal direction, but positive and negative frequencies in the vertical direction pass, an interference phase distribution with only increasing phases in the horizontal direction, but increasing and decreasing phases in the vertical direction results. For a filter with passband only in the +v-halfplane these directions interchange. This dependence of the interference phase distribution on the filter orientation can be used for the detection of sign changes: Two phase distributions determined from the same pattern, but with orthogonally oriented passbands are compared to resolve the sign ambiguity, Eq. (2).

Fig. 2c displays the interference phase distribution as determined using a filter with a passband only in the +u-halfplane. In this Fig. $-\pi$ is displayed as black, $+\pi$ is white, the other phase values are linearly mapped to gray-values. After sign correction the demodulation based on the sampling theorem is performed. If the difference of the phase values at adjacent pixels is greater than π, 2π has to be added or subtracted from this pixel on /7, 9/. The differences in vertical direction after correction by adding or subtracting 2π are given in Fig. 2d in a gray-scale display. This image may be interpreted as a shadowcasting of the bumps and holes of the deformation field, in this example caused by debonds of the surface layer to the core.

A pseudo-perspective line by line plot of the interference phase distribution after sign correction and demodulation is given in Fig. 2e. Due to the nearly constant sensitivity vectors of the arrangement in this experiment, the phase distribution is nearly proportional to the normal component of the displacement vector field.

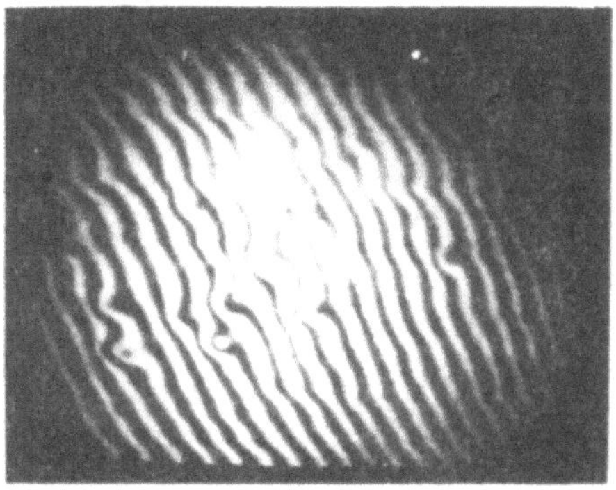

Fig. 2a. Holographic interferogram

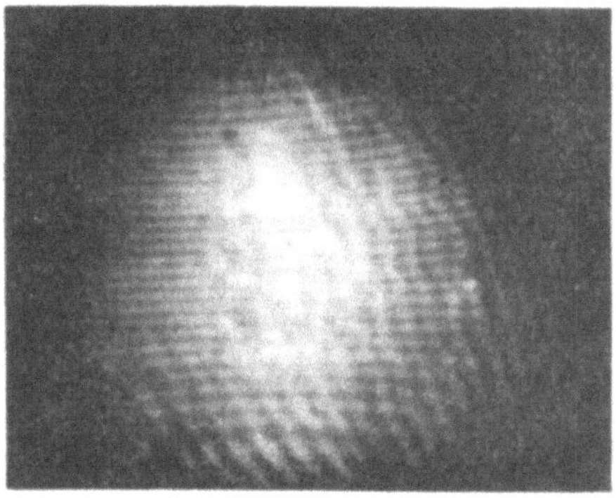

Fig. 2b. Background illumination

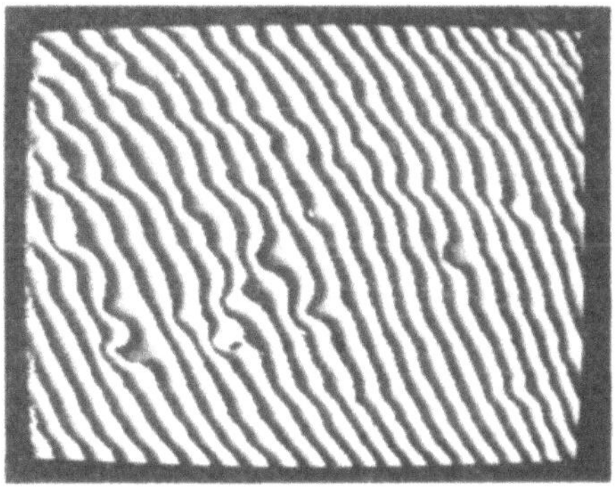

Fig. 2c. Interference phase modulo 2π

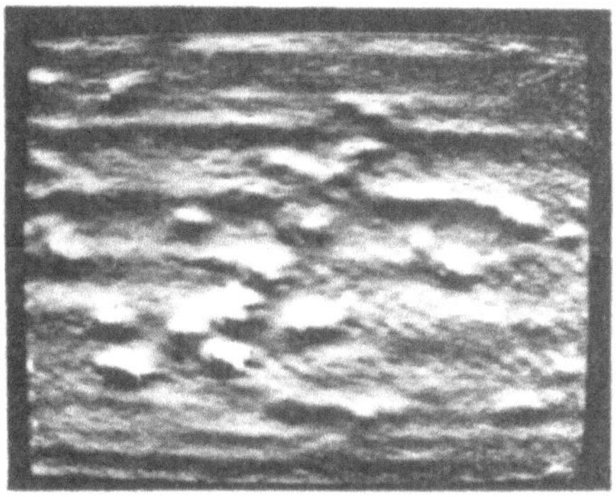

Fig. 2d. Interference phase differences

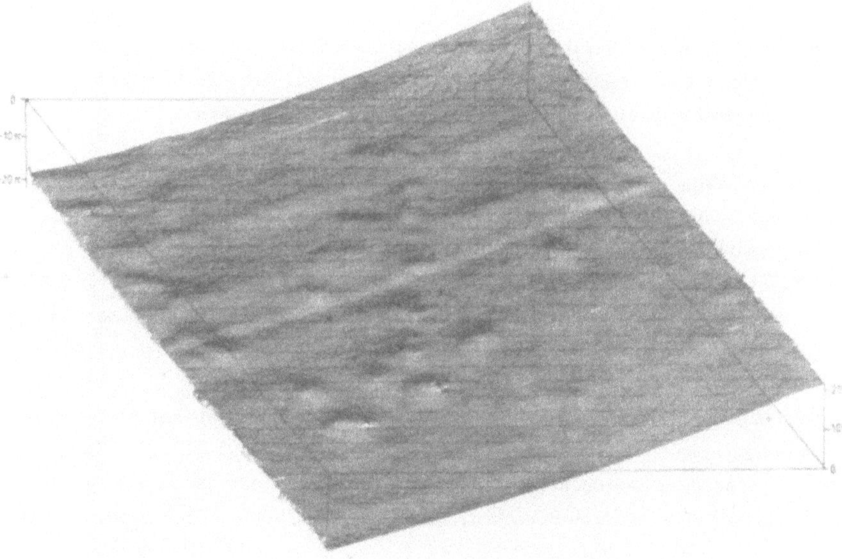

Fig. 2e. Interference phase distribution evaluated by Fourier-transform method

If an interference pattern not covering the whole rectangular frame has to be evaluated, the area of the interferogram must be used as a background /3/. The artificial interference phases outside this area, that occur in the determination, have to be eliminated by masking in the spatial domain.

Conclusions

The Fourier-transform method for interference phase determination offers a number of advantages. It pointwisely determines the interference phase even in the sub-wavelength range from a single interferogram. No multiple recordings, e.g. with phase shifts, are necessary. So the method can be used with pulsed lasers. Archival material, stored as photographs or holograms, can be evaluated.

Image enhancement and noise suppression are performed inherently by filtering out distortions in specified spectral ranges. Previously recorded background patterns are recognized.

The method can be used with all images formed by cosine-related fringes, arising in classical interferometry, holographic interferometry, speckle interferometry, speckle photography, moire topography, projected fringe contouring and other metrologic techniques.

References

/1/ W. Osten, J. Saedler, H. Rottenkolber: Quantitative Auswertung von Interferogrammen mit einem digitalen Bildverarbeitungssystem, Technisches Messen-tm, vol. 54, 285-290 (1988)

/2/ W. Jüptner, Th. Kreis, H. Kreitlow: Automatic evaluation of holographic interferograms by reference beam phase shifting, Proc. SPIE, vol. 398, 22-29 (1983)

/3/ Th. Kreis: Automatic evaluation of interference patterns, Proc. SPIE, vol. 1026 (1988)

/4/ R. Thalmann, R. Dändliker: Strain measurement by heterodyne holographic interferometry, Appl. Opt., vol. 26(10), 1964-1971 (1987)

/5/ Th. Kreis: Quantitative evaluation of interference patterns, Proc. SPIE, vol. 863, 68-77 (1987)

/6/ M. Takeda, H. Ina, S. Kobayashi: Fourier transform method of fringe pattern analysis for computer based topography and interferometry, Journ. Opt. Soc. Amer., vol. 72(1) 156-160 (1982)

/7/ Th. Kreis: Digital holographic interference phase measurement using the Fourier-transform method, Journ. Opt. Soc. Amer. A, vol. 3(6), 847-855 (1986)

/8/ Th. Kreis: Auswertung holografischer Interferenzmuster mit Methoden der Ortsfrequenzanalyse, VDI-Fortschritt-Berichte, Reihe 8, vol. 108, VDI-Verlag, Düsseldorf (1986)

/9/ Th. Kreis: Fourier transform evaluation of holographic interference patterns, Proc. SPIE, vol. 814, 365-371 (1987)

PATTERN SEQUENTIAL ANALYSIS OF SECOND-ORDER MOIRE INTERFEROGRAMS

Kühnert, Rolf and Michel, Bernd [1)]

ABSTRACT

By the example of moireinterferometric deformation analysis in a scanning electron microscope it is represented, how the use of 2nd-order moire patterns can be employed to record additional information in the process of pattern generation as well as to simplify pattern recognition and processing.
A short survey of the theoretical fundamentals of scanning moire analysis is given paying particular attention to the advantages of 2nd-order interferograms.
Finally, the practical application of the measurement technique is demonstrated by the example of its use for the analysis of a certain mechanical problem in fracture mechanics and micromechanics as well.

KEYWORDS

Scanning Electron Microscopy; Scanning Micro Moire Technique; 2nd-Order Moire Patterns; Fracture Mechanics; Fracture Criterion; J-Integral.

NOTATION

r	position vector
R	extrema position vector
L_n	fourier coefficients of the l-structure
$\hat{l}=e_1 \hat{l}=e_1/l$	spatial frequency of the l-structure
s_1	phase shifting vector of the l-structure
u_1	displacement vector of the l-structure
M	interference fringe order
$\hat{f}=e_f \hat{f}=e_f/f$	spatial frequency of the interference structure
a_1	sampling coefficient
L,l	P,p for the object structure
	B,b for the reference structure

[1)] Academy of Sciences of the G.D.R.
The Institute of Mechanics Karl-Marx-Stadt
P.O.B. 408
Karl-Marx-Stadt
G.D.R.-9010

INTRODUCTION

Since it was first recognized and used for measuring purposes on the end of the last century, the moire effect became widely accepted as a handy measurement tool for the experimental determination of relative displacements and related quantities since suitable preparation and recording techniques are available.

In addition to the almost optical realization of the measuring principle several electron-optical modifications have been published in the last years. In connection with the extension of powerfull image processing computers this results in the opening of new, almost pretentious, applications.

In the present paper by the example of moireinterferometric deformation analysis in a scanning electron microscope it should be outlined how the combination of interferograms can be used to simplify recognition and processing as well as interpretation of moire patterns.

Furthermore, the application for analyzing the nearest crack-tip surroundings for the verification of fracture concepts is introduced.

FUNDAMENTALS

As known the superposition of quasiperiodic structures leads to the generation of interference phenomena if a suitable mismatch has been realized.

Their use for measuring purposes is based on a quantitative analysis of the interference structure phase distribution, since its position dependence contains the pointwise information about the relative displacement between the superimposed object (active) and reference structure in the image plane.

In the wide range of metrological applications the so-called scanning moire techniques take a relatively exceptional position. Thereby an electron-optical deflection system realizes the superposition of the reference mode (see e.g. Idesawa et al., 1977).

Especially for the investigation of the nearest crack-tip region in fracture mechanics the so-called micro moire technique (Kühnert and Michel, 1985) has been applied successfully.

Scanning Electron Microscopy.

In a scanning electron microscope (SEM) a primary electron probe -ejected from the electron gun by thermionic or field emission- is focused on the surface of a bulk specimen by an objective coil and scanned over the cut out under investigation by means of scanning coils.

The secondary electrons which are released by the interaction between the

primary probe and the specimen (as well as backscattered, absorbed or transmitted electrons) can be collected by special detectors and transformed into electrical signals.
Their intensity is amplified and represented on the screen of a cathode ray tube that works in the same scanning mode.
So, a magnified image of the investigated surface cut-out can be seen that represents the intensity distribution of the detected signals that correlates to certain properties of the scanned region.
Thus, if the yield of secondary electrons is modulated periodically by a suitable preparation, moire-like intensity distributions can be accepted by the detector, respectively displayed on the screen as interference pattern.
(For further information about Scanning Electron Microscopy see e.g. Goldstein, 1981).

Scanning Moire Interferometry.

Pattern Generation. If the periodic structures $S_p(r)$ and $S_b(r)$

$$S_p(r) = \sum_n P_n(r)\exp\{2\pi in\hat{p}[r+\mathbf{s}_p]\} \tag{1}$$

$$S_b(r) = \sum_m B_m(r)\exp\{2\pi im\hat{b}[r+\mathbf{s}_b]\} \tag{2}$$

with local extrema at R_p and R_b are superimposed additionally or multiplicativelly as well, interference extrema will arise in the image plane with the outward unit normal $\mathbf{e}_a || \mathbf{e}_p x \mathbf{e}_b$ at the positions

$$\{R\} \subseteq \{R_p\} \cap \{R_b\} \tag{3}$$

Now, if the recording device interpolates between the intensities of nearest extrema R_i and R_j with $[R_i - R_j] = \mathbf{D}$ an interference structure with the spatial frequency $\hat{f}$ can be observed. Thereby for $\mathbf{e}_p\mathbf{e}_b < 1$ $\hat{f}$ can be expressed as

$$\begin{aligned}\hat{f} &= \mathbf{D} \times [\hat{p} \times \hat{b}] = \hat{p}[\mathbf{D}\hat{b}] - \hat{b}[\mathbf{D}\hat{p}] \\ &= a_1\hat{p} - a_2\hat{b}\end{aligned} \tag{4}$$

respectively for $\mathbf{e}_p\mathbf{e}_b = 1$

$$\begin{aligned}\hat{f} &= [\hat{p} - \hat{b}]/[\mathbf{D}\hat{p} - \mathbf{D}\hat{b}] \\ &= a_3\hat{p} - a_3\hat{b}\end{aligned} \tag{5}$$

what takes into consideration that with $\mathbf{e}_p\mathbf{e}_b \to 1$ a steady turn of the interference pattern only will appear for $a_1 = a_2 = a_3 = 1$.
Thus, the interference fringe order, M, is obtained as

$$M(R) = R\hat{f} = R[a_p\hat{p} - a_b\hat{b}] \tag{6}$$

with $a_p = a_1, a_3$; $a_b = a_2, a_3$.
(So only if $[a_p s_p \hat{p} + a_b s_b \hat{b}]$ is zero or integer also M will be integer.)
However, in practice at least one of the spatial frequencies $\hat{p}$ and $\hat{b}$ are positiondependent in most of the cases. By setting

$$\hat{p}'(R) = \hat{p}[R - u_p(R)] \quad | \quad \hat{p} = const \tag{7}$$

$$\hat{b}'(R) = \hat{b}[R - u_b(R)] \quad | \quad \hat{b} = const \tag{8}$$

M can be rewritten as sum of a mismatch and a displacement term in the form

$$M(R) = R[a_p\hat{p} - a_b\hat{b}] - [a_p u_p(R)\hat{p} - a_b u_b(R)\hat{b}] \tag{9}$$

<u>Pattern Processing.</u> To use equation (9) for measurment problems it is advisable to satisfy $a_p = a_b = 1$ and independence on position of defined items.

<u>-1st-order patterns.</u> If the superscript k denotes any analysing increment and the subscript i=x,y the plane component, the object structure displacement $u^k(R) = u_p{}^k(R)$ can be derived componentwise as

$$u_i{}^k(R) = p_i[M_i{}^o(r)\big|_{r=R} - M_i{}^k(R)] \tag{10}$$

for $e_{pi} \| e_i$.
Presumed an accuracy of fringe centre detection of 5% this leads to an accuracy in displacements of about 1.0 E-03mm.

<u>-2nd-order patterns.</u> The designation 2nd-order pattern was choosen to illustrate the superposition of two any-like fringe patterns (Kühnert <u>et al.</u>, 1987) what does not need to result in a higher-order fringe pattern in every application. There are many imaginable realizations to utilize the larger information content of such interferograms; here only the componentwise superposition of $M_x{}^k(R)$ and $M_y{}^k(R)$ should be introduced in detail.
It is clear from equation (9) that for $e_{pi} \| e_{bi} \| e_i$ the object structure displacement at the nodes R^k of the interference fringe mesh of such a pattern now can be derived as

$$\begin{aligned} u_i{}^k(R^k) &= [1 - p_i/b_i][R_i{}^k - R_i{}^o] \\ &= [1 - p_i/b_i]\, U_i{}^k \end{aligned} \tag{11}$$

Therefore, in microscopic regions of about $1mm^2$ an accuracy in displacements of about 2.0 E-04mm can be reached.
Consequently, the requirements of pattern recognition and processing can be reduced to the recording of the interference nodal trajectories in the image plane. While the density of the interference mesh (also for separated components) can be calibrated by the interferometric magnification $[1-p_i/b_i]^{-1}$ the direction of the displacement vector $u^k(R^k)$ is fixed by that of $U^k(R^k)$.
Additionally, the migration of the interference nodes R^k unambiguously differs from that of other intensity extrema.
For these reasons and because no assumption is made to the phase response of the superimposed structures the 2nd-order approach seems to be suited, especially for the computer aided analysis of deformation processes

APPLICATION IN FRACTURE MECHANICS

Fracture mechanics has in view to estimate the reliability of engineering materials and structures with cracks or crack similar defects.
The basic approach used for this purpose is the comparision of a fracture parameter (fracture criterion) that only depends on component and crack geometry and the applied load with a fracture thoughness beeing a material constant.
While the choosen fracture parameter can be numerically calculated , the fracture thoughness value has to be determined experimentally.
Often used criteria like the J-integral in its various formulations also for non-linear material behaviour is based on a near-crack-tip energy balance. So, the knowledge of mechanical fields like displacements and related quantities in this region is of most importance.
This analysis can be done with sufficient accuracy by means of the 2nd-order micro moire technique described above in a handy way.
Additionally, since the analytical solutions for the plane displacement components on the crack tip are known, the onset of energy dissipation by yielding processes in the crack surroundings can be controlled by the local curvature of the interference node trajectories.

REFERENCES

Goldstein, J.I. (1981). Scanning Electron Microscopy, Plenum Press, New York, 1981.
Idesawa, M., T. Yatagai and T. Soma (1977). Appl. Opt., 16, 2152-2162.
Kühnert, R. and B. Michel (1985). Phys. stat. sol. (a), 89, K163-165.
Kühnert, R., B. Michel and K. Haberland (1987). Patent DD 247507 A1 08.07.1987.

DIGITAL IMAGE PROCESSING AS A PREREQUISITE FOR THE ANIMATION OF DEFORMATIONS MEASURED BY MEANS OF HOLOGRAPHIC PROCESSES

Dr.-Ing. H. Marwitz*

0. ABSTRACT

From the combination of DIGITAL IMAGE PROCESSING of holographic interferograms using the PHASE-SHIFT process and non-coherent optical contour generation based on the PROJECTED FRINGE method, it is possible with the aid of COMPUTER ANIMATION to reproduce deformations of components which have been measured by means of pulse holographic processes in the form of a moving picture.

1. INITIAL SITUATION

If lightweight design priciples are to be optimally applied, it is necessary to have a profound understanding also of the deformations of components when subjected to various loads which determine their operation and their service life.

Preference is given to the use of holographic methods nowadays for the analysis of real-life deformations, although such methods display the following paradox:

The density and coding of the holographic information are structured so highly an in such a complicated manner that an excess of information distorts the look at the essential relationships. This demands more than the human imaginative faculty can cope with, which in turn results in only a fraction of the available information being used.

Our colleagues on the stress analysis side were basically confronted by the same problem. They, too, had to present the results of their stress analyses in a plausible manner to their clients. As this is not easily achieved with columns of figures, they turned at a very early stage to using animation of computed deformations as an aid in their work.

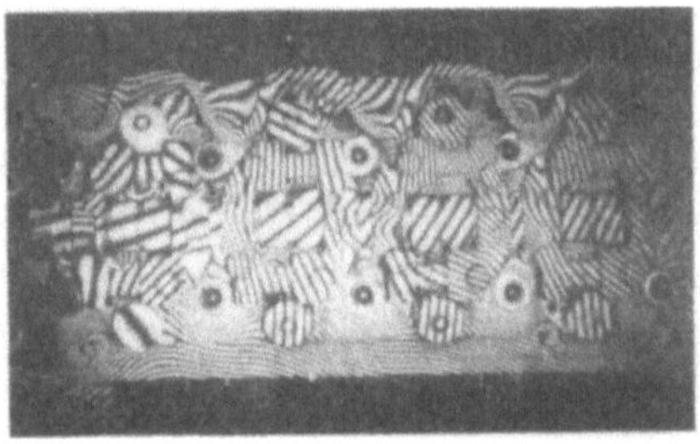

Fig. 1
Hologram of a cylinder head subjected to bolting forces

A computer develops the deformed body contour in stages from a lattice structure of the body under examination. As this is done with an adequate number of intermediate steps and with an exaggerated deformation scale, the end result of the condensed presentation give the impression of a moving picture of a virbration.

The aim of our endeavours was to provide the same presentation technique for holographic interferometry, in order to overcome the paradox referred to above.

* DAIMLER-BENZ AG, D-7000 Stuttgart 60, Mercedesstraße

2. DIGITAL IMAGE PROCESSING OF HOLOGRAPHIC INTERFEROGRAMS

This process is based on the use of a double exposure hologram which can be image-processed using the PHASE-SHIFT method. It is immaterial in this connection whether use is made of a continuous-wave (CW) laser for static exposures or of a pulsed laser for dynamic problems. In practice, the two processes differ only in the type of hardware used.

In the case in question, the task was to determine the mode shape of a commercial vehicle fan:

Following initial electronic analysis to determine the natural frequencies, the respective oscillation forms were excited by a shaker.

Image-processable mode shape holograms can be produced in different ways:

* Both reference beams are operated synchronized to the particular exposure with Pockels cells.
* The pulses are triggered at large intervals such as to be initiated at a defined amplitude of the harmonic oscillation (Fig. 2).
* A CW laser is operated with an acusto-optical modulator such that it always only illuminates two defined positions in the manner of a stroboscope.

Excitation amplitude and trigger point are selected with the aim of achieving optimum fringe density.

Fig. 2
Pulse hologram of mode form of a fan

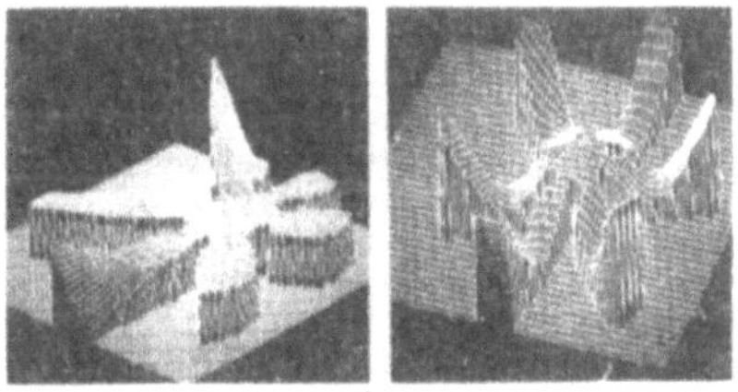

Fig. 3
Deformation plots of the mode forms of a fan

Once the image-processable holograms are available, it ist state-of-the-art to then process them to produce deformation plots. Even animation of the pure, unidimensional deformation vector is a feature offered nowadays by commercially available PCs.

3. CONTOUR GENERATION

Animating the body contour instead of the deformation vector of the body under examination requires not only the deformation array but also a second data set, that of the body geometry.

There are a number of requirements which apply in respect of this data set, which rule out use of traditional contour generation methods:

1. The deformation hologram and the contour image must be so well harmonised as to allow a deformation and a geometrical depth value to be assigned to each pixel

2. The process must permit deformation measurement and contour generation in a single setup.

3. The system must be automatable.

These restrictions reduce the number of suitable possibilities to two basic processes in different variants:

3.1 "DIFFERENCE IN WAVE NUMBER" METHOD

Image-processable interferograms meeting the above conditions can be produced by a holographical comparison of two wave fronts, the individual light paths of which display differences in wave numbers which are proportional to the geometrical depth of the body which is the subject of the measurements.

* The two wave length method
  The body is holographed with two slightly differing wave lengths using the phase-shift process.

* The two media method
  Between the two exposures of the double exposure hologram, the refractive index of the surrounding medium is slightly altered, producing interference structures as a result of the difference in the length of the optical paths.

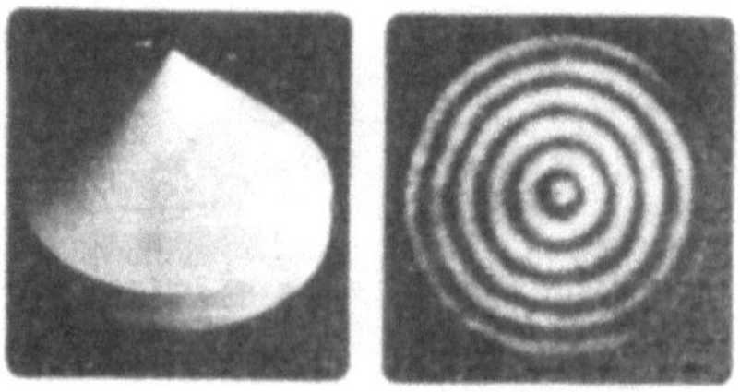

Fig. 4
Cone and contour hologram

Both patterns contain the depth information relating to the body.

The stratified interference surfaces intersect with the body under examination and produce contour lines on it.

The surfaces of identical intensity which intersect with the real bodies, are as a rule not planes with parallel faces, perpendicular to the observation direction, but are generally curved three-dimensional surfaces.

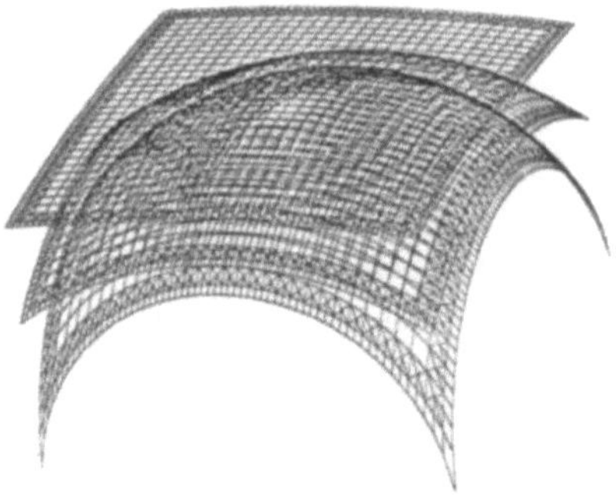

Fig. 5
Correction planes

Appropriate correction algorithms should be used to back-calculate the intersection curves in such a way that they simulate an intersection with two-dimensional surfaches. The benefits of this process lie in the optimum sensitivity for the depth dimension and the best possible utilization of the image.

The drawbacks lie in the experimental realisation:

* The immersion tank method has limited application.

* The wave length method founders on the availability of a practical laser which can be activated to emit adequate energy at a suitable difference in wave length.

3.2 "TWO OBJECT BEAM" METHOD

The image of the projection of a harmonic, lattice-like intensity distribution on a body is distorted as a function of its expansion of depth.

The projection can be performed with holographic or coherent-optical means or even with white light. This process harbours the conflicting aims, though, that maximum fringe sensitivity results in minimal image utilization and, vice versa, with maximum image utilization, the sensitivity for the depth dimension approaches zero.

It is immaterial what is the physical origin of the interference fringes for the algorithm of the phase-shift method. It is, therefore, also possible to project a white light sine lattice onto the body, the local phase can be shifted and the remainder of the processing conducted with the phase-shift method.

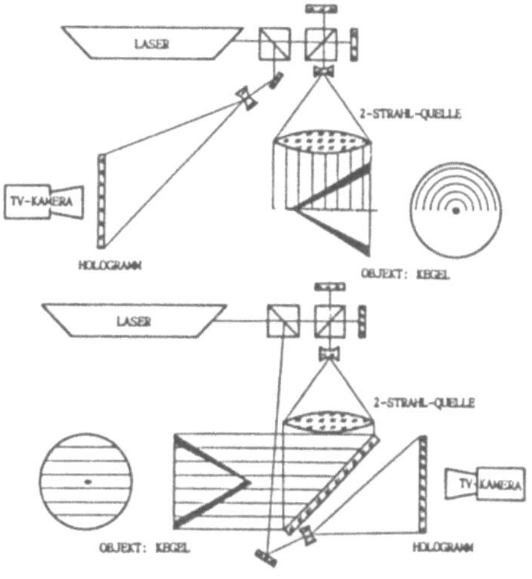

Fig. 6
Conflicting aims between sensitivity and image utilization

It was not feasible to consider this extraordinarily practical process for industrial applications until the following problems had been solved:

* The actual contour information is embedded in a ramp.

* Resolution is restricted in view of the fact that the 8-bit deep useful signal contains both the ramp as well as the object contour.

* Overcoming the conflicting aims between image utilization and depth sensitivity.

4. WHITE LIGHT CONTOUR GENERATION

As a result of illuminating the body at an angle, which is the means of at all producing the intersection curves with the depth information, a ramp-like expansion of depth of the body is simulated, which is of no significance for its relative expansion. The numerical separation of the contour from the ramp proved to be hypercritical as it is not possible to sufficiently accurately measure the structure geometry relations which are needed for this operation. The goal was finally achieved by following a different path:

The self-calibrating correction systematic consists in the fact that two complete data sets of the object from different perspectives are obtained from a symmetrical illumination setup.

If both exposures are overlapped they can then calibrate each other or close shading gaps.

The result ist

* A complete contour description of the visible part of the body.

* Enhanced accuracy by averaging the halftones in areas with overlapping and

* Resolution of the depth dimension with the entire image storage depth by skilful formation of additions based on halftones on a modulo-pi image plane followed by demodulation.

Fig. 7
White light illumination of a cone

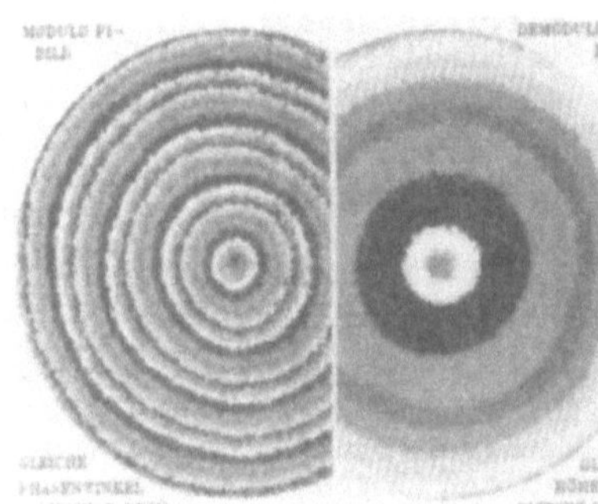

Fig. 8
Demodulation with cone as example

5. MAINFRAME COMPUTER PROCESSING

Following holographic and contour-technical image processing

* the deformation data set and

* the contour data set

are available in the dimension 512*512*8 bits at the PC level. These two data sets are now transferred to the mainframe computer in each case with 262144 dots.

Following numerical data processing, the quantity of data must be reduced on a problem-oriented basis as it is only practical to animate with up to 5 000 nodal points at the most.

A problem- and surface structure-oriented lattice or surface element description, known as the "topology", is derived from the contour data set, the intersection points of this topology being filed in the "nodal point list" with the geometry description.

6. ANIMATION

For the animation of measured deformations, the same topology is taken as the basis for the deformation data set. In other words, the shift vectors are removed from the deformation data set for all the nodes of the nodal point list and filed in a reduced shift data set.

This is followed by a comput ing step in which any desired number of image phases of the harmonic oscillation is calculated from the

* contour topology, the
* geometry nodal point list

  and the
* reduced shift data set

with a randomly selectable amplitude increase and filed as an animation data set.

The animation computer composes these intermediate image phases so rapidly that it produces the illusion that the component (in this case, the fan) is continuously oscillating.

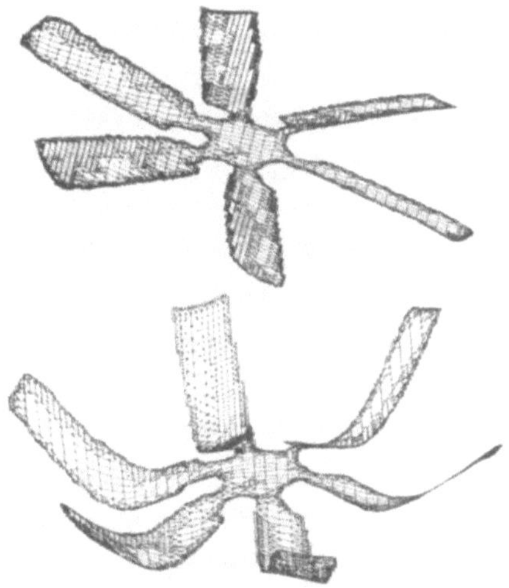

Fig. 9
Mode form of a fan

HIGH-SPEED ARITHMETICAL SUPPORT IN PHASE-SHIFTING INTERFEROMETRY

H.-H. Meyer, M. Goessel

1. Problem

In phase-shifting interferometry it is of practical importance to compute the expression

$$\phi(i,j) = \arctan \frac{I_2(i,j) - I_4(i,j)}{I_3(i,j) - I_1(i,j)} \qquad (1)$$

fast and with the accuracy of at least one degree, where $I_k(i,j)$, $j=1,\ldots,4$, are the grey scale values for the corresponding images (s. e. g. [1]).

In this paper we show how $\phi(i,j)$ can be calculated by the pipeline processor A 6472. For an image range of 512 x 512 with each $I_k(i,j)$ having an eight bit grey scale value the computation of the 2^{18} values of $\phi(i,j)$ according to (1) takes about two seconds.

2. Hardware

The basic component of the display processor system is a processing pipeline with four eight bit input ports and one eight bit output port (see fig. 1). Every two of the input ports are connected by an arithmetical logical unit (ALU) via look-up-tables (LUT) While passing the input-look-up-tables the image data can be extended up to ten bits. The execution of the first arithmetical or logical operation leads to an eleven bit value.

Processing the output streams of the first two ALUs, a third arithmetical logical unit yields twelve bit data which are taken to a shifter unit.

The data leave that shifter unit in ten bit format.

Finally, each data item has to pass an output-look-up-table with an output wordlength of eight bits. (For more details we refer to [2]).

Academy of Sciences of the G. D. R.,
Central Institute of Cybernetics and Information Processes,
P.O.Box 1298,
DDR - 1086 Berlin

3. Solution ([3])

At first the absolute values

$$J_1(i,j) = | I_2(i,j) - I_4(i,j) |, \tag{2}$$

$$J_2(i,j) = | I_3(i,j) - I_1(i,j) | \tag{3}$$

and the sign of the quotient are computed with the sign bit being stored separately.

It is impossible to compute

$$K = \frac{J_1}{J_2} \tag{4}$$

in a first step and arctan(K) in a second step because of the restricted wordlength of the pipeline processor. This will become obvious by the following example:

In order to distinguish between

$\tan(0°) = 0$

and $\tan(0° 30') = 0.0087$

we need numbers less than 2^{-6}.

On the other hand,

$\tan(89° 30') = 114.59$

can only be represented by a number greater than 2^{6}.

Hence, the solution to this problem is to compute arctan(J1/J2) in one step using the output-look-up-table of the pipeline processor. Simple "floating point numbers" are introduced in order to guarantee the desired accuracy.

The input wordlength of the mentioned look-up-table is ten bits. Therefore we have chosen a five bit mantissa for J_1 and J_2, respectively.

All grey scale values greater than 31 have to be shifted and rounded up to the five most significant bits.

The amount of shift we call exponential characteristic.

f1(x) is the shift of x defined for the dividend (plus an offset of 4)

$| I_2(i,j) - I_4(i,j) |$

f2(x) is simply the shift of x for the divisor

$| I_3(i,j) - I_1(i,j) |$

The difference between the exponential characteristics controls the calculation of the arcustangens.

By use of an offset of four for f1(x), negative differences can be avoided.

$$f1(x) = \{ \begin{array}{ll} 4 : & 0 \le x \le 31 ; \\ 5 : & 32 \le x \le 62 ; \end{array} \tag{5}$$

$$
\begin{aligned}
&6 : \quad 63 <= x <= 125 \;; \\
&7 : \; 126 <= x <= 251 \;; \\
&8 : \; 252 <= x <= 255 \;\}
\end{aligned}
$$

$$
f2(x) = \{ \begin{aligned}
&0 : \quad 0 <= x <= 31 \;; \\
&1 : \quad 32 <= x <= 62 \;; \\
&2 : \quad 63 <= x <= 125 \;; \\
&3 : \; 126 <= x <= 251 \;; \\
&4 : \; 252 <= x <= 255 \;\}
\end{aligned} \tag{6}
$$

In dependence on the value of $f1(x) - f2(x)$ the two five bit mantissas, which are the input of the output-look-up-table, have to be interpreted in different ways. This will be done by use of nine distinct configurations of output-look-up-tables in nine successive steps.

In each step the incoming data are transformed by input-look-up-tables to obtain a five bit mantissa as follows:

$$
f3(x) = \{ \begin{aligned}
&x*32 && : \quad 0 <= x <= 31 \;; \\
&int((x+1)/2)*32 && : \quad 32 <= x <= 62 \;; \\
&512 && : \quad x = 63 \;; \\
&int((x+2)/4)*32 && : \quad 64 <= x <= 125 \;; \\
&512 && : \; 126 <= x <= 127 \;; \\
&int((x+4)/8)*32 && : \; 128 <= x <= 251 \;; \\
&512 && : \; 252 <= x <= 255 \;\}
\end{aligned} \quad \text{for } | I_2(i,j) - I_4(i,j) | \tag{7}
$$

$$
f4(x) = \{ \begin{aligned}
&x && : \quad 0 <= x <= 31 \;; \\
&int((x+1)/2) && : \quad 32 <= x <= 62 \;; \\
&16 && : \quad x = 63 \;; \\
&int((x+2)/4) && : \quad 64 <= x <= 125 \;; \\
&16 && : \; 126 <= x <= 127 \;; \\
&int((x+4)/8) && : \; 128 <= x <= 251 \;; \\
&16 && : \; 252 <= x <= 255 \;\}
\end{aligned} \quad \text{for } | I_3(i,j) - I_1(i,j) \tag{8}
$$

The resulting mantissas are combined in the corresponding ALU by "logical OR" where the mantissa of the dividend becomes the upper five bits and the mantissa of the divisor the lower five bits of a ten bit word to be processed in the output-look-up-table.
Nine distinct configurations of output-look-up-tables transform these combined five bit mantissas for matching pixels to eight bit angle values.

For a good visual presentation the range of the resulting angle values has to be stretched from a range of

$$-90° \le \phi \le +90°$$

to $0 \le g(\phi) \le 255$

with $g(\phi) = (\phi+90) * 255/180$ (see fig. 2(b)).

Afterwards, the saw-tooth phase image may be scanned as in ([4]).

Acknowledgement

This investigation was stimulated by W. Osten and we thank G. Hess for preparing the figures 2 a - 2 d.

References

[1] OSTEN, W., HOEFLING, R., SAEDLER, J.
"Two computer-aided methods for data reduction from interferograms"
SPIE, Vol. 863, Industrial Optoelectronic Measurement Systems Using Coherent Light (1987), pp. 105-113

[2] LUTH, W., VILSER, R.-J., EICHHORN, N., GOESSEL, M.
"Bitgenaue schnelle Arithmetik mit dem Bildverarbeitungssystem BVS A 6472"
Angewandte Informatik (applied informatics), 3/1988, S. 110-115

[3] MEYER, H.-H., GOESSEL, M., OSTEN, W., HOEFLING, R.
"Verfahren zur Verknuepfung zweier Grauwertbilder"
DD-Patentanmeldung, 1988

[4] HOEFLING, R., LINDNER, E.
"A parallel fringe-scanning algorithm for phase-shifting interferometry"
Journal of Modern Optics, 1988, Vol. 35, No. 5, pp. 843-846

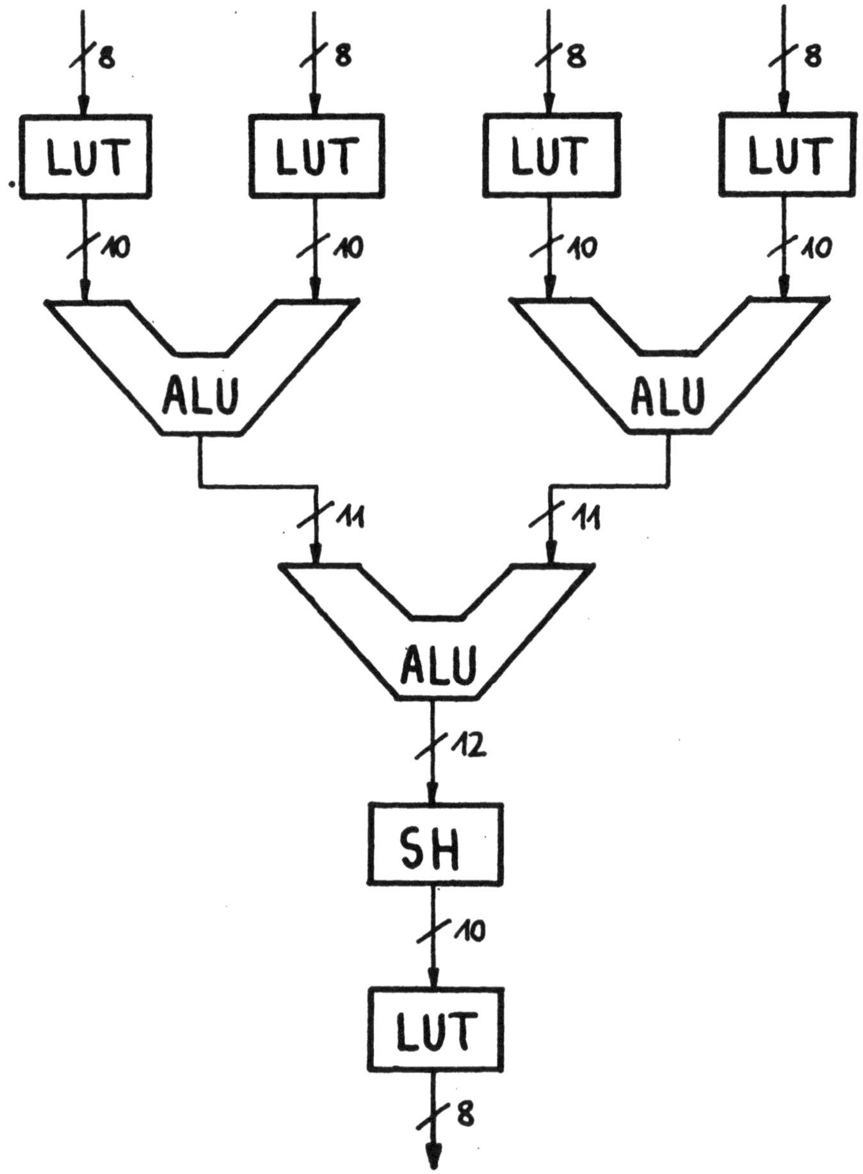

Fig. 1 Display processor system

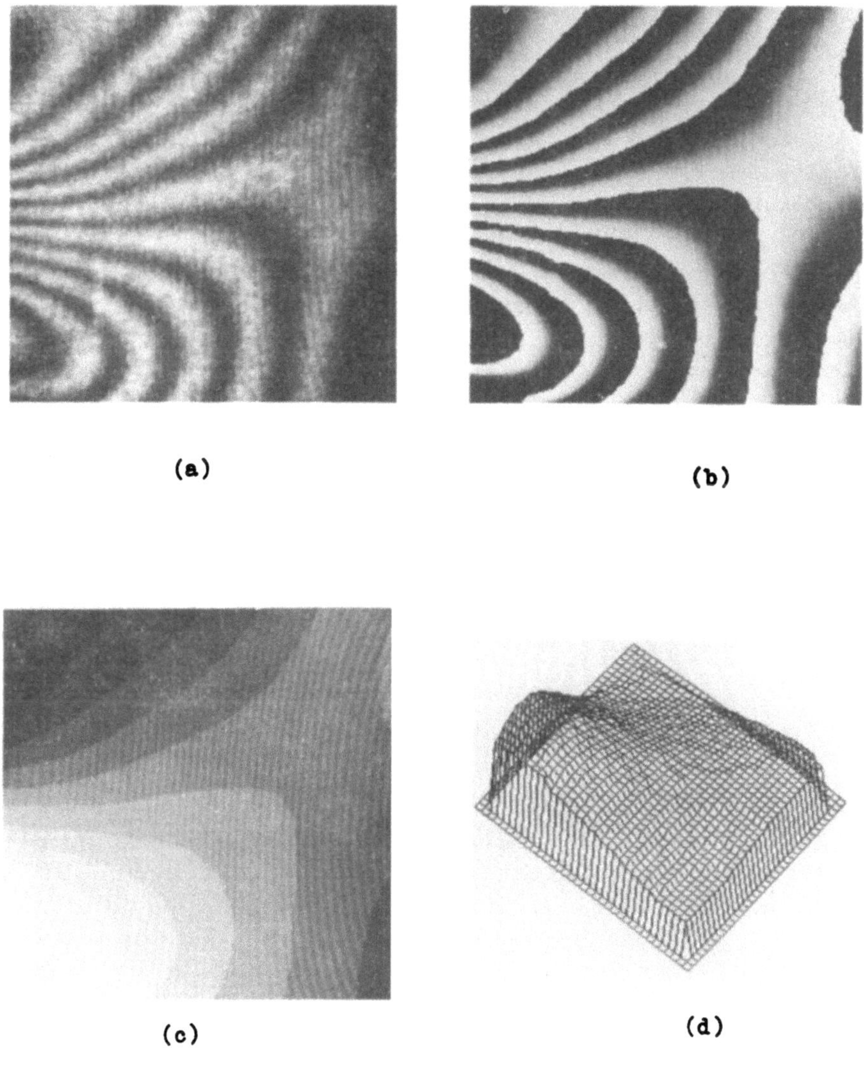

Fig. 2. (a) I_1(1:512, 1:512) (b) ø - image (0 ≤ g(ø) ≤ 255)

(c) result of fringe-scanning algorithm ([4]) (d) pseudo-3D-plot

THREE METHODS FOR THE INTERPOLATION OF PHASE VALUES BETWEEN FRINGE PATTERN SKELETONS

Mieth,Ulrike[1]
Osten,Wolfgang[2]

1. Introduction

The holographic interferometry is widely used for measuring deformations of solid objects. It yields images of the object covered with interference fringe patterns.
For the analysis of the interferogram a skeleton of the fringe pattern is derived (skeleton method) and the phase distribution and the displacement field are evaluated from the skeleton. The skeleton constructed as a result of the computer-aided digital image processing is an image where the places of the interference maxima (bright fringes) and the interference minima (dark fringes) are approximated by lines.
After assignment of the interference order to each line the phase values are known along the skeleton lines. For these points, the displacement can be determined by the basic equation of the holographic interferometry

$$\lambda N = \vec{S} \vec{d}$$

with N - interference order,
λ - wave length of the used laser light,
$\vec{S}$ - sensitivity vector,
$\vec{d}$ - displacement vector.

---

[1]
Academy of Sciences of the GDR
Institute of Informatics and Computing Technique
Rudower Chaussee 5
GDR-1199 Berlin

[2]
Academy of Sciences of the GDR
Central Institute of Cybernetics and Information Processes
Kurstrasse 33
GDR-1086 Berlin

The task to determine the phase value and the displacement for each image point corresponds to the problem of recovering a function from its contour lines. The irregular distribution of the points with known values (nodes) makes it difficult to evaluate the phase value for any other point situated between the skeleton lines. The required interpolation would be easier in the case of a regular grid of nodes or in the case of nodes situated on parallel lines. Two-dimensional splines (Hayes [1], Späth [2]) or orthogonal polynoms (Clenshaw [3], Cadwell [4]) could be used.
By using B-splines Hayes ([1]) developed methods working for irregularly distributed nodes too. But these methods and also the interpolation using surface splines by Harder ([5]) require the solution of large systems of linear equations, which is very computing time consuming. There are also suitable interpolation methods for one-dimensional problems (for example Matczak [6]).
In this paper the solution of the problem is divided into two steps:

1. evaluation of the phase values for a regular grid of nodes,
2. evaluation of the phase values for all points by using the (in the first step) determined values of the grid nodes.

In the following several methods for both solution steps will be described and discussed.

2. Description of the methods

In the first interpolation step the image is covered by a regular mesh and for all grid points the phase values are interpolated. Three interpolation methods have been developed :

1. sophisticated bilinear interpolation,
2. mixed one-dimensional spline interpolation,
3. interpolation by triangulation.

All three methods have been tested for the example of a synthetic interferogram of a centrally loaded and tilted plate. For the interferogram and its skeleton see figure 1 and figure 2, respectively.
In the second interpolation step, the calculated phase values of the grid points can be used to the determination of the phase values for the whole image by some interpolation. It can be done very quickly by bilinear interpolation in the rectangular parts or aiming for a smoother image at the expense of the computing time by two-dimensional splines.
In the following the three mentioned interpolation methods for the first interpolation step will be described more detailed.

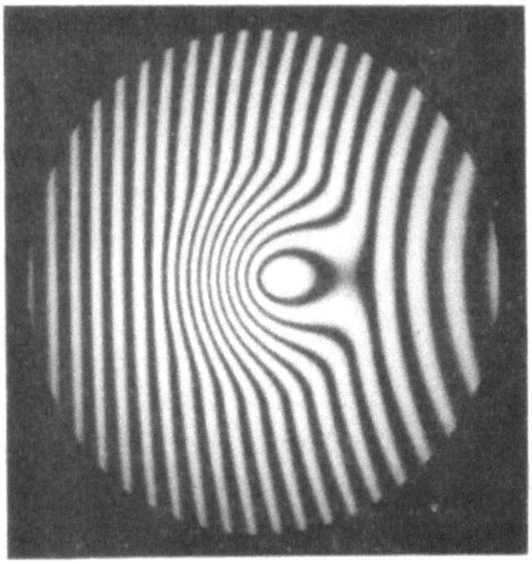

Fig.1 Synthetic interferogram of a loaded plate

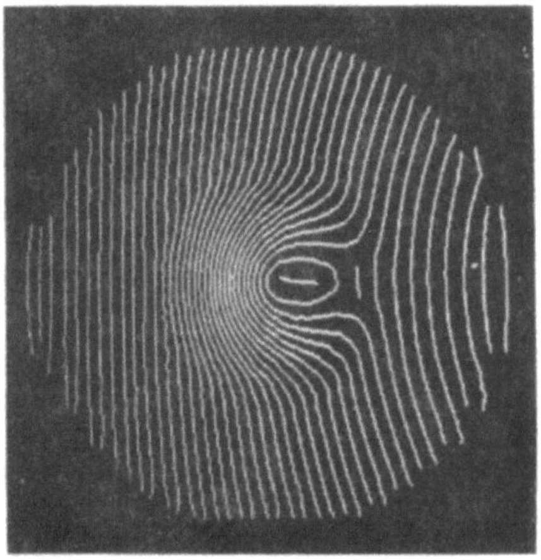

Fig.2 Skeleton of a loaded plate

2.1.Sophisticated bilinear interpolation

This method and also the much more expensive interpolation by triangulation take into consideration the special geometrical position of the skeleton lines in the given interferogram.
For each grid point the least quadrangle containing this point and posessing vertices on skeleton lines is determined. To evaluate the phase value of the grid point the values of the next skeleton lines in horizontal and vertical direction are considered in a bilinear interpolation. For this aim, the fixed quadrangle is transformed onto the unit square, the value of the quadrangle point corresponding to the grid point is evaluated and the inverse transformation of the square onto the quadrangle is carried out.

2.2.Mixed one-dimensional spline interpolation

The combination of one-dimensional cubic splines yields a very simple method (at the expense of the precision). We get the phase value for each grid point as the arithmetical mean value of both values evaluated by one-dimensional cubic splines for the grid lines and the grid columns, respectively.

2.3. Interpolation by triangulation

The whole skeleton is covered with triangles, like in the finite-element-method. The triangles are placed so between the skeleton lines that the vertices and one side are situated on the lines. That's why the phase values of the vertices of all triangles are known. In the interior of the triangles a linear interpolation can be used. For each grid point at first the triangle containing it has to be determined, then the phase value can be evaluated by using the corresponding linear function.

The required triangulation of the image is carried out automatically step by step for interactively fixed image parts. Figure 3 shows the triangulation of the skeleton of the loaded plate.

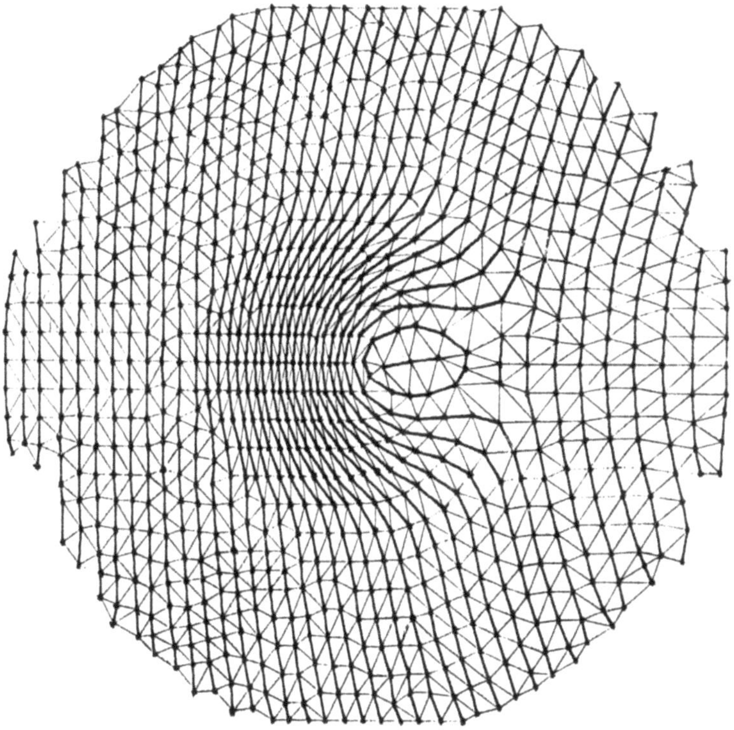

Fig.3 Triangulated skeleton of a centrally loaded and tilted plate

3. Comparing remarks

In the test of the three described interpolation methods with the synthetic interferogram the triangulation method proved to be the best one regarding accuracy. Its disadvantage is the relative high computing effort. The used spline and bilinear interpolation are very fast and robust, but not so accurate as the triangulation. For a comparison of the considered methods see the in figurés 4 and 5 presented results concerning the determined phase values in chosen grid lines and columns. For noncomplicated skeletons an accuracy of 1/10 of wave length can be achieved for all three methods. That gives the possibility to measure displacements in the order of magnitude of 100 nm.

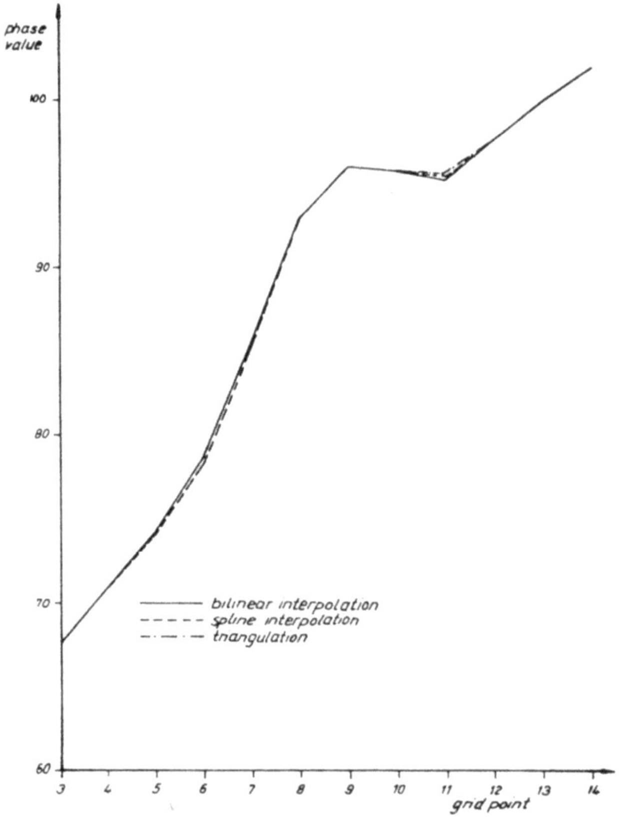

Fig.4 Results of three interpolation methods for a chosen grid line

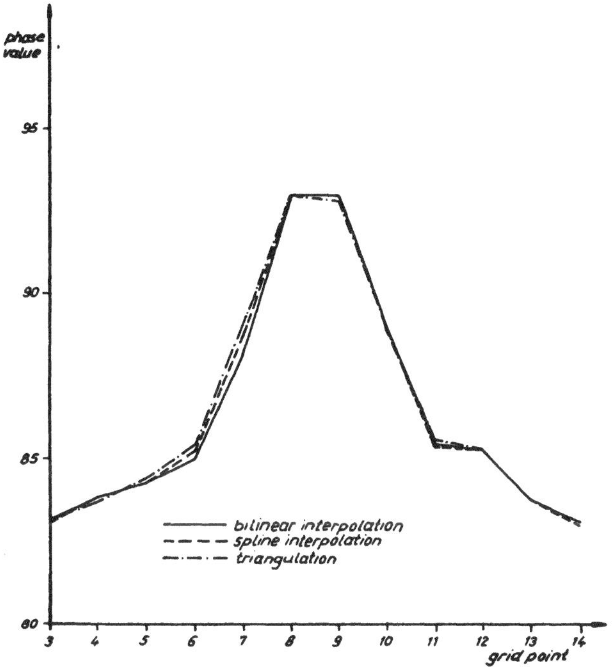

Fig.5 Results of three interpolation methods for a chosen grid column

4.Literature

[1] Hayes,J.G.,Halliday,J., The least-squares fitting of cubic spline surfaces to general data sets, Journ. Inst. Maths.Applics14(1974), pp.318-324

[2] Späth,H, Spline Algorithmen zur Konstruktion glatter Kurven und Flächen,R.Oldenburg Verlag München Wien 1973

[3] Clenshaw,C.W., Hayes,J.G., Curve and surface fitting,Journ.Inst. Maths.Applics(1965),pp.164-183

[4] Cadwell,J.H., Williams,D.E., Some orthogonal methods of curve and surface fitting,The computer Journal,(1961,62),pp.260-264

[5] Harder,R.L.,Desmarais,R.N.,Interpolation using surface splines,Eng. notes(1972),pp.189-191

[6] Matczak,M.J.,Stupnicki,J.,A new method of experimental data interpolation minimizing error of final results,Symposium Optika '84

ALGORITHMS FOR AUTOMATIC OBTAINING OF PREPARATIONS USED FOR THE COUNTING OF PHASE DIFFERENCE OF HOLOGRAPHIC INTERFEROGRAMS

Mnatsakanyan E.A., Nefyodov S.V.[1].

In optic measurements related to interferometric methods (both in holographic interferometry and in conventional one) it is necessary to reproduce phase differences of interfering light beams along the surface of fringe localization. In general the light intensity along the image plane of interferogram can be set by the following expression:

$$I(x,y)=I_0(x,y) \times M(\varphi(x,y)) \qquad (1)$$

where I(x,y) is the intensity along the image plane,

$I_0(x,y)$ - some background intensity,

$M(\varphi)$ - a positively defined function(modulation or characteristic fringe function,

$\varphi(x,y)$- phase difference of interfering light beams along the image.

In general case characteristic functions are not single-valued in relation to phase. Thus, for instance, in case of time average holographic interferometry of sinusoidally vibrating objects the modulation function is the squared Bessel function of the first kind, zero order, and the equation (1) acquires the following form:

$$I(x,y)/I_0(x,y)= M(\varphi(x,y))=J_0^2(\varphi(x,y) \qquad (2)$$

For a correct determination of the $\varphi(x,y)$ function it is necessary to know the single-valued regions of modulation function arguments, where the solution of equations (1) and (2) is searched (the diagram of $M(\varphi)$ for the case (2) is shown in Fig.1a).

In the paper the method of preparation constructing is proposed, it allows to practically completely automate the solution of equations (1) and(2) in relation to the phase for a wide group of interferograms with a sufficiently complicated fringe pattern.

The preparation of two types are proposed . The first type serves for a direct phase determination in all the points proceeding from the values of the $M(\varphi)$ function in these points and the function form. This preparation is preferable on condition that the devices allow to determine I(x,y) and $I_0(x,y)$ precisely enough and local phase changes are important. The preparation represents a two-dimensional array in which the regions of single-valued $M(\varphi)$ function are coded by a correspon - ding number.

Extracting the intensity value in the initial interferogram image and then determining the corresponding region of the phase change on the preparation we may find the true values of the $\varphi(x,y)$ function, having solved equations (1) and (2), as far as the phase change range for

1).Lebedev Physical Institute of the USSR Academy of Sciences,
Kuibyshev Branch. 443020 Kuibyshev , Sadovaya Street,61

a given point of the interferogram is known from the $M(\varphi)$ function form In Fig.1b the diagram of $J_0(\varphi(x,y))$ function preparation along a certain line $l(x,y)$ of the interferogram image plane is presented.

The usage of the second type preparation is reasonable in case when it is either difficult to exactly determine $I(x,y)$ and $I_0(x,y)$ functions or the errors committed in the determination of local phase changes are not decisive. The preparation of this type represents a two-dimensional array in which the maximum and minimum centres of the interferogram fringes are coded by a corresponding number. As a matter of fact this is an interferogram skeleton in which maximum and minimum lines have their codes corresponding to the fringe orders (Fig.1b). As far as the phase values for a specific $M(\varphi)$ function on these lines are known then chosing certain points on these lines and with the help of various interpolation methods we may reproduce with a sufficient degree of accuracy the $\varphi(x,y)$ function along the interferogram image surface. It should be emphasized that in a general case this method does not allow to register local phase changes, especially far from the skeleton lines. After the initial optical information filtering of various noises the preparation obtaining is realized by two stages.

Stage 1. Skeletonizing of interferogram image.

A skeleton is prepared in which the maxima and minima are coded by different numbers, for example, 255 and 254 correspondingly(Fig.1c).

Stage 2. Preparation obtaining.

In order to produce a preparation the interferogram skeleton is scanned by an expanding spiral leading off from an arbitrary point lying on the zero order fringe and indicated by an operator(Fig2). In case of the first type preparation obtaining the codes are automatically disposed at the covered points in accordance with the being scanned region of the single-valued characteristic function starting from zero (Fig.1b). When the intersection of the skeleton points occurs then the check of these points with the inner points of the scanned region of the interferogram skeleton is carried out. As a result of the obtained information it becomes possible to determine whether another region of single-valuedness is encountered or not and how the filled-in code is modified in case if it really is encountered.

In case of the second type preparation obtaining the regions between the skeleton lines are not marked. When the skeleton line is encountered the latter is being retraced together with its code modification. If the scanning revealed a line with already modified code then the modification code is correspondingly changed. The preparation is ready when the skeleton is completely scanned. In case of complicated modes and if there is more than one zero-order fringe at the interferogram then firstly the preparation with one given zero-order fringe is made.

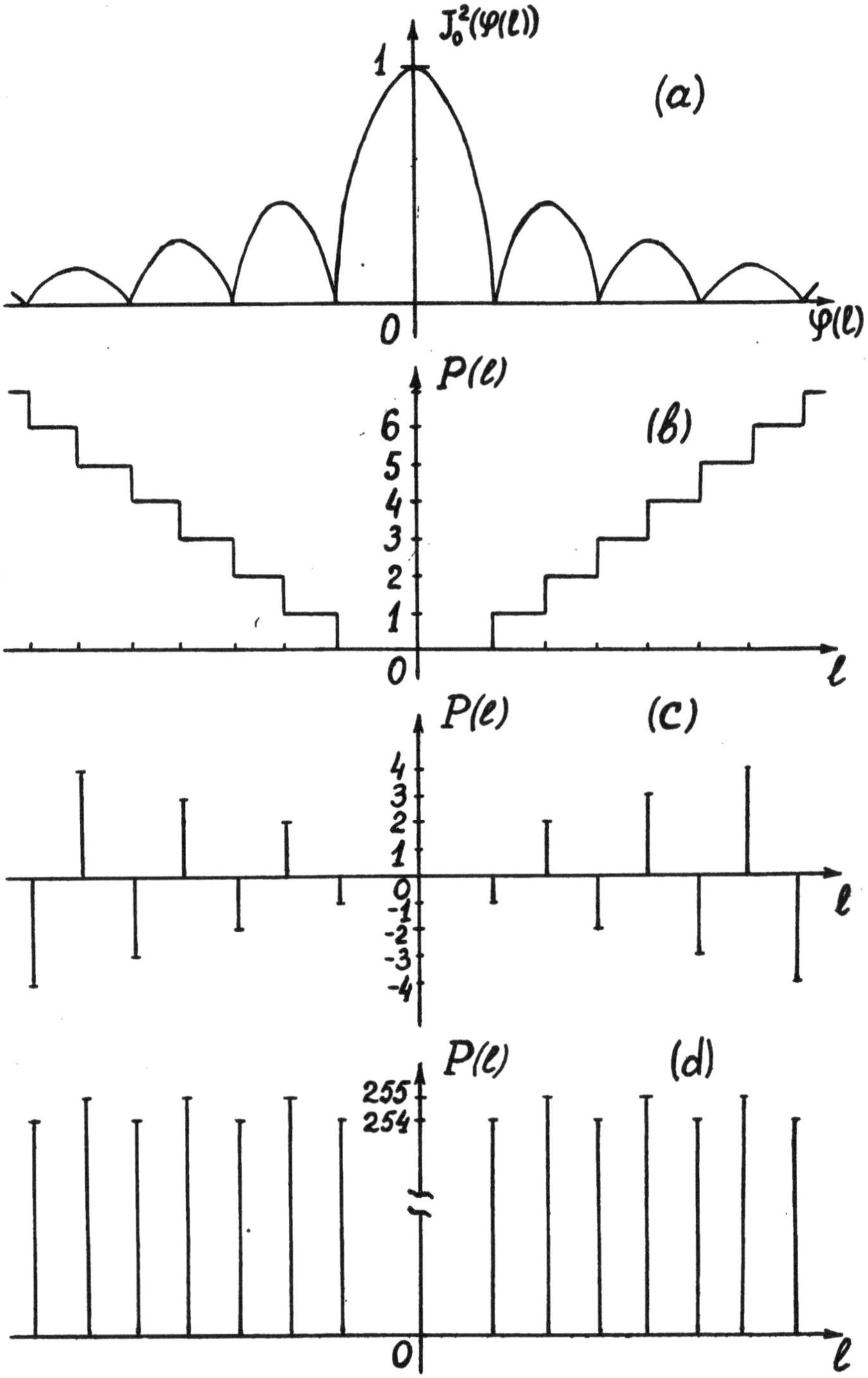
$J_0^2(\varphi(l))$
1
(a)
0
$\varphi(l)$
P(l)
(b)
6
5
4
3
2
1
0
l
P(l)
(c)
4
3
2
1
0
-1
-2
-3
-4
l
P(l)
(d)
255
254
0
l

Fig. 1.

Then the co-ordinates for one arbitrary point belonging to other zero-order fringes are introduced successively , after that the determined marking codes are modified. Thus the algorithm allows to make preparations for a wide variety of interferograms.

The advantage of the offered methods consists in the fact that at the stage of the fringe counting an operator participation is excluded. As far as the decision about the filled-in code change is reached after the check inside the scanned region where the code has already been determined, then the algorithm allows to "count" fringes of a complex structure. The described algorithms function succesfully even in the presence of a split zero-order fringe. If there is splitting of other fringes this difficulty can be overcome by a slight complication of the algorithm. In fact this complication comes to the joining up of both types preparations obtaining methods. A specific algorithm realization is of course more complicated than the described method since during the scanning it is necessary to take into account the image bounds, the type of the skeleton lines connectivity, the peculiarities of the hardware, etc.

The proposed methods were tested on the interferograms of real objects vibrating sinusoidally. In order to realize this method a software has been developed working under the control of the operating system RSX-11M, version 4.1, in the ASIP-complex (Automated System of Image Processing) on the basis of SM-4 computer. The format of the used initial image was 256 x 256 x 8 bit, the average processing time including the noise filtering and the skeleton constructing was several minutes.

Literature

[1] Mnatsakanyan E.A., Nefyodov S.V.:Some Notes on Automated Quantitative Decoding of Interferograms with Time Average. Materials of the All-Union science-technic conference "Photometry and its Metrological Providing,Moscow,1988

[2] Pasian F., Santin P.:Shape Information Extraction in Noisy Environments. Pattern Recognition Letters, vol.2, December 1983,p.109-116

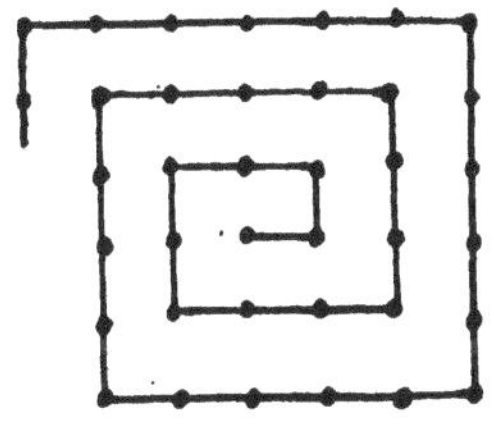

Fig. 2.

COMPUTERIZED INTERFERENCE MEASUREMENTS

Nyarsik, Ľ. - Burdík, K. - Keppert, M. - Ertlová, J.[1)]

1. Introduction

Digital evaluation of interference information principally increases the accuracy of interference measurements and enables introduction of interferometers into automatic measuring systems. The paper deals with some methods of digital interferometry, we presently deal with at our Institute. These methods are determined first of all for flatness measurement of optical surfaces.

2. Heterodyne interferometer with rotating half-wave plate

The basis of heterodyne interferometry consists in transformation of optical phase shift on a phase shift of electrical sine signals, which are received as beat signals, if two optical signals with different frequencies are mixed. It is possible to measure the phase shift of sine electric signals with resolution better than $2\pi/1000$.

There are various methods for creation of heterodyne signals. For our experiments we have employed the method of rotating half-wave plate, which uses supplementary periodical time modulation of transmitted circular polarized laser beam. Many ways how to arrange a heterodyne interferometer with a rotating half-wave plate are described in literature [1,3,4,5].

For experimental verification of the above-mentioned method we have used the Twyman-Green interferometer with a quater-wave plate (45° orientation) in reference arm. Linearly polarized laser beam (0°) passed through a modulator composed of a quater-wave plate (45°), rotating half-wave plate (50 Hz) and a quater-wave plate (45°). A polarizer (0°) and a dividing prism for a fixed reference and scanning photodetector (PIN photodiode) are placed on the interferometer output.

---

1) Institute of Measurement and Measuring Technique, Centre of Electrophysical Research of the Slovak Academy of Sciences, 842 19 Bratislava, Czechoslovakia

The scanning photodetector was placed on a x-y table controlled by means of a manual and motorizing micrometer (MIKE fy Oriel) with an encoder for reading the position. The motorizing micrometer was controlled by an 8-bit microcomputer, which also reads the position and measures the phase shift of photodetector signals.

Electric signals from photodefectors are defined by following relations:

reference signal - $U_o(x_o,y_o) = A(x_o,y_o) + B_o(x_o,y_o)\cos(4w_o t)$

measuring signal - $U_m(x,y) = A_m(x,y) + B_m(x,y)\cos(4w_o t+\phi(x,y))$

where w_o is an angle velocity of the half-wave plate, $\phi(x,y)$ is relative phase in point (x,y) of the interference patterns with respect to (x_o,y_o) and A(x,y),B(x,y) depend on intensity distribution in the laser beam, R/T ratio on the beamsplitters and reflexivity of objects in the measuring and reference arm of the interferometer. By electric signals shaping in analog-digital electronic unit we receive two TTL pulse signals with durations T and t, corresponding to a period of heterodyne signals and to a mutual time shift. Quotient t/T determines the searched phase $\phi_1(x,y) = (\phi(x,y) - \phi(x_o,y_o)) \bmod 2\pi$.

Signals T and t are connected to digital inputs of the 8-bit microcomputer. Pulses durations are software-measured with the phase resolution is $2\pi/1024$ that in the realized interferometer corresponded to the height change 1/2048 of used wavelenght on the measured object.

During the measurement each phase value in the point was an average from 20 succeeding phase measurements (i.e. every 40 msec 1 value). Measurements were realized both in positive and negative direction of the motorized micrometer motion, while the resultant difference of the measured phase was less than $2\pi/100$ caused by a backlash in the x-y table.

Taking into account the slow evaluation of the phase on the whole surface, the above described high accuracy method for phase measurement is be mainly usefull for laboratory aims.

3. Interpolation method

In this part experiences with automatic evaluation of interferogram by means of the interpolation method for flatness measurement of optical **surfaces are described.**

The searched phase field ϕ_r from intensity distribution in fringes of a two-beam interferometer, without a knowledge of some supplementary conditions and considering, is not unambiguous. This indeterminancy is eliminated by introducing of a reference phase ϕ_r. At the same time it is necessary to fulfill the condition, that the overall phase function $\phi = \phi_m - \phi_r$ is a monotonic function in the direction of evaluation. The evaluating process itself can be summarized in subsequent four steps:

- localization of the extremes of the intensity distribution function by second-order polynomial approximation
- phase allocation to these points
- interpolation of phase values in equividistant raster of 64x64 points
- filtering of linear component from evaluated phase values.

The accuracy of the evaluation method was tested on simulated interferograms. The evaluating program allows to predefine the shape of the modelled surface. This enables to evaluate and illustrate the error as a difference between the real and evaluated surface shape. We found out, that with growing amplitude of surface unflatness A, the absolute evaluation error is increasing. It is caused by growing error of the applied approximation of the extremes localization in intensity distribution function, as a result of non-uniform fringes density (failure disturbance of their symmetrical profile). Comparing the relative error, i.e. the error related to A, it is more appropriate to measure surfaces with higher A value. If A is higher than $\lambda/10$, it follows that 95% of the surface is evaluated with the relative error up to 5%. Influence of the interferogram quality (levels of random noise and intensity amplitude in interferogram) is mainly obvious on surfaces with small A value (orderly $\lambda/10$ and smaller).

On our minicomputer SM 52-11 a complete patterns evaluation took about 30 sec.

4. Fourier transform method

Evaluation of 2-D interference patterns by means of 1-D Fourier transform (FT) proposed by Takeda et al. [6,7] is suitable from the standpoint of full utilization of digitalized information, because we directly receive phase values in each picture pixel.

Similarly, as in above -described interpolation method, we use auxiliary carrier frequency f_0 in order to receive a resultant interferogram with monotonic fringe orders in x-direction. Interference patterns are then defined by a general relation:

$$u(x,y) = a(x,y) + b(x,y)\cos(\phi_1(x,y)),$$

where $\phi_1(x,y) = 2\pi f_0 + \phi_0(x,y)$ and $\phi_0(x,y)$ is the measured phase. For correct evaluation it is necessary that the folowing relations are valid $|\partial\phi_1(x,y)/\partial y|<\pi$ and $0<\partial\phi_1(x,y)/\partial x<\pi$. Previous relation and its Fourier spectrum can be expressed in the form:

$$u(x,y)=a(x,y)+c(x,y)+c^*(x,y) \longleftrightarrow U(f,y)=A(f,y)+C(f,y)+C(-f,y),$$

where $c(x,y) = (1/2)b(x,y)\exp(i\phi_1(x,y))$.

In the case that individual components of the Fourier spectrum do not overlap, it is possible to separate the term $C(f,y)$ and after reverse FT we receive $c(x,y)$, from which we can calculate the phase $\phi_2(x,y)$ as

$$\phi_2(x,y) = \phi_1(x,y) \bmod 2\pi = \tan^{-1}(\mathrm{Im}(c(x,y))/\mathrm{Re}(c(x,y))),$$

for $\phi_2(x,y)<0$ we add 2π and we receive $\phi_2(x,y)$ in $\langle 0;2\pi\rangle$ range. During filtering in Fourier spectrum it is possible to eliminate the carrier frequency by shifting the $C(f,y)$ into the origin, but f_0 is not to be always generally known, and thus it is more appropriate to eliminate the linear term from phase distribution $\phi_1(x,y)$ by the least square method. For transition from wrapped phase ϕ_2 towards unwrapped phase ϕ_1 it is necessary to choose one reference point (x_0,y_0) and to allocate to it a zero fringe order $N(x_0,y_0) = 0$ and gradually determine fringe orders in neighbouring points according to the relation:

$$N(x,y,l,k) = N(x,y) + \begin{cases} +1 & \text{for } \pi < DIF \\ 0 & |DIF| \le \pi \\ -1 & DIF < -\pi, \end{cases}$$

where $DIF(x,y,k,l) = \phi_2(x+k,y+l) - \phi_2(x,y)$ and $l,k = \pm 1$. For unwrapped phase then holds $\phi_1(x,y) = \phi_2(x,y) + N(x,y)$.

The choice of reference point (x_0,y_0) in interferogram is arbitrary, strategy of filling $N(x,y)$ depends on x-y shape of the valid interferogram area. Developed software can also evaluate fringe patterns with central obscurations.

Testing of evaluating method on simulated interferograms confirmed the RMS from differencies between simulated and evaluated surfaces below $2\pi \cdot 10^{-2}$.

5. Conclusions

The paper deals with some aspects of digital evaluation implemented at our Institute. Emphasis was given on methods evaluating static fringes, however mainly these methods allow easy updating of classical interferometers commonly used in practice replacing visual observations by optical sensor with picture digitizer.

In practice we employed a CCD 256x256 pixels matrix based camera with digitizer on 256 grey-levels, frame-memory of 256x256x8 bits and planinterferometer [2].

Heterodyne method is determined for accurate calibration in laboratory conditions. Further it can be used for calibrating of interferometers with phase sampling employing piezocrystals for phase adjustment.

6. Literature

[1] Crane, R.: Interference Phase Measurement. Appl. Opt. 8 (1969) 3, 538-542.

[2] Keppert, M., J. Buzási and J. Sudek: PI 115-4 planinterferometer for flatness measurements. Nauch. Apparat. 2 (1987) 3, 65-70.

[3] Kothiyal, M. P. and C. Delisle: Optical frequency shifter for heterodyne interferometery using counterrotating wave plates. Opt. Lett. 9 (1984) 8, 319-321.

[4] Shagan, R. N. and J. C. Wyant: Optical frequency shifter for heterodyne interferometers using multiple rotating polarization retarders. Appl. Opt. 17 (1978) 18, 3034-3035.

[5] Sommargen, G. E.: Up/down frequency shifter for optical heterodyne interferometry. J. of Opt. Soc. Am. 65 (1975) 8, 960-961.

[6] Takeda, M., H. Ina and S.Kobayashi: Fourier-transform method of fringe-pattern analysis for computer-based topography and interferometry. J. of Opt. Soc. Am. 72 (1982) 1, 156-160.

[7] Takeda, M. and K. Mutoh: Fourier transform profilometry for the automatic measurement of 3-D object shapes. Appl. Opt. 22 (1983) 24, 3977-3982.

INTERACTIVE FRINGE PROCESSING USING PSEUDOCOLOURING

V. Parthiban and Rajpal S. Sirohi

ABSTRACT

An algorithm for interacive analysis of interferogram fringes is presented. This algorithm, based on a PDP 11/23 microcomputer, uses a pseudo colour mapping technique. The pixels are coded sequentially, according to their graylevel, by different colours, which enables the operator to select suitable threshold values. This pseudocolour coding can also be used effectively while labeling closed loop fringes. This algorithm also incorporates an interactive fringe tracking algorithm to connect discontinuities in the fringe peak contours.

INTRODUCTION

Interferometry has for long been regarded as a somewhat academic and experimentally difficult technique. This stems partly from the difficulty which lies in the interpretation of the interferograms. During the past several years, a number of image processing techniques have been introduced to investigate the possibility of analysing interferograms automatically[1].

In an interferogram, a phase information is available in the form of irradiance distribution. The phase information can be extracted by the following methods :

(i) heterodyne interferometry,
(ii) phase shifting interferometry and
(iii) from recorded interferograms.

The first two methods have the advantage of operating in real time and of being fast and very accurate. When interferometric techniques are used for repetitive calibration, non-destructive testing or inspection, it is sometimes possible to design a comparatively simple fringe analysis system. After identifying the charactaristics of the fringe pattern which are peculiar to the application, the capabilities of the analysis system can be confined to those required for the measurement in question. Robinson[2] has described a number of fringe analysis procedures for use in engineering applications of interfrometery and in speckle metrology.

Until artificial intelligence is applied to fringe processing, there is little hope of producing a fully automated system. The basic information in an interferogram is the intensity distribution given by,

---

Applied Optics Laboratory, Physics Department,
Indian Institute of Technology, Madras 600 036,
INDIA.

$$I = I_1 + I_2 + 2\sqrt{I_1 I_2}\ \cos \varnothing \qquad \ldots.(1)$$

from which the phase $\varnothing$ is computed. Unfortunately, the intensity distribution in a real interferogram is much more complicated than that expressed in this equation, because optical noise and parasitic interference render the intensity distribution much more complex. A fully automated fringe processing system would fail in most cases when encountered with an interferogram with complex intensity pattern. The operator's intervention and guidance is required in most cases. Image processing systems fortunately allow direct interaction from an operator. Interactive algorithms which use light pens[3], and keyboards[4,5] are described in the literature.

In this paper we propose an interactive algorithm which can be used on any general purpose computer with image display and digitizer hardware. Fig. 1 shows the system configuration. This algorithm has been developed on a PDP 11/23 microcomputer with 256 kb buffer memory. For image display a CUB R G B monitor is used. The digitized image is stored in a single frame buffer of 512 X 512 X 8 bit resolution.

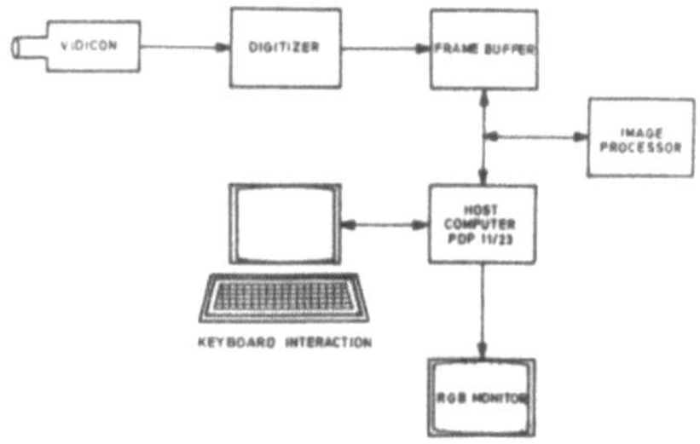

Fig. 1.

The algorithm has five components: (i) noise reduction and averaging, (ii) thresholding, (iii) peak detection, (iv) on-line editing, and (v) fringe scanning and labeling.

(i) Noise reduction

When the background is non-uniform over the whole interferogram, several problems are introduced in fringe peak detection. The digitized interferogram provides the computer with the intensity information of each pixel, and these can be scanned sequentially to detect sudden change in slope as the position of the peak. But the noise due to speckle or dust can mislead the machine to assume a peak or valley where there is none. When severe noise is present, the interferogram has to be preprocessed. When the spatial frequency of the noise is significantly higher than that of the fringes, low pass filtering can be performed. Low pass filtering is carried out by replacing the intensity value at each pixel by the average, or weighted average, or the median of the intensties measured at the pixel and its neighbours. The convolution array for low pass filtering can be written as[6],

$$H = \begin{vmatrix} 1 & 2 & 1 \\ 2 & 4 & 2 \\ 1 & 2 & 1 \end{vmatrix} \qquad \ldots..(2)$$

(ii) Thresholding

An easy way to find out the fringe peak is to convert the gray scale image into a binary image by application of a suitable threshold. If the interferogram has uniform background, providing a fringe profile of constant sinusoidal variation, it is a trivial task to set a mid gray threshold. Practical problems occur, however, when the interferogram is subject to noise or when both the fringe pattern and the backgraound assume the same broad range of gray scale.

We follow a combination of edge detection and thresholding to extract the binary picture from the interferogram. The interferogram is pseudo colour coded to enable the operator to chose a rough threshold value. The 256 gray levels are divided into eight sectors and each sector is coded sequentially as gray, blue, cyan, green, yellow, red, magenta, and white.

After pseudo colour mapping the interferogram, the computer asks for maximum and minimum threshold gray values corresponding to the bright and dark regions of the interfrerogram. The pixels are compared to the two gray values and made zero or 255 depending on whether they are below or above the minimum threshold. All pixels above the maximum threshold are made 255. Also when the luminace value begins to fall from the peak created by a bright fringe, its value is made zero regardless of the threshold. The threshold values can be changed by the operator until all the fringes are retained in the binary picture.

(iii) Peak Detection

The fringe peaks are detected from the binary picture by finding out the locus of midpoints of the dark fringes. This is done sequentially, line by line, by vertical scanning. When the fringes are not closed and are perpendicular to the direction of scanning, this method is highly effective. When the interferogram has components parellel to the direction of scanning. the locus of midpoints will be a line perpendicular to the scan line, whereas in reality, the peak contour runs parallel to the scan line. So this method is not effective while processing closed loop fringes.

(iv) On-line Editing

The peak contours may have discontinuities due to noise and there may be some unwanted peaks which are to be deleted. This can be done by the on-line editing subroutine. This helps the operator to place the cursor at any pixel and to either write or erase the pixel by a key board command.

(v) Fringe Tracing and Labeling

The discontinuities can be connected by a fringe tracing algorithm. The operator places the cursor at the beginning of a peak contour, and the computer tracks the fringe. When it encounters a discontinuity, it pauses and asks for the operator's help. The operator should then to decide on the correct path and should direct the machine.

Interferograms of closed loop fringes pose numerous difficulties during numbering. Automatic fringe numbering routines usually assign fringe numbers on an assumption of linear unit increase in finge number along each scan line. Such a routine will fail when a closed loop fringe pattern is encountered during evaluation. To help the machine to identify the fringe order, the operator pseudo colour codes each contour line by changing the gray value of each fringe by tracing them individually and tells the machine the gray value and the order it represents. Thus the computer can identify each fringe order and store it in a data file for further evaluation. When the fringes are in the form of loops, each order can be identified by the computer by its gray value. Fig. 2 shows the fringe contours of the interferogram.

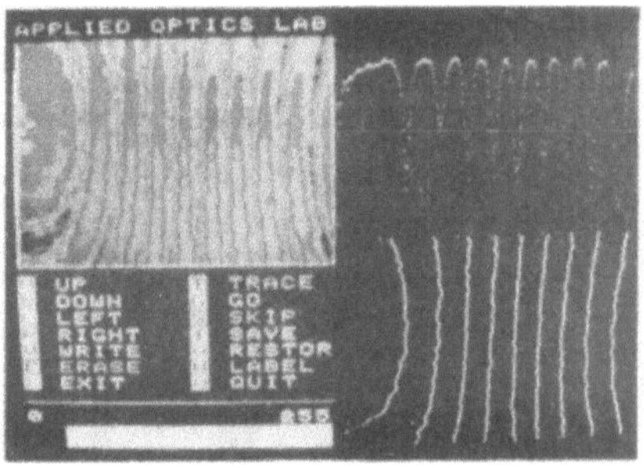

Fig. 2

REFERENCES

1. G.T. Reid, 'Automatic fringe pattern analysis: A review', Opt.& Lasers in Eng., 7 (1986/87) 37 - 68.

2. D.W. Robinson, 'Automatic fringe analysis with a computer image processing system', Appl. Opt., 22 (1983) 2169 - 76.

3. T. Yatagai, M. Idesawa, Y.Yamaashi, and M. Suzuki, 'Interactive fringe analysis system: application to moire contourgram and interferograms', Opt. Eng., 21 (1982) 901 - 6.

4. E. Bernel and J. Loomis, 'Interactive video image digitiser - Application to interferogram analysis', Proc. SPIE, 126 (1977) 143 - 151.

5. V. Parthiban, and R.S. Sirohi, 'Interactive fringe processing algorithm for interferogram analysis', submitted to Opt. & Lasers in Eng. (1988).

6. W. K. Pratt, 'Digital image processing', Wiley, New York (1978).

REAL-TIME METHODS IN OPTICAL TESTING INTERFEROMETRY

R. Spolaczyk, K.-E. Elssner [1]

1. Introduction

Interferometric methods are often the only way to achieve high precision in testing of optical elements. The invention of the laser has led to the development of several new techniques in interferometry. Other technological developments in the early 70th contributed to a considerable expasion of interferometry, namely, solid-state detector arrays and fast microprocessors.

Nowadays, a modern interferometric measurement device works in real time, including a detector array to aquire the interferometric data and an on-line microcomputer for evaluation and interferometer control using techniques like, for example, phase-shifting or heterodyning [1,2,3,4].

Among the interferometers two-beam devices are the most common. Real-time interferometers have been applied to nearly all test situations prevailing in optics. The most common two-beam interferometer types are the Fizeau, Twyman-Green and Mach-Zehnder interferometer.

The aim of this paper is to give a short survey of application of real-time two-beam interferometers to some of the most important cases of optical testing. References can be found in [1]. But holographic interferometry and speckle interferometry will not be considered in this survey.

2. Plane surfaces

Phase-shifting Fizeau interferometers are especially suited in testing plane surfaces. The big advantage of a Fizeau design is its stability against shock and vibration and its immunity against dust diffraction if parallel adjustment is maintained during the measurement. The interferometer can be applied to absolute testing.

3. Optical systems, prism and gratings

These elements are mostly tested in a Twyman-Green design because of its configuration variability and adaptability to different reflexion coefficients. Preferably the interferometer is of the polarising type. The need for calibration becomes evident since a multitude of optical elements contributes to the interferometer aberrations.

---

1) Akademie der Wissenschaften der DDR, Zentralinstitut fuer Optik und Spektroskopie, Berlin, 1199, German Democratic Republic

4. Asphericѕ

Testing aspheric surfaces can be carried out with the help of computer-generated holograms (CGH). To overcome problems arising from warping wavefronts generated by aspherics the CGH has to be placed inside one arm of the interferometer. Mach-Zehnder and Twyman-Green interferometers have been applied to the testing. Using shearing interferometers there is no need for a CGH.

5. Technical flats

Testing technical flats, e.g. semiconductor wafers, the neccessary depth resolution (about 0,1µm) is much smaller than that necessary for testing optical surfaces and the range of surface deviations can be in the order of some 10µm. By means of a grazing incidence Fizeau interferometer the effective wavelength can be enlarged and adapted to this range of deviations. Alternatively, a rather dense sampling can also solve this problem.

6. Microstructure

Interferometric profilometers for microstructure testing work by various principles. One possibility is to compare the reflected wave from the tiny measuring spot with a wave reflected from an extended region in the neighbourhood of the measuring point. Interference microscopes of the Michelson, Mireau or Linnik type are different solutions. To diminish the influence of coherent noise the use of incoherent light is advantageous in the latter case. Fizeau interferometers combined with polarizing means have also been applied.

7. Shape of ground surfaces

This measurement is the counterpart to microstructure studies. One method to get the surface profile is infrared interferometry with wavelengths in the um region.

A different possibility is to use two neighbouring laser wavelengths for interferometry. So, from the superposition of these wavelengths an increased effective wavelength results and can be adjusted to the measuring task.

8. Refractive index distributions

Small inhomogeneities in high quality optical glass plates can be determined using real-time interferometers, e.g. from the Twyman-Green type. To separate the influence of the glass body inhomogeneities from the surface deviations a combination of four interference patterns has to be evaluated.

Also for the determination of the refractive index profile of preforms and fibres interferometric methods have been applied.

9. Wavefronts

A further field of application is the testing of wavefronts in linear adaptive optical systems. Here a very fast measurement is necessary to run the system in real-time.
The wavefront testing gives an important information also for the characterisation of the output of semiconductor lasers.
Lateral and radial shearing interferometers as well as point reference interferometers are suitable for these tasks.

10. Literature

[1] Autorenkollektiv, "Real-time methods in optical testing interferometry", Preprint 88-6, AdW der DDR, ZOS, Juni 1988.

[2] P.Hariharan, "Interferometry with Lasers", in Progress in Optics, Ed. E.Wolf, North-Holland Publ. Co., Amsterdam, 1987, Vol.24, p.103-164.

[3] K.Creath, "Phase-measurement interferometry techniques", in Progress in Optics, Ed. E.Wolf, North-Holland Publ. Co., Amsterdam, 1988, Vol.26, p.350-393.

[4] D.Malacara (Ed.), "Optical shop testing", John Wiley and Sons, New York, 1978.

APPLICATION OF DIFFERENT TYPES OF LOCAL FILTERS FOR THE SHADING CORRECTION OF INTERFEROGRAMS

G. Stanke and W. Osten [1]

1. Introduction

Shading correction is an important step in preprocessing of images. This step is necessary to compensate imperfections of visual sensors or illumination. Generally, linear and nonlinear local filters are applied, whereby linear filters are often prefered for their good implementation properties for parallel processors [1]. In this paper our interest is focused on a class of non linear filters - rank order filters (ROF). The main properties and two different algorithms implemented on a parallel video processor are described. An interesting application field for shading correction is interferometry. Interferograms made with laser light usually show clear irregularities in the background intensity distribution originating from the expanted and projected gaussian profile in the laser beam, object shape and local varying surface reflectivity. Consequently, bright fringes show in some regions of the interferogram smaller intensity values than dark fringes in other regions and simple binarization without sliding threshold will fail. For the derivation of local intensity extrema which follow the centre lines of bright and dark fringes a normalization of background intensity is necessary.

2. Properties of rank order filters

Rank order filters represent a widely used class of local nonlinear operators. The median is the best known. A description of their properties and application fields is given by [2],[3] and [4]. Some important properties are:

- ROF smooth noise; exception to this: the minimal or maximal rank is choosen.
- The application of ROF change the mean image intensity; exception: median to images with symmetrical noise distribution.
- ROF preserve the shape of edges (also of corners if 1-dimensional windows are used). Small lines can be bloted out, what is useful for shading correction.
- The application of ROF shift the position of edges; exception: the median is selected.
- No new intensity values are generated by application of ROF; this property is explicity used in algorithms described below

---

[1] Academy of Sciences of the GDR, Central Institute of Cybernetics and Information Processes, POB 1298, Berlin, 1086, GDR

- Using ROF the image algebra can be simulated (binary images, programmable windows)
- ROF for programmable windows provide the possibility to detect and to label "features" in images
- The difference of two rank ordered images gives a gradient like result.

3. Parallelization by stepwise gray value comparision

The idea of that method is to test all gray values accuring in the image as possible median of the window. Using the histogram unit of the video processor the whole scale of gray values in an 8-bit image can be reduced to the actual number GW of gray values. The procedure starts with the lowest gray value and is finished after the highest gray value was tested. If we denote the gray value of the pixel with GP and the momentary test value with GT then we find the temporary rank order of GT for the window by the operation

```
if (GP.ge.GT) then GP=1  else GP=Ø
```

That means, if GP is greater or equal than GT the pixel in a temporary image memory is marked with 1 otherwise with Ø. The sum Σ_w of all marked pixels within the window shows if the momentary test value GT is a new candidate for e. g. the median or if the previous test value can be fixed as median. For this purpose the sum Σ_w is compared with the median rank order RMED of the window. If we use for instance $3^n x 3^n$-windows (n=1, 2, 3...) to calculate Σ_w very fast with the pipeline processor [1] it follows

$$RMED = \frac{3^{2n}+1}{2}$$

and we get for the operation in FORTRAN 77 notation

```
if(Σw.ge.RMED) then
MEDIAN = GT
else
MEDIAN = MEDIAN
endif
```

That means, only if Σ_w is smaller than RMED the test value of the previous run is confirmed and masked for all further runs.
All operations described above are homogeneous and uniform for all pixels in the image. Therefore they are able to parallelize on a special purpose processor modelling the SIMD principle [4].

4. Bit-slice implementation of ROF in a parallel processor

The parallel processor of the image processing system robotron A6472 is not designed for ordering in pixel windows. Bit-slice techniques are useful to implement ROF [2], [3]. Basically the procedure proposed below is simple. An image with up to 256 different gray levels (8 bit-slices) is considered. In difference to the method of stepwise gray value comparison the shape of the filter window does not play any role. The bit-slices are processed step by step.

The first step is identical to the reduction of the scale of actual occuring gray values described above. Obviously, as a result we get the number of relevant slices (SLICE).

In a second step all pixels of an image memory containing the so called updated rank value are set to 2**(SLICE-1). A second image memory that serves as accumulator is labeled with zero.

In the third step a pixelwise comparison is made between the gray values in the processed image and the pixels in the memory for the updated rank values. If the value of the image pixel is greater the according accumulator pixel value is increased by 1 otherwise by 0. Then the original image is shifted accordingly to the shape of the operator window to make the comparison for the next position of the operator window. Step 3 is repeated until all positions of the operator window are processed.

In a forth step the values of the accumulator pixels are compared to the demanded rank number. If they are greater, the value 2**(SLICE-2) is added to the value in the according position of the updated rank memory, and subtracted in the opposit case.

Finally, SLICE is decreased by 1 and if equal or greater 1 the accumulator image memory is set to zero and the procedure jumps back to step three for the next slice. Otherwise the procedure is finished.

As the result we get the rank order filtered image in the updated rank memory.

5. Shading correction of holographic interferograms

If we follow the intensity distribution in holographic interferometry

$$I(x,y) = I_0(x,y)\cdot(1+V(x,y)\cdot\cos[\delta(x,y)]) \qquad (1)$$

then a shading correction is performed by pixelwise division of the intensity $I(x,y)$ in the interferogram through its mean intensity $I_0(x,y)$. This mean intensity distribution can be derived from a holographic reconstruction of the single illuminated object or from the interferogram using spatial averaging. Because it is often impossible to refer to the real background intensity we prefer here the approximation of $I_0(x,y)$ from the interferogram by spatial filteration within a square window. In this case it is necessary to use window dimensions of at least one fringe period. Mean filters are mostly used for this purpose because of their simple implementation and short running times on special or general purpose processors. But they always result in blurring of object shape (as for instance sharp edges) what gives bad approximations of I_0 in such regions.

Figure 1a shows an interferogram of a central loaded plate and figure 1b the result of binarization without shading correction (threshold level 84). The approximations of the background level reached by median filtering and linear mean filtering are given in figure 1c and figure 1d respectively. Obviously the edge information in the mean filtered image is more vague. Both corrected images, figure 1e and figure 1f seem to be quite similar but the the intensity profiles show clearly the differences in the edge regions. The image corrected by help of rank order filtering gives a more natural result. This is convincingly underlined by the results after binarization, figure 1g and figure 1h. The binary image in 1g corrected by help of median filtering is an unlike better base for further quantitative analysis than the image in figure 1h.

Literature

[1] Kovalevsky, V.; Luth, N.: Parallel Algorithms in Image Processing and Computer Graphics. In: T. Legendi et. al (Eds.). Akademie-Verlag, Berlin 1986, S. 163-171.

[2] Hodgson, R.M.; Bailey, D.G.; Naylor, M.J.; McNeill, S.J.: Properties, Implementations and Applications of Rank Filters. Image and Vision Computing, Vol. 3(1985)1., S. 3-14.

[3] Wilhelmi, W.: Beiträge zur Datenorganisation und zur Entwicklung von Programmierwerkzeugen für die interaktive rechnergestützte Bildverarbeitung. Dissertation B (1983), Berlin, AdW.

[4] Stanke, G.; Osten, W.: Rangordnungsoperatoren auf einem parallelen Bildprozessor. Bild und Ton, (to be published)

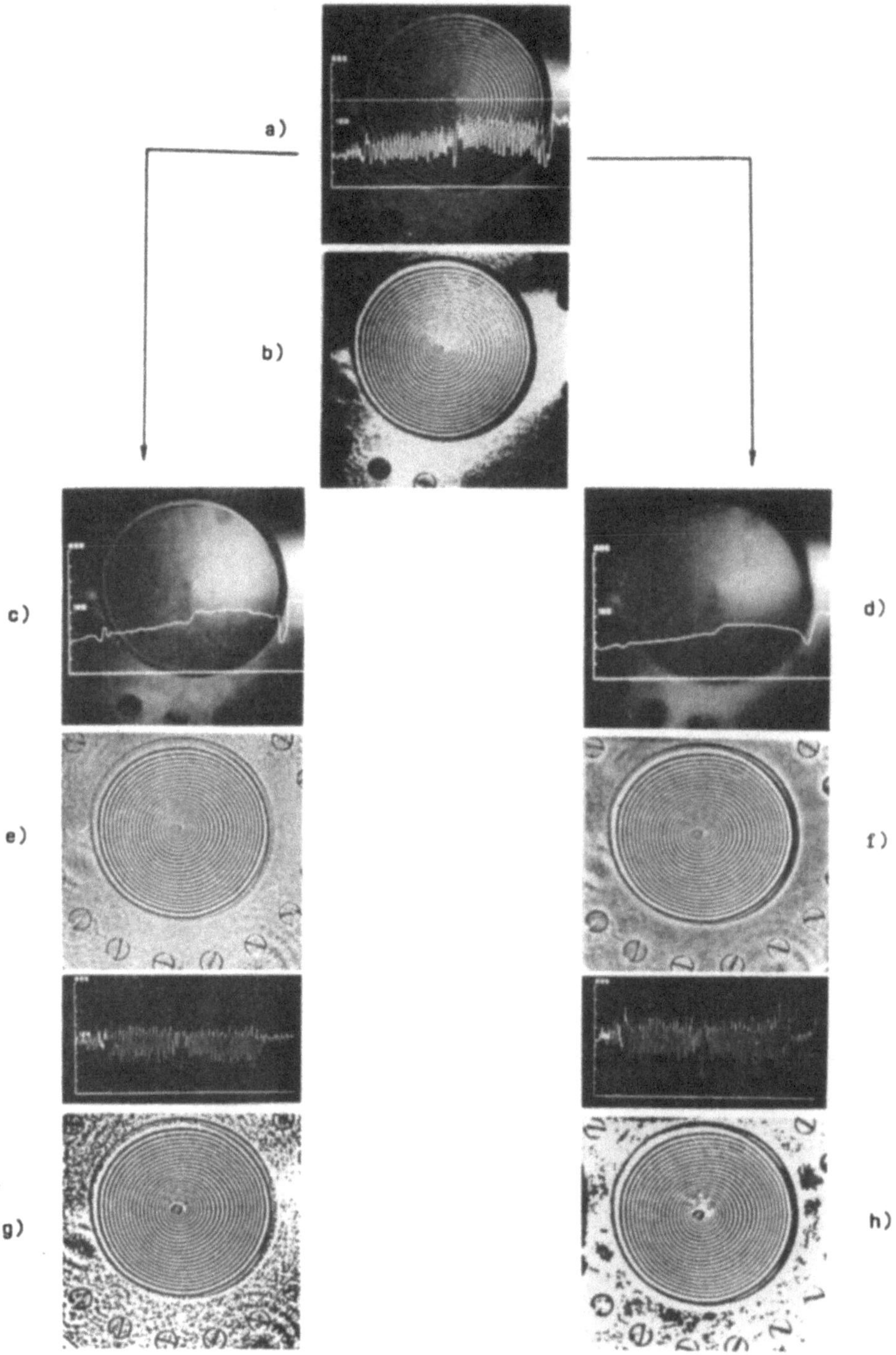

Figure 1: Shading correction and binarization of an interferogram (a, b) using median (c, e, g) and mean (d, f, h) filters.

SPECKLE METROLOGY OF PROPERTIES OF ROUGHNESS AND INHOMOGENEOUS PHASE SAMPLES

A.G.Ushenko and S.B.Yermolenko[1)]

A microrelief of a rough surface formed as a result of arbitrary factors can be reasonably described by the following probability distributions of heights (h) and inclination angles (γ) of microirregularities[1]:

$$g(h) = \frac{1}{\sqrt{2\pi}h_0} \exp\left(-\frac{h^2}{2h_0^2}\right) \tag{1}$$

$$q(\gamma) = \frac{ctg\gamma_0}{\sqrt{\pi}\cos^2\gamma} \exp\left(-\frac{tg^2\gamma}{tg^2\gamma_0}\right), \tag{2}$$

where h_0 and γ_0 are the corresponding average values.

A plane wave front passing through such a surface becomes polarization and phase modulated. The period l_i of the full phase change of the wave from 0 to 2π over a quasi-plane surface area is related to its angular orientation by

$$l_i = \frac{\lambda}{\cos\gamma_i} \tag{3}$$

where λ is the incident beam wavelength.

The distribution $R(l)$ of the periods of phase change due to all surface irregularities is obtained from eq.(3) in the form of inverse function $S^{-1}(\gamma)$ to which the following procedure[2] is applied:

$$R(l) = \left| \frac{d\{q[S^{-1}(\gamma)]\}}{d\gamma} \right| q[S^{-1}(\gamma)] \tag{4}$$

As a result, the following expression for the phase change on a rough surface is obtained:

$$R(l) = \frac{l \exp\left(-\frac{l^2-\lambda^2}{l_0^2-\lambda^2}\right)}{\sqrt{\pi}\sqrt{l_0^2-\lambda^2}}, \tag{5}$$

where $l_0 = \dfrac{\lambda}{\cos\gamma_0}$.

The phase difference between partial beams refracted by a surface area l_i can be written as

$$\Delta\varphi_i = \frac{2\pi}{\lambda} n l_i \sin\gamma_i \tag{6}$$

The probability distribution associated with eq.(6) is rather cumbersome and is obtained by numerical methods taking into account distributions

1) Chernovtsy State University, 2 Kotsyubinsky Str., 274012 Chernovtsy, USSR

(2) and (5) in the form

$$U(\Delta\varphi) = \int_{-\infty}^{\infty} R\left(\frac{\Delta\varphi}{t}\right) q(t)\,dt \tag{7}$$

Along with the phase modulation due to local refraction events which cause rotation of incident wave polarization plane, there is also statistical modulation of the orientation of the light vibration plane. The amount of arbitrary rotation ε of the polarization plane is defined by

$$\varepsilon = \operatorname{arctg}\left[\frac{tg\,\varkappa_0(\Delta P - 1)}{tg^2\varkappa_0\,\Delta P + 1}\right] \tag{8}$$

where $\Delta P = \frac{P_s}{P_p}$, P_s and P_p being the Fresnel transmission coefficients, and $\varkappa_0$ the polarization azimuth of the incident wave.

The probability distribution of all rotations of the polarization plane will have the form

$$W(\varepsilon) = \frac{2}{\sqrt{\pi}}\sqrt{\frac{2N+1}{N+1}}\left|\frac{dN}{d\varepsilon}\right| \exp\left\{-\frac{N[N(\varepsilon_0)+1]}{(N+1)N(\varepsilon_0)}\right\}^2 \tag{9}$$

where

$$N = \frac{b_1 tg^2\varepsilon + b_2 tg\varepsilon}{b_3 tg^2\varepsilon + b_4 tg\varepsilon + b_5} \tag{10}$$

Thus, a plane coherent wave passing through arbitrarily inclined micro-irregularities creates a "fine" polarization and phase structure.

When a reference wave is applied to the speckle structure thus created, a local interference pattern is formed within each correlation zone its contrast being defined by

$$V_i = \frac{a_i A_0 \cos(\varepsilon_i - \theta)}{a_i^2\cos^2(\varphi_i - \theta) + A_0^2\cos\theta + a_i A_0 \cos(\varphi_i - \theta)} \tag{11}$$

where A_0 is the reference wave amplitude, a_i is the amplitude within a correlation zone, θ is the orientation of the analyzer transmission axis, ε_i the arbitrary polarization azimuth, φ_i the phase difference between the interfering beams.

Thus the contrast of partial speckle interferograms is determined by the polarization state and the amplitude of light vibrations in a given correlation zone of a rough surface.

It follows that by changing the polarization state of the reference wave one should be able to adjust the contrast of speckle interferograms. Therefore by changing the reference field amplitude up to a level $A_0^{(k)} \equiv a_i$, the contrast can be increased up to a level

$$V_i' = \frac{\cos^2(\varepsilon_i - \theta)}{\cos^2(\varepsilon_i - \theta) + \cos(\varepsilon_i - \theta) + \cos\theta} \tag{12}$$

and a set of local values of correlation zone amplitudes $\{a_i\}$ can be found.

Then by rotating the analyzer transmission axis, a maximum increase in contrast can be achieved

$$V_i''\Big|_{\theta=\varepsilon_i} = \frac{1}{3}, \tag{13}$$

thus accumulating data on the polarization azimuth distribution $\{\varepsilon_i\}$.

Finally, by changing the optical length of the reference beam a situation is created when

$$V_i''' \equiv 0 \tag{14}$$

This situation takes place when

$$\Delta\varphi_k = \varphi_i + \frac{\pi}{2} \tag{15}$$

Having accumulated the statistical ensembles of (a_i), (ε_i) and (φ_i) values, one can evaluate the following parameters of an optically inhomogeneous sample:

(i) steepness of microirregularities

$$\gamma_i = \arcsin\sqrt{\frac{d_1 tg\varepsilon_i + d_2 tg\varepsilon_i\sqrt{d_3 tg^2\varepsilon_i + d_4 tg\varepsilon_i + d_5}}{d_6 tg^2\varepsilon_i + d_7 tg\varepsilon_i + d_8}} \tag{16}$$

(ii) local value of the refractive index of a rough interface

$$n_i = \sqrt{\frac{b_1 + \sqrt{b_2^2 - 4b_1 b_3}}{2b_2}} \tag{17}$$

where $b_1 - b_3$ are the functionals depending on the incidence angle α and the amplitudes a_i;

(iii) local value of the birefringent index

$$\Delta n_i = \frac{\varphi_i \lambda}{2\pi l_i \cos\gamma_i} = \frac{\varphi_i \lambda}{2\pi L_i} \tag{18}$$

where d_i is the set of constants, L_i the interferogram width.

The above analysis was used to design an automatic system for processing of speckle interferograms which is shown in Fig.1.

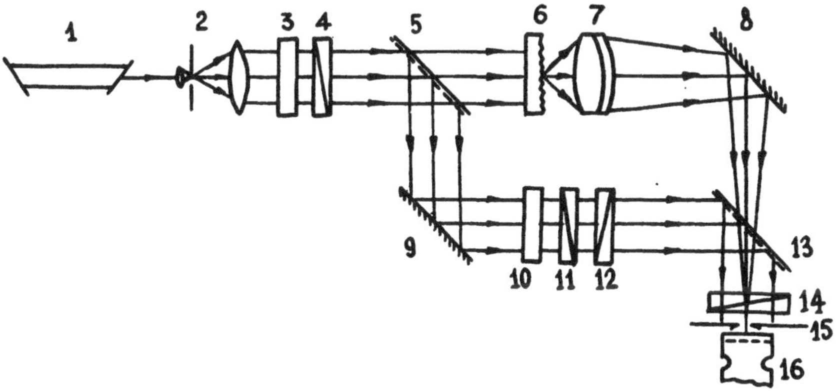

Fig.1. 1-laser; 2-collimator; 3,10-quarter-wave plates; 4,11,12,14-polarizers; 5,13-beamsplitters; 6-sample; 7-objective; 8,9-mirrors; 15-slit; 16-photodetector.

The speckle interferogram processing is carried out as follows. The contrast of the partial interference pattern is first measured by scanning the slit 15. Then polarizer 12 is rotated until maximum contrast V_i' is obtained, followed by rotation of polarizer 14 until level V_i'' is obtained.

For an arbitrary azimuthal orientation of a microirregularity, slit 15 is automatically rotated about its axis until maximum V_i value is obtained, and then the system proceeds to the above described automatic polarization correction. The angle of slit rotation thus obtained gives information on the azimuthal orientation of the microirregularity.

The above described procedure for processing speckle interferograms gives information on angle distributions of microirregularity orientations as well as anisotropy parameters of rough and inhomogeneous phase samples.

---

[1] Ushenko, A.: On the space polarizational characteristics of the object field of a rough surface scattering layer. Ukr.fiz.Zh.26 (1981) 1969-1974.

[2] Frieden, B.(Ed.): The Computer in Optical Research Methods and Applications. Springer -Verlag, Berlin/Heidelberg/New York 1980.

A CONTRIBUTION TO A SIMPLE DETERMINATION OF THE SENSITIVITY VECTOR $\vec{K}$

Dipl.Ing.Jaroslav Václavík [1)]

1. INTRODUCTION

When making finer measurements of the general displacement vector $\Delta\vec{r}$ using the holographic interferometry method, it is necessary to determine with sufficient accuracy the sensitivity vector $\vec{K}$. Solving the equation

$$\vec{K}\cdot\Delta\vec{r} = \vec{N}\cdot\lambda \quad ; \quad \vec{K} = \vec{k}_1 - \vec{k}_2 \tag{1}$$

for 3 or more directions of $\vec{K}$, we obtain the components of the displacement vector $\Delta\vec{r}$ using the zero order method e.g..

The present method proposes to determine this vector $\vec{K}$ at each image point of the evaluated holographic interferogram and could be adopted to a computerized evaluation of holographic interferograms using picture processing.

2. DESCRIPTION OF METHOD

To determine the sensitivity vector $\vec{K}$ we find the relations for the direction cosines of the individual iluminating $\vec{k}_1$ and viewing $\vec{k}_2$ unity vectors. The surface points of the measured object will be represented by an optical system at viewing angles in the image plane of the recording camera. Let the maximum image angle σ be assigned to the boundary of the squard image plane in the directions x,y (Fig.1). In the case of a nontelecentric image-forming system with a focus f, we shall carry out the correction of the angle σ with respect to the object distance z

$$\mathrm{tg}\,\sigma' = \mathrm{tg}\,\sigma \left(1 - \frac{f}{z} \right) \tag{2}$$

For the image angles of the remaining points within the image plane, and for the directions x,y there holds

$$\mathrm{tg}\,\delta = \frac{2\,\mathrm{tg}\,\sigma'}{a}\cdot x = A\cdot x = X \tag{3}$$

1) Central Research Institute - VZM, ŠKODA Plzeň, Concern Enterprise, 316 00 Plzeň, Czechoslovakia

$$\mathrm{tg}\,\tau = \frac{2\,\mathrm{tg}\,\sigma}{a}\cdot y = A\cdot y = Y$$

2.1 Derivation of the vector $\vec{k}_2$

From the viewing angles δ, τ, it is posible to derive directly the angles α_2, β_2, γ_2 of the vector $\vec{k}_2$ with respect to the coordinates

$$\mathrm{tg}\,\alpha_2 = -\frac{1}{\mathrm{tg}\,\delta_2 \cos\tau_2} = -\frac{\sqrt{1+Y^2}}{X}$$

$$\mathrm{tg}\,\beta_2 = -\frac{1}{\mathrm{tg}\,\tau_2 \cos\delta_2} = -\frac{\sqrt{1+X^2}}{Y} \qquad (4)$$

$$\mathrm{tg}\,\gamma_2 = -\sqrt{\mathrm{tg}^2\delta_2 + \mathrm{tg}^2\tau_2} = -\sqrt{X^2+Y^2}$$

For the cosines of these angles there holds

$$\cos\alpha_2 = -\frac{X}{\sqrt{1+X^2+Y^2}}$$

$$\cos\beta_2 = -\frac{Y}{\sqrt{1+X^2+Y^2}} \qquad (5)$$

$$\cos\gamma_2 = -\frac{1}{\sqrt{1+X^2+Y^2}}$$

2.2 Derivation of the vector $\vec{k}_1$

The derivation is carried out for a messured plane perpendicular to the viewing direction. In a general case, it is necessary to consider the deviations of the coordinate z from the plane of measurement. However, it is necessary, again in the image system, to measure also the shape of the object and to carry out the correction of z automatically with the aid of a computer system. From Fig.1 for the angle of illumination with respect to the xy-plane, the following relations hold

$$\mathrm{tg}\,\delta_1 = -\mathrm{tg}\,\Theta_x + \mathrm{tg}\,\xi_x \qquad (6)$$

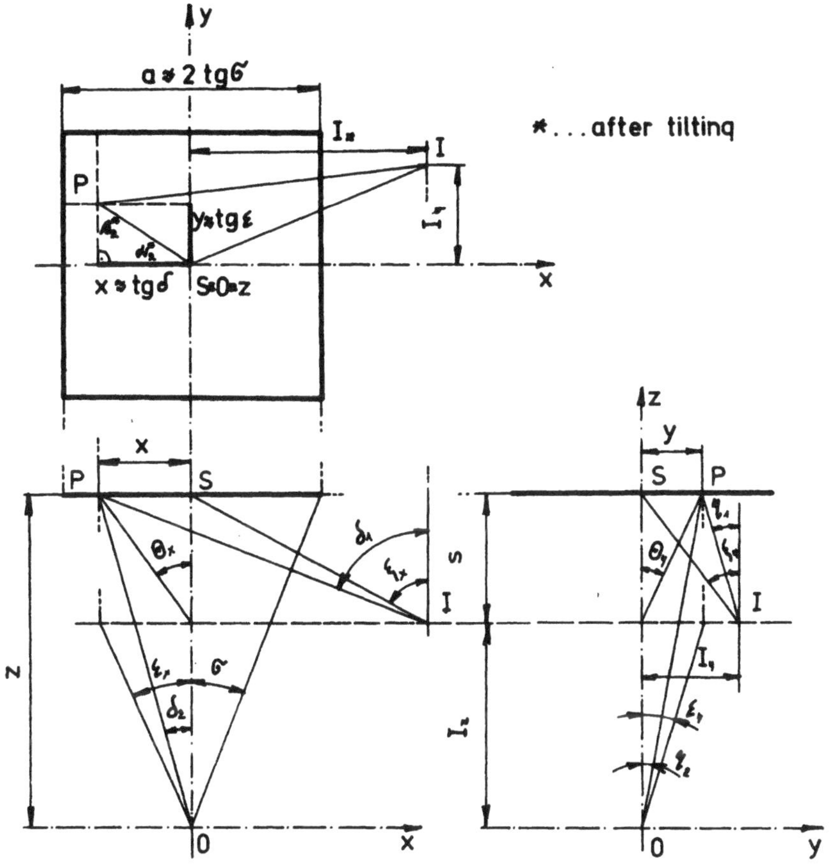

Fig.1 Diagram of the arrangement for the determination of relations

$$\operatorname{tg}\theta_x = \frac{\operatorname{tg}\delta_2}{1 - \dfrac{\operatorname{tg}\delta_2}{\operatorname{tg}\varepsilon_x}} = \frac{z}{z - I_z}\cdot\operatorname{tg}\delta_2 \tag{7}$$

$$\operatorname{tg}\xi_x = \frac{I_x}{z - I_z} \tag{8}$$

By substituing (7) and (8) into (6) we get

$$\operatorname{tg}\delta_1 = \frac{z}{z - I_z}\cdot\operatorname{tg}\delta_2 - \frac{I_x}{z - I_z} = B\cdot\operatorname{tg}\delta_2 - C = X \tag{9}$$

Similary for the angle η_1 with respect to the xy-plane we would obtain

$$\mathrm{tg}\,\eta_1 = \frac{z}{z - I_z} \cdot \mathrm{tg}\,\eta_2 - \frac{I_4}{z - I_z} = B \cdot \mathrm{tg}\,\eta_2 - D = Y' \qquad (10)$$

Again, as to (4) and (5), for the angles of $\vec{k}_1$ with respect to the coordinates there holds

$$\cos\alpha_1 = \frac{X'}{\sqrt{1 + X'^2 + Y'^2}}$$

$$\cos\beta_1 = \frac{Y'}{\sqrt{1 + X'^2 + Y'^2}} \qquad (11)$$

$$\cos\gamma_1 = \frac{1}{\sqrt{1 + X'^2 + Y'^2}}$$

The relations (5) and (11) define uniquely the vector $\vec{K}$:

$$\vec{K} = (\cos\alpha_1 - \cos\alpha_2;\ \cos\beta_1 - \cos\beta_2;\ \cos\gamma_1 - \cos\gamma_2) \qquad (12)$$

3. USE OF THE METHOD

The method has been designed to evaluate holographic interferograms by means of computer picture processing. In order to determinate the common vector displacement $\Delta\vec{r}$, 3 or more direction of the vector $\vec{k}_1$ are necessary.

The method can also be used for "manual" evaluation of one holographic interferogram for more viewing directions. For instance, the evaluation of the vector $\vec{K}$ is carried out on a negative obtained from a camera or again directly by image processing of course. The point of intersection of the camera optical axis with the image plane will be denoted by O. The vector $\vec{k}_2$ is then calculated for this point. For other viewing points given with respect to the point O in the image plane by the position vector $\vec{e}=(e_{xi}, e_{yi})$, we shall displace the origin of the coordinate system by the value $\vec{E}_i = (E_{xi}, E_{yi})$, where E_{xi}, E_{yi} are the tangents of the viewing angles of the components of the i-th displacement vector $\vec{e}$. Thus

$$E_{xi} = \mathrm{tg}\,\mu_i = \frac{e_{xi}}{z}\ , \qquad \begin{array}{l} i = 1,2,\ldots,n \\ \text{(number of viewing points)} \end{array}$$

$$E_{yi} = tg\,\mathcal{X}_i = \frac{e_{yi}}{z} \tag{13}$$

For the tangents of the viewing angles from the i-th viewing position the following expressions will hold

$$\begin{aligned} 'X^{(i)} &= X - E_{xi} \\ 'Y^{(i)} &= Y - E_{yi} \end{aligned} \tag{14}$$

Then from 2.1 , the components of the vectors $\vec{k}_{1i}$ can be determined.

4. CONCLUSION

The paper presented a proposal for a simple determination of the components of the sensitivity vector $\vec{K}$ from the image representation of a measured object. In addition to the constant value given by the parameters of the image forming system and by the position of the ilumination sources, the only necessary external value for its determination is the distance of the measured object. The proposed method has been compared with the conventional measuring method for the coordinates and the precision of the results has been satisfactory.

Even though this method can also be used with advantage for manual evaluation of holographic interferograms, its importance is in the area of computerized evaluation of holographic interferograms.

5. REFERENCES

[1] Ennos A.E., J. Phys.E (J. Sci. Instrum.) 1 (1968) 731-4

[2] Dhir S.K., Sikora J.P., Experimental Mechanics 7 (1972) 323-7

IMPROVEMENT OF VISUAL INTERPRETATION OF INTERFEROGRAMS IN HOLOGRAPHIC INTERFEROMETRIC MICROSCOPY

Dr. sc. techn. G. Wernicke, Dipl.-Phys. H. Gruber [1)]

1. Introduction

Holographic microscopy has been a major subject of investigation since the invention of holography by Gabor. In spite of efforts by Gabor and others, the original drawbacks of the Gabor in-line holographic microscopy could not be satisfactorily solved. Leith and Upatnieks applied their off-axis technique of holography also to holographic microscopy /1/. Following Gabor's lead, they dispensed with the objective and obtained image magnification by use of divergent reference and reconstruction beams. Although lensless magnification in holographic microscopy had been previously demonstrated, they used the new approach to obtain a resolution of 7-10 μm at magnifications of 60 - 120 x.
Apart from noise, the technique of lensless holographic microscopy suffered, in general, from aberration due to the use of divergent reference and or reconstruction beams. The problem of aberration was bypassed by the introduction of a hybrid technique in which the conventional objective is used to form a magnified real image of the object field which is then combined with a suitable off-axis reference beam for holographic recording. Although the attractive feature of lensless imagery was not used, the holographic ability to record a substantial depth as well as the phase information in the object field could be preserved. It was also demonstrated that the techniques of microscopy, such as dark-field imagery and interferometry, which are used in conventional microscopy, could also be used in hybrid holographic microscopy. A further investigation also reemphasized the fact that lens-assisted holographic microscopy gives better resolution than the lensless technique. From all these works it appears that the hybrid technique is most likely to be successful by achieving good image quality and flexibility in processing the reconstructed image and by retaining some of the useful properties of holography.
However, one major problem in realizing this potentiality is posed by noise which is present in all holographic imagery. The image degradation due to noise has the most serious effect on resolution in holographic interferometric microscopy and must be reduced to a very low level for

1) Humboldt-Universität Berlin, Sektion Physik, Bereich Exp. Biophysik u. Spektroskopie, Invalidenstr. 42, Berlin 1040, DDR

successful use of holographic interferometric microscopy with low contrast and especially biological microscopic objects. A few methods have been used for reducing noise in holographic imagery/2/. None of these methods is suitable for application in holographic microscopy except that of van Ligten/3/. He illuminated the object with a few spatially separated collimated beams each of which was mutually coherent with the reference beam. All the beams were contained within the pupil of the optical system. During reconstruction, a mask with an aperture in it was used in the Fourier plane conjugate to the plane containing the object illumination for isolating the images and adding them together incoherently. Metelkin/4/ proposed to reduce noise by changing the angle of incidence of the laser beam on the object plane continuously during the exposure by means of a rotating parallelepiped. All these techniques are difficult to apply in practice and are mostly restricted to transmission microscopy.

2. Investigations on the surface dynamics of small biological objects

The application of holographic microscopy and holographic interferometric microscopy is mostly restricted to the investigation of transmission objects, e.g. the growth of cells or the freezing and thawing of blood cells.
In our experiments surface deformations in the region denominated as Hilum of seeds of Festuca altissima were investigated holographically using the hybrid holographic microscope shown in Fig. 1. The seeds, originally 0.3 mm in extension, were steeped for two days. Humidity changes were obtained by means of water evaporating from a little piece of paper. Holographic interferograms were made by the double exposure technique with time intervals between the exposures of 1,2,4,6 and 12 minutes, respectively. A deformation of the seed surface was visible on the Hilum. The image quality is highly affected by speckle granulation. The best way for an improvement of image quality for the visual interpretation of the interferograms seemed to be the application of digital image analysis.

3. Image improvement of the interferograms

For the improvement of the identification of interference fringes in interferograms of seeds disturbed by strong speckle noise and irregular intensity distribution we used the image processing system A 6472 at

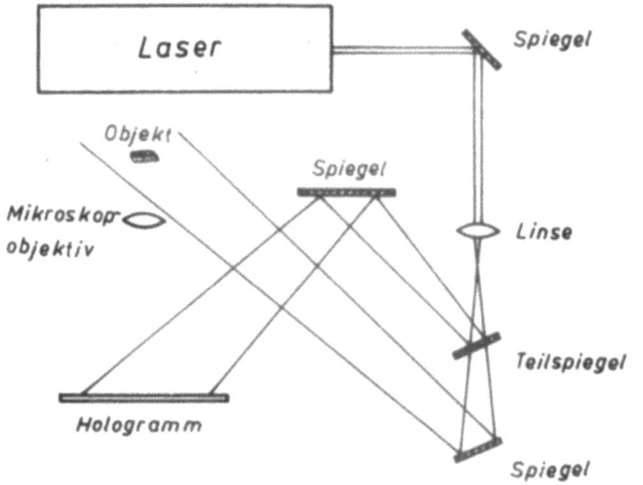

Fig. 1 Experimental arrangement

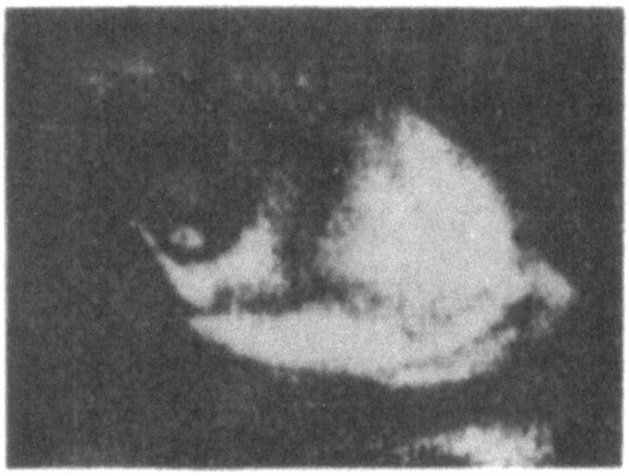

Fig. 2 Original interferogram double exposure time interval 4 minutes

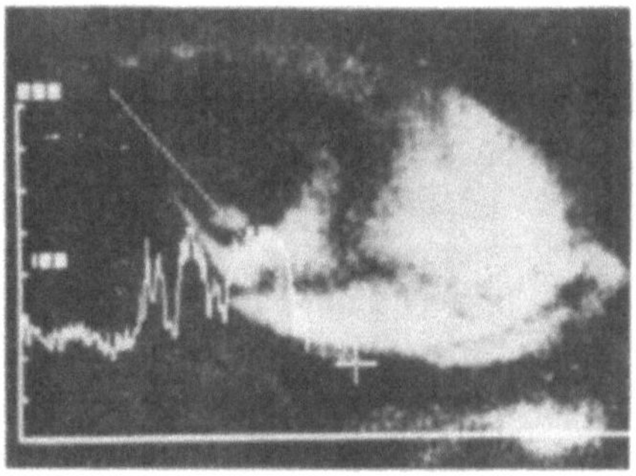

Fig. 3 Original interferogram intensity profile

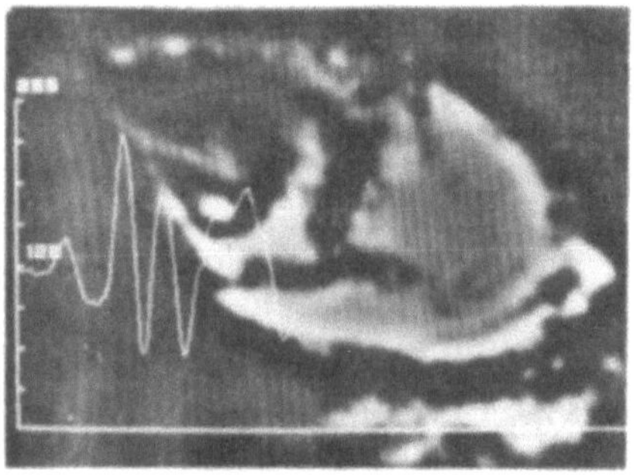

Fig. 4 Improved image intensity profile

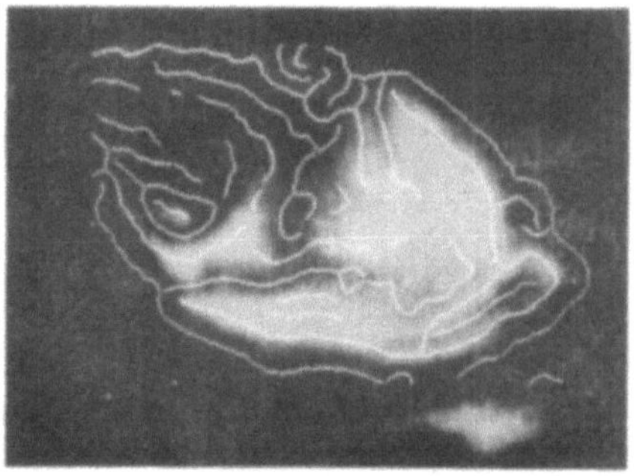

Fig. 5 Original interferogram overlaid with the non-interactively improved skeleton of the derived fringes

the Central Institute of Cybernetics and Information Processing. The system robotron A 6472 using high performance video processor enshures rapid processing to images with 512 x 512 pixels. After storing the image the improvement was carried out in the following steps:

- Shading correction for homogeneous distribution of the background intensity.
- Smoothing process with medium value filters.
- Contrast enhancement.

The result of the image improvement is shown in Fig. 5. The original interferogram is overlaid with the noninteractively improved skeleton of the derived fringes. The shading correction took a time of 2 seconds including the approximation of the background intensity and a space domain filtration also took some seconds only.

4. Summary

We have attempted image processing for the improvement of visual interpretation of holographic microscopic interferograms of seeds. Experimental results show the effectiveness of this method.

Acknowledgement

The authors would like to express their gratitude to Dr. W. Osten for his generous help in carrying out the image improvement. Many thanks are also to G. Hess for taking the photographs.

References

/1/ E.N. Leith, J. Upatnieks; J. Opt. Soc. Am. 55 (1965) 569
/2/ J.C. Dainty (Ed.): Laser Speckle and Related Phenomena. Berlin, Heidelberg, New York, Tokyo: Springer Verlag 1984
/3/ R.F. van Ligten: Appl. Opt. 12 (1973) 255
/4/ A.N. Metelkin: VI Vsesojus. biofiz. konf. Krasnojarsk 1978

THE APPLICATION OF ADAPTIVE AND ANISOTROPIC FILTERING FOR THE EXTRACTION OF FRINGE PATTERN SKELETONS

Winter, H.; Unger, S.; Osten, W. [1)]

Abstract

The extraction of valleys, ridges and slopes in the intensity profile of a fringe pattern may be difficult under the conditions of strong varying line sizes and the presence of noise and shading. In this cases the described methods including size-adaptive line detection with operators of Pseudo-Laplace-Type and anisotropic enhancement can give better results. All proposed algorithms are fitted for parallel processing and implemented on the high speed image processing system robotron A6472. Experimental results are given.

1. Introduction

In /1/ a segmentation algorithm was described, which may be used for the fast derivation of line structures from interferograms. These binary line structures can be thinned to a skeleton of dark and bright fringes. The special features of that algorithm were its local principle of operation, the consideration of characteristic neighbourhood relations and its inherent ability for parallelization. For the extraction of ridges and valleys in the intensity relief, for each pixel (i,j) the gray level difference between that pixel and the eight neighbouring pixels which are central symmetrically located around (i,j) at a distance R was computed. Taking into account broad and narrow fringes in an interferogram the same procedure was carried out with two different distances R and the results were overlayed. Problems may arise in regions where the results of both segmentation procedures are contradictorily. In such a case it is to decide between the valley or the ridge and such an alternative decision may be false.
In this paper we propose an other method for extraction of ridges and valleys to achieve better results in such cases. All proposed algorithms are fitted for parallel processing on special purpose processors of SIMD-type and implemented on the high speed image processing system robotron A6472. The mainly steps of this method are:

1. Adaptive line detection:
- Line detection by n Pseudo-Laplace-Operations with different prespecified size according to the possible line size in the interferogram.

---

1) Academy of Science of GDR, Central Institute of Cybernetics and Information Processes, Kurstr. 33, P.O.Box 1298, Berlin, 1086, GDR

All operators use a threshold S to make them less sensitive to noise and shading. The resulting images have a position-invariant scale of the local line intensity variations.

- Combination of the filtered images by a simple combining rule.

2. Anisotropic filtering
   - We estimate the local line direction in the combined line image by fitting some level crossings of the intensity with 3x3 masks followed by smoothing of the direction image.
   - To improve the resulting line image of step 1 an anisotropic smoothing controled by the direction image is used. Regions with an uncertain direction can be excluded from anisotropic smoothing.

3. Segmentation:

   The segmentation can be performed by two universally definable thresholds. As the result we get an image which contains three different labels:

   ridge points, valley points and slope or homogeneous points.

   Further processing to get a skeleton of dark and/or bright fringes can be done now using methods described in /1/. Anisotropic thinning and skeleton restoration methods contains paper /2/.

2. Adaptive Line Detection by Pseudo-Laplace-Operators

Pseudo-Laplace-Operators are highly nonlinear operators (also called "logical operators"), which are used for edge and line detection /3,4/. Known advantages of these operators are:

- they are simple to implement using subtractions, counting, look-up's and comparison only without multiplication and division
- they can be tuned to respond to any defined image feature (directional operators, edges and lines of defined size)
- thresholding or non-linear functions can make them less sensitiv to noise and other disturbances.

It is usual to include in the definition of such an operator a decision about the presence or absence of the defined feature. Like in /1/ the operator output can produce e. g. four labels: ridge point, valley point, slope point and unrecognized point.

In this case undecisonable situations may arise if the results of different operators must be combined. In our approach the operator output is only a result of counting the sign of intensity differences and the decision about ridge, valley or other point is done after combining several output images and anisotropic filtering of the combined result. Size and shape of our operators are defined by a sampling set

$$\{((SX_i,SY_i),\ (CX_i,CY_i))\}\ ;\ i=1,\dots,N$$

which contains the coordinates of N pairs of points between them the intensity differences are calculated. The coordinates are related to the central point (Ø,Ø), whereby the distance between (Ø,Ø) and (CX_i, CY_i) is always less than between (Ø,Ø) and (SX_i, SY_i). Besides that we use a threshold S ($S \geq Ø$) to classify an intensity difference as significant or nonsignificant. Our operator of Pseudo-Laplace-type applicated on input image f at point (x,y) works in the following nonrecursive and homogeneous way:

$$d_i = f(x+SX_i, y+SY_i) - f(x+CX_i, y+CY_i); \quad i=1,\ldots,N$$

$$g1 := \text{number of differences } d_i \text{ with } d_i < -S \; ; \; i=1,\ldots,N$$

$$g2 := \text{number of differences } d_i \text{ with } d_i > S \; ; \; i=1,\ldots,N$$

$$g(x,y) = g1 - g2$$

The output image g has a scale from -N until +N.
It is well known, that line detection (ridges and valleys) can be performed by several directional operators. With regard to computation time and to the necessity to use operators of several sizes we prefere the undirected case.
Finally, we decide to use ring-shaped operators of several sizes being nearly rotational invariant and achieve a maximum of sensitivity to the corresponding line size. To study the properties of such operators and to verify our considerations we have performed some simulations on an universal computer with synthetic continuous images. In the sampling set all (CX_i, CY_i) were choosen as (Ø,Ø) and the points (SX_i, SY_i) were densely sampled on a circle with a radius R around (Ø,Ø).
Fig. 1 gives some results in form of one-dimensional intensity profiles. All operator outputs are transformed at the same scale, so that they do not depend on N. The input image in fig. 1a) is a two-dimensional periodical sinusoidal intensity function with wave lenght D, wherein the intensity depends on one dimension only. The input image 1d) is a linear shaded version of a). Results are shown for three radii and two cases of threshold S.
The operator has the following properties:

1. In the case of optimal size of R=D/2 at all positions the absolute value of the operator output is greater than in the case of too small and too large sizes (except of a little shading effect in fig. 1e)).
2. If we use a threshold S greater than zero, the output of too large and too small operator is much more depressed than the output of the optimal one (compare fig. 1b) and c)) and shading effects can be reduced (compare fig. 1e) and f)).
3. In the optimal case of the operator size the absolute value of the output does not depend on the amplitude A of the input wave if $2A \gg S$ (compare fig. 1b) and e)).

According to this properties we can define the following simple rule to combine the outputs of different operators (with constant N or transformation to an uniform scale of $\{-N,\dots,+N\}$):

$$g(x,y)=\begin{cases} g1(x,y) & \text{if } |g1(x,y)| \geq |g2(x,y)| \\ g2(x,y) & \text{otherwise} \end{cases}$$

Several versions of ring-shaped operators with different sizes are implemented. With the object to reduce additionally the influence of noise, shading, and other disturbances we can use not only the differences between the central point (x,y) and some points located on a concentric circle with radius R, but also differences between points on a circle with a small radius C ($C < R$) and points on a circle with radius $R' \in \{R, R+1,\dots,R+C\}$. In our experiments we have used a runtime effective operator with a constant number of differences (N=32), which shape and size is defined by two parameters R and C (see fig. 2). Perhaps its shape must be named as star-shaped in the case of $R \geq 5$.

3. Anisotropic filtering

In /1/ region growing is used to improve the segmented image. In some cases this isotropic method can produce false connecting links between equal labeled regions.
An alternative way to avoid this disadvantage is anisotropic filtering /5,6/. We propose anisotropic smoothing in the direction of the line flow to close small disconnections and to get smoothed line borders in the combined line image. Anisotropic smoothing can be applied more than once. It is performed with 8 directed convolution operators as shown in fig. 3.
The selection of one directed operator in each point of the image must be controled by a direction image. To estimate the line directions we fitt at first some level crossings of the intensity in the combined line image with 3x3 masks. The resulting image contains 8 direction values and one value for an undefined direction. Secondly we smooth the direction with a method based on vector addition as discribed in /5,6/, whereby nearly all points with undefined direction get a defined value. The absolute value of the resulting vectors is a measure for the significance of the direction. So points with an unsignificant direction can be excluded from anisotropic filtering.

4. Segmentation

According to the above mentioned properties of the line detection step the transformed intensities have on ridges and valleys near constant positive and negative values throughout the image. Segmentation can now be done with a single threshold M ($M \geq 0$):

ridge point: $g(x,y) > +M$
valley point: $g(x,y) < -M$
slope or homogeneous point: $-M \leq g(x,y) \leq +M$.

5. Results

The experimental results proved the efficiency of our method. Fig. 4 shows an example. Fig. 4a) is an fringe pattern with 512x512 points and 8 bit intensity values. The adaptive line detection was executed by four operators as represented in fig. 2 with the parameters $C_1=1$, $R_1=3$, $C_2=1$, $R_2=5$, $C_3=2$, $R_3=10$, $C_4=3$, $R_4=15$, and S=6 in all cases. Fig. 4b) shows the output of the smallest operator and c) until e) the stepwise combination results. The direction image in fig. 4f) is a result of two direction smoothing steps, first with a 29*29 window and secondly with a 17*17 window. One anisotropic smoothing step on image 4e) controlled by 4f) gives the image 4g). Image 4h) is the result of segmentation with M=N/3 (only the ridges are presented in the figure). The skeleton of the ridges (bright lines) in fig. 4i) we got by isotropic thinning. In fig. 4j) and k) the corresponding results of the methods presented in /1/ are shown, which contain a deffect in the center and at the border of the fringe pattern. The better result must be paid with a higher run time. The hole procedure (without thinning) tooks about 25 seconds. But this time is acceptable in much applications.

Acknowledgments

The autors wish to thank C. Feist for collaboration in programming, P. Hänßgen for writing the manuscript, G. Heß for making the photographs, and I. Lekscha for performing the graphic works.

References

/1/ Eichhorn, N., and Osten, W.: An algorithm for the fast derivation of the line structures from interferograms. J. Mod. Opt. (in press)

/2/ Unger, S., Winter, H., Feist, C., Marzok, U., and Zedler, L.: Program package for processing line flow like images by BVS A6472 using adaptive and anisotropic methods. In: Yaroslavskij, L. P., Rosenfeld, A., Wilhelmi, W.: Computer analysis of images and patterns. Akademie-Verlag, Berlin 1987, 255-265

/3/ Nadler, M.: Effective and cost-effective real time picture operators for medical imagery. In: Dombal, F. T. and Gremy, F.: Decision making and medical care. North-Holland, Amsterdam 1976

/4/ Letellier, Nadler, and Abramatic: The telesign project. Proc. of the IEEE, 73(1985)4, 813

/5/ Knutsson, H., Wilson, R., Granlund, G. H.: Anisotropic filtering operations for image enhancement and their relation to the visual system. IEEE Computer Conf. on Pattern Recognition and Image Processing, Dallas, Aug. 1981

/6/ Knutsson, H., Wilson, R., Granlund, G. H.: Content dependent anisotropic filtering of images. Int. Conf. on Digital Signal Processing, Florence, Sept. 1981

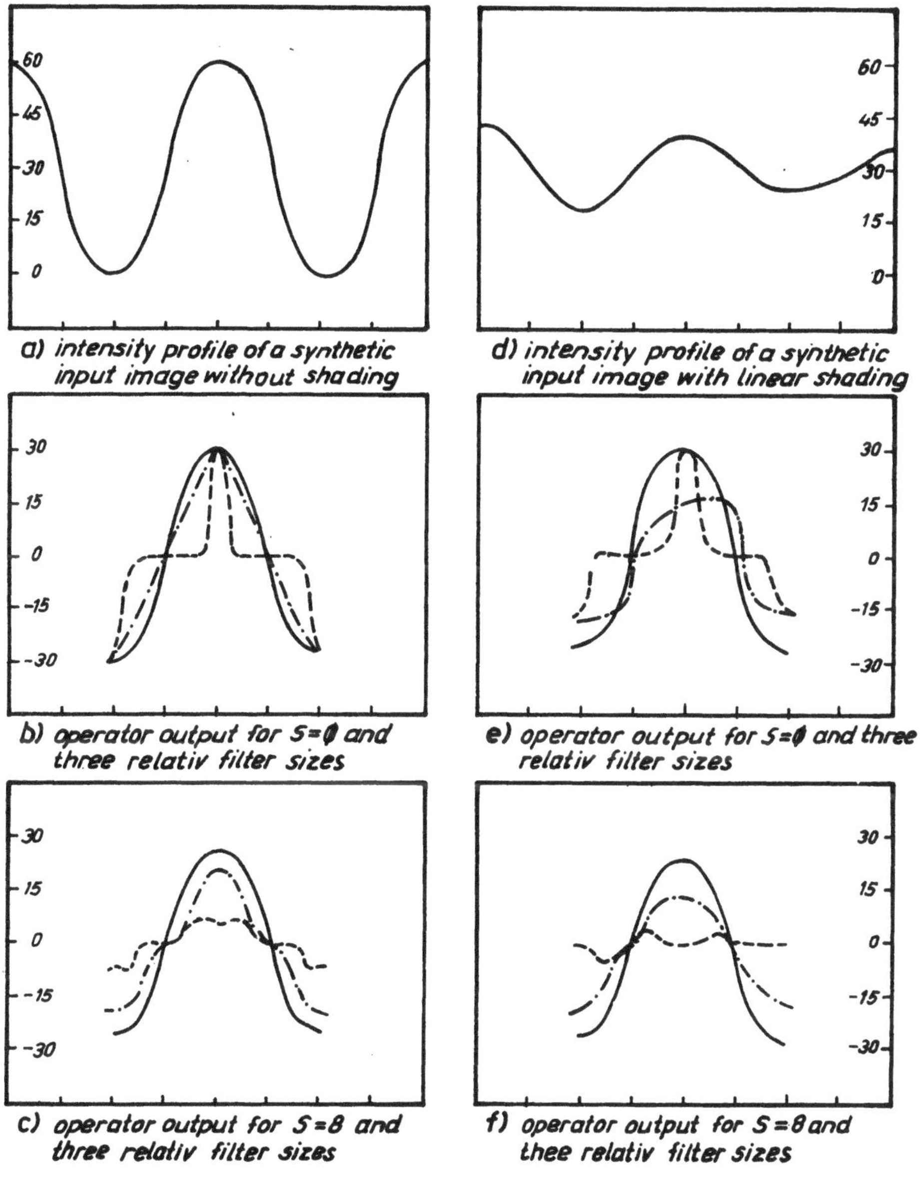

relativ filter size :

- ·— R/D = 4 (filter size too large)
—— R/D = 0,5 (optimal size)
--- R/D = 0,125 (filter size too small)

R: filter size (radius)
D: wave length of the sinusoidal intensity profile
S: threshold

Fig. 1 Properties of Pseudo-Laplace-Operators with different size and different value of threshold

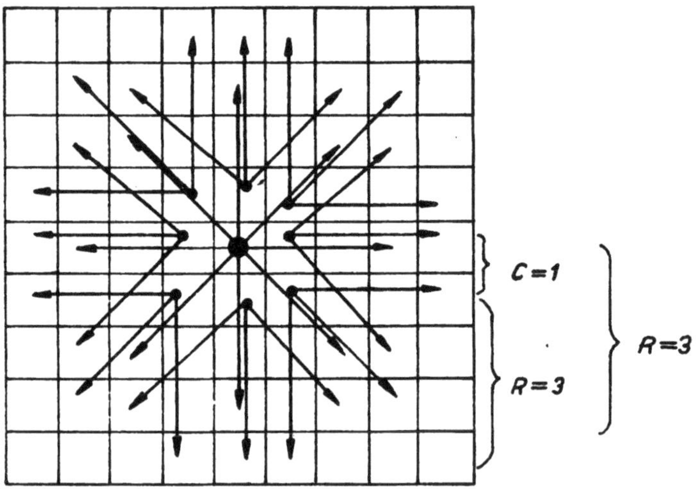

Fig. 2 A Pseudo-Laplace-operator with radius R and central radius C

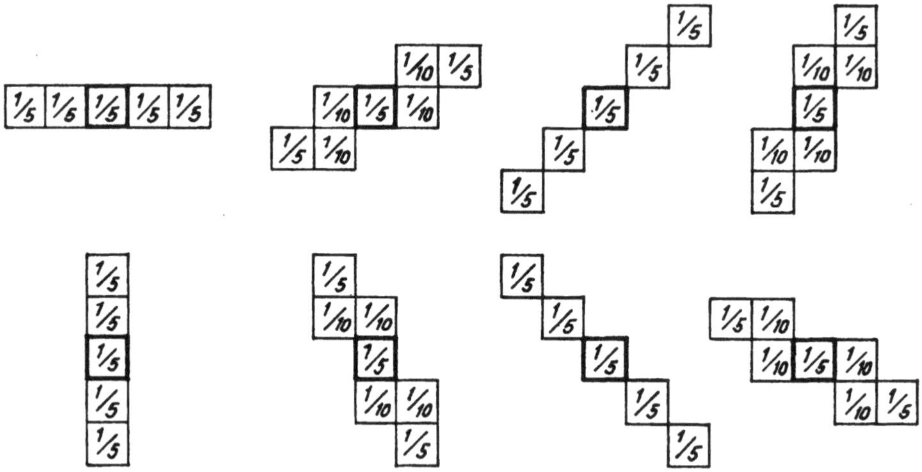

Fig. 3 Directed convolution operators for anisotropic smoothing

Fig. 4: Fringe pattern and results of processing

a) unprocessed fringe pattern

b) output of the smallest line detecting operator

c),d),e) results of stepwise output combination

f) direction image

g) result of anisotropic filtering of e)

h) result of segmentation (only bright lines)

i) skeleton of h)

j),k) results of the operator described in /1/

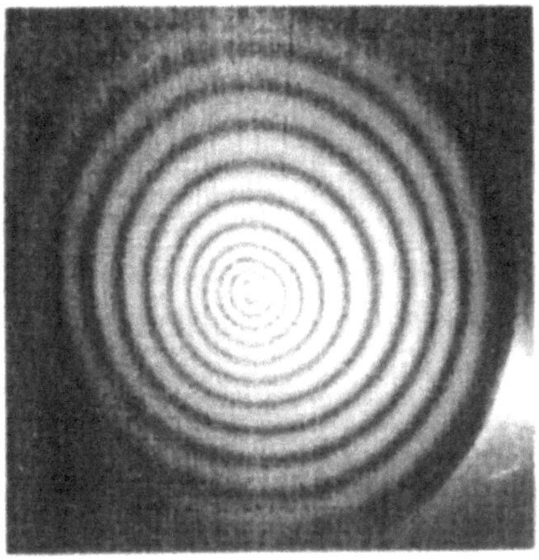

a)

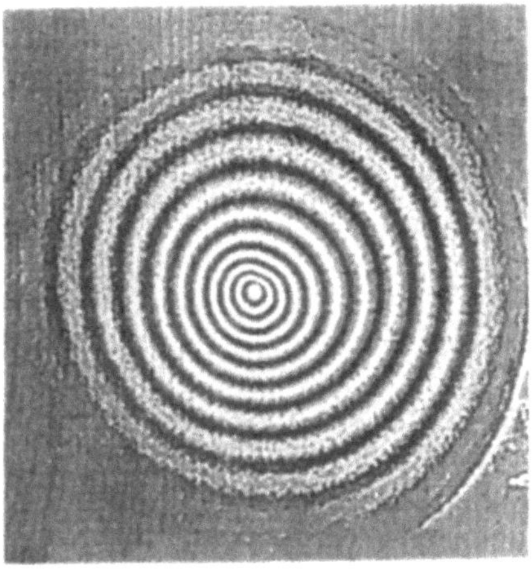

b)

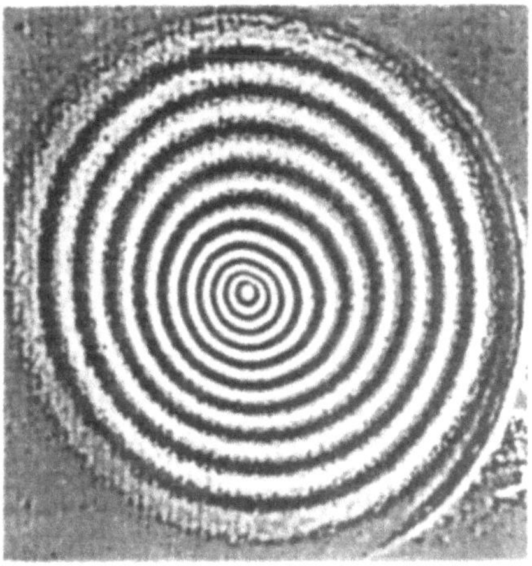

c)

d)

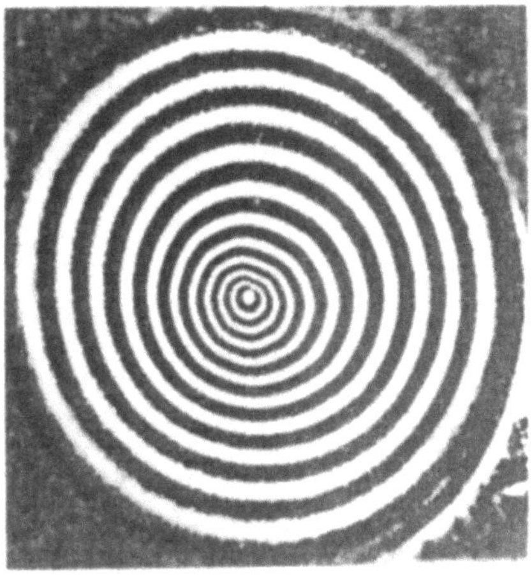

e)

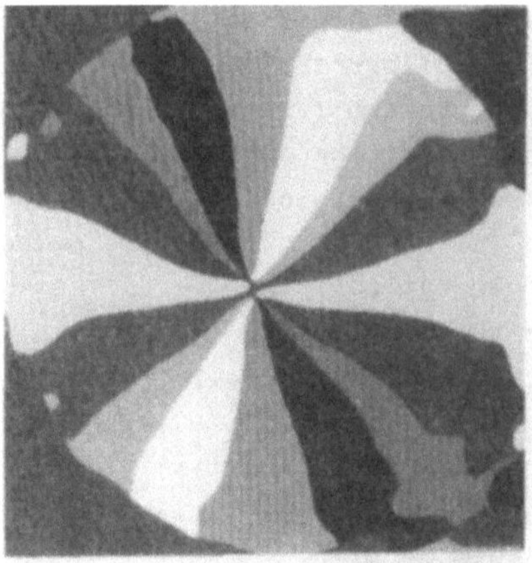

f)

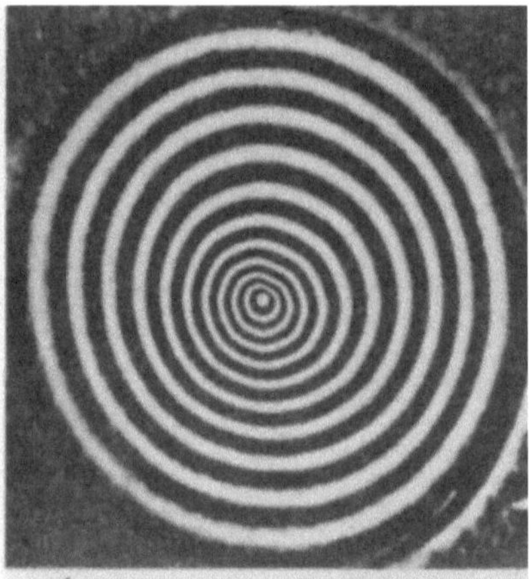

g)

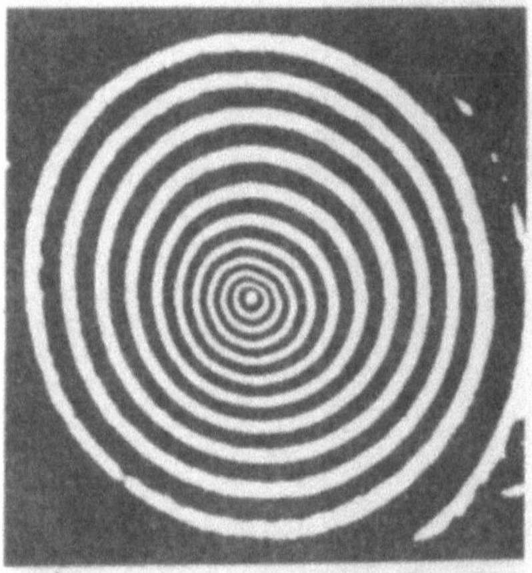

h)

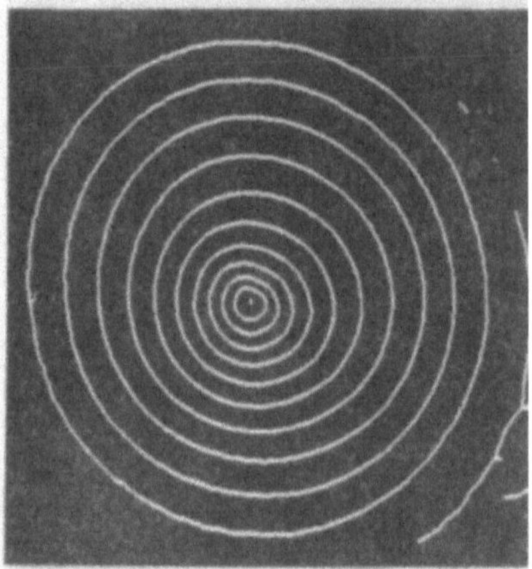

i)

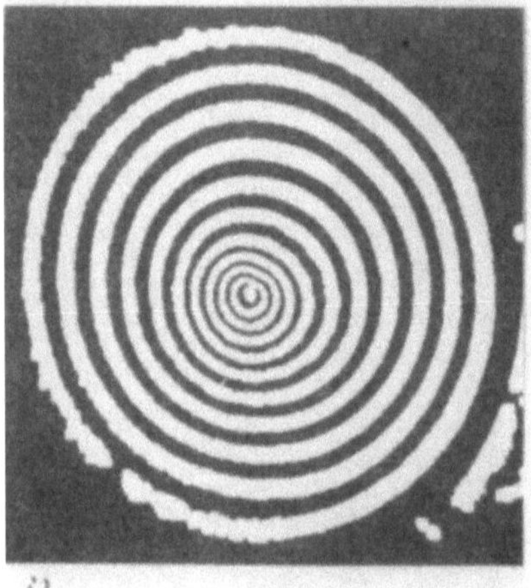

j)

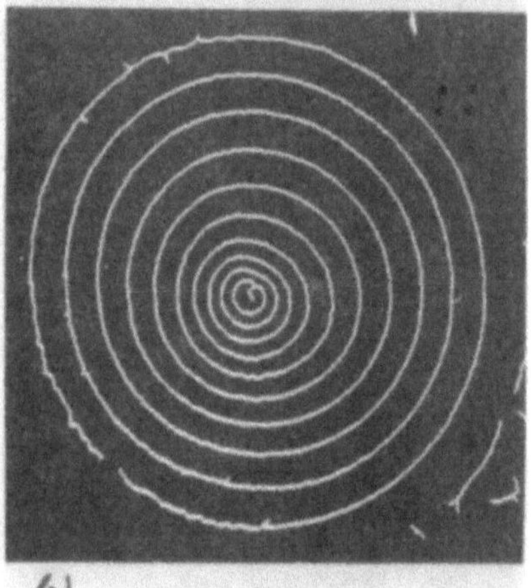

k)

MEASURING COMPLEX

Yu.B.Koverkin, P.P.Kuzmin, T.V.Lyashenko,
P.I.Novikov, N.O.Reinhand, E.S.Volodin I)

New directions in the field of measuring technique are needed because of the wide and complex field of engineering technological problems of machine building. One of them is the creation of modular measuring computer complexes. The kernel of the difficult measuring systems lies now in the computers development. The measuring and equipment parts will be standard.

In our modular measuring complex we use space-time optical structures as a basis of adaptive tie-in of the standards and the studied part. We also use opto-electronic measuring methods instead of electrical methods.

The advantage of the optical methods is firstable their most informativity in comparison with the other information sources. They supply us opportunity of the simultanious control of the whole studied surface and the parallel development of the receiving information. The high speed of light propagation makes the optical first transformers sluggishnessless. Thus, dynamic characteristics of our complex are limited by the further transformers.

The measuring computer complex may be used for the optical non-destructive measurements of geometric and mechanic parameters of different machines, diagnostic control of difficult equipment. Besides that it may be used for the solving of the different problems of analysis, comparison, filtration, optimization of technological processes and receiving devices quality.

This complex may be used at different structure levels depending of the class and difficulty of the problems. The basic element of the complex structure at the every level is the measuring module. It consists of a light source and a detector, optical elements, measuring table and studied object itself. Scheme of the modular measuring complex may be seen on the picture.

Measuring module may be used itself for the easy tasks, when the difficult development of data is not needed. All the results may be seen on the registrating apparatus.

Further development of the measuring complex structure may be either by introduction of new measuring modules, or by the entering of new functions to the blocks of information controlling, transforma-

I) Leningrad Branch of Machine Science Institute,
Academy of Sciences USSR,
199178, USSR, Leningrad, Vas.ost., Bolshoy pr.,61

tion and display.

Modular measuring computer complex is completed by the software of the digital development of video information.

This system may work on the basis of the personal computers, which may be joint to the plant computer system.

This complex must ensure:

- image introduction in digital form,
- interactive work regime,
- the solution of automatization problems,
- information exchange between the processor and the external systems,
- possibility of modification and improvement of the program depending of specific conditions.

The system of the optical elements: fiber optical conductors, optical connectors and others may be introduced on the next structure levels.

Modular measuring complex may be used in the different fields of the national economy: power plant industries, transport, agriculture machine engineering and others. Thanks to the modular principle of the complex structure it may solve different problems.

Bei Fragen zur Produktsicherheit wenden Sie sich bitte an:
If you have any questions regarding product safety,
please contact:

Walter de Gruyter GmbH
Genthiner Straße 13
10785 Berlin
productsafety@degruyterbrill.com